MISSION CRITICAL

The 7 Strategic Traps that Derail Even the Smartest Companies

JOSEPH C. PICKEN

GREGORY G. DESS

IRWIN
Professional Publishing®
Chicago • London • Singapore

Times Mirror
Higher Education Group

Library of Congress Cataloging-in-Publication Data
Picken, Joseph C.
   Mission Critical : the 7 strategic traps that derail even the smartest companies / Joseph C. Picken, Gregory G. Dess.
      p.   cm.
   Includes index.
   ISBN 0-7863-0969-5
   1. Strategic planning.   2. Corporate turnarounds.   I. Dess, Gregory G.   II. Title.
HD30.28.P44 1997
658.4'012—dc20   96–23782

Printed in the United States of America
1 2 3 4 5 6 7 8 9 0 DO 3 2 1 0 9 8 7 6

PREFACE

Why do strategies fail? Is it planning? Is it leadership? Is it execution, or do some managers just fail to look before they leap? Is it just fate? Are some strategies doomed to failure before they ever get off the ground?

Is there a common thread in strategic failure, or is every case unique? Peter Drucker once observed that "entrepreneurship is 'risky' mainly because so few of the so-called entrepreneurs know what they are doing. They lack the methodology. They violate elementary and well-known rules." And so it is with strategy. We believe that most strategic failures are avoidable. At the same time, there is consistency in failure, as strategists seem to fall into the same strategic traps, over and over again, apparently unable to learn from the mistakes of those who have preceded them.

So, how can strategic failures be avoided? Over the years, we have assisted hundreds of companies and their top managers—observing, coaching, advising, and participating—as they wrestled with the complex and often difficult processes of strategy formulation and implementation. And as we compared notes and reflected on our experiences, we arrived at a couple of observations:

- The best of strategies, poorly implemented, is of little value. A sound strategy, implemented without error, wins every time.
- A flawed strategy—no matter how brilliant the leadership, no matter how effective the implementation—is doomed to failure. A sound strategy, implemented without error, wins every time.

It seemed so obvious it was almost trivial—and the punch line was the same in both cases. On the other hand, it had a touch of elegance in its simplicity: *a sound strategy, implemented without error, wins every time!*

As we looked at more and more companies, the lesson was clear: the strategy need not be brilliant, just as long as it was sound, well conceived, and avoided the most obvious strategic errors. We also found that it doesn't take the world's greatest leader to succeed in implementation, just one who doesn't make any really dumb mistakes. And, the most important lesson of all is that it's not that hard to avoid the most common strategic traps—*if you know what to look for*.

There seems to be a consistent pattern. Strategic managers at all levels, perhaps blinded by the misguided notion that their situation is somehow unique, tend to ignore the lessons of past failures and blunder into the same strategic traps over and over again. This book is about some of the most common and dangerous strategic pitfalls and how to avoid them. It is about what to look for and how to minimize your risks so that the corporate ship, or your division or department, doesn't end up on the rocks *on your watch*.

Our list is representative, not exhaustive. We don't pretend to have addressed all the mistakes that have ever been made in the formulation or implementation of strategy. We know first hand that the task is complex, and that every situation is a little different. And we believe that, although the lessons of this book will help to point the way, in the end the task is yours alone. *You're in charge, the mission is critical and—as your boss or shareholders have warned you—you'd better not screw it up!*

This book is not just for CEO's. It's intended to be of interest and value to anyone involved in the formulation or implementation of strategy at any level—and these days, almost everyone is involved in one way or another. It really doesn't matter whether you see the world from the top rung of the ladder, or the bottom, or somewhere in between. The challenges and difficulties of strategy formulation and implementation are much the same regardless of the size or nature of the organization. If you have a stake in organizational strategy—how to formulate it, how to implement it, and most importantly, how to avoid messing it up—this book is for you.

This book reflects a unique collaboration between two individuals who, in the beginning, saw the world through very different lenses. One, a professor, enjoyed the relatively detached perspective of an external observer. The other, a former senior executive and turnaround manager now turned management consultant, had just enrolled in a Ph.D. program and saw things from the insider's point of view, conditioned by 25 years of experience in the rough-and-tumble world of the competitive arena. Over a span of five years, as they struggled to find common ground and reconcile their very different points of view, a friendship and professional collaboration has emerged. Both have learned from each other and from the executives they've encountered in their research. This book is based on the strengths of that collaboration: the perspective of an external observer combined with the action-oriented, no-nonsense approach of a seasoned executive and management consultant.

The organization of the book is fairly straightforward. Ask any guru, and he'll tell you there are three steps in the strategy-making process: understanding the environment, formulating a strategy, and managing its implementation. We'll pretty much follow the same path, with a couple of chapters devoted to the kinds of things that can go wrong along the way in each of these key areas. Each chapter begins with a brief vignette or two—stories of organizational disasters—followed by an analysis that shows how each organization tripped themselves up by blundering into what should have been an obvious strategic trap. Timely examples of both successes and failures are used to highlight common patterns and expose the root causes of strategic failure. Turning then to the solution, we provide a set of practical guidelines that combine our professional experience with the latest in academic research to help you steer your organization clear of the most obvious strategic traps.

ACKNOWLEDGMENTS

The creation of a book is not a solo effort—there are many people to acknowledge and thank for their contributions, both to this project and to our personal and professional development. In the course of our research, we've had the opportunity to exchange ideas with the CEOs of a number of leading companies, each of whom has contributed, in various ways, to the ideas reflected in this book. We acknowledge and appreciate the contributions of Les Alberthal of EDS, William Howell of the J.C. Penney Company, Vin Prothro of Dallas Semiconductor, Ed Schollmaier of Alcon Laboratories, Keith Hughes of the Associates Corporation, Gary Hegna of OpenConnect Systems, Stephen Polley of Interphase Corporation, George Platt of Intecom Corporation, John McHale of Networth, Inc., Bill Ogle of STB Systems, Inc., and David Rowley of Digital Techniques, Inc.

Thanks also to our colleagues from the Department of Management and the Department of Information Systems & Management Sciences at the University of Texas at Arlington. Their friendship, encouragement, and helpful suggestions have enriched not only our work, but our lives as well. A special thanks to Abdul Rasheed, Richard Priem, Lawrence Schkade, David Harrison, Stephanie Newport, Leonard Love, Vinay Garg, Tom Lumpkin, and John Lundin; and to the outstanding business librarians at UTA, Ms. Ruthie Brock and Ms. Tommie Wingfield, whose cheerful and enthusiastic assistance in the research for and preparation of this book was "above and beyond." And finally, our thanks to Jeffrey Krames, Caroline Carney, and the staff at Irwin Professional Publishing, without whose efforts this book would not have been possible.

Over the years, many individuals—colleagues, teachers, students and clients—have contributed to our understanding of organizations, their strategies, and the leaders and workers that make them tick. Others have supported us, inspired us, and motivated us to keep going—or to make that leap of faith we all need to make from time to time.

Joseph would like to acknowledge the support and encouragement of his wife, Mary Dee; his children, to whom this book is dedicated; and the support and counsel of his parents, Joseph and Dorothy Picken. Over the years, a number of individuals have served as mentors, role models and sources of inspiration. Professor James Brian Quinn is at the head of the list. He created excitement in the classroom and with his work that has stimulated a lifelong interest in strategic management. Dr. Robert C. Dean, Jr. planted a seed that grew into a fascination with technology and entrepreneurship. Dr. Robert J. Potter has been a mentor, friend and counselor over the years. Thanks also to the clients of my consulting practice, who have provided a stimulating environment to test and refine many of the ideas reflected in this book. And, in everyone's life there are special friends who have counseled and inspired. Dean Pratt is one of those, as are the members of the Dallas Junto who, individually and as a group, have contributed in many ways.

Greg would like to acknowledge the colleagues and mentors who have provided support and encouragement over the years, including Professors Nelson Rogers and Cecil Johnson at Georgia Tech and Don Beard, Monty Kast and the late Charles Summer at the University of Washington. All played key roles in priming his interest in a career in academics. Along the way, he has benefitted, both personally and professionally, from his associations with

Clark Holloway, Nancy Origer, Peter Davis, Mark Martinko, Mike Hitt, Duane Ireland, Bill Anthony, Alan Bauerschmidt, Jeff Covin, and Alex Miller. On a more personal note, he owes a special debt of gratitude to his wife Margie, daughter Taylor, and the two people who *really* made it all possible, Bill and Mary Dess.

Joseph C. Picken
McKinney, Texas

Gregory G. Dess
Lexington, Kentucky

To David, Matthew, Anna and Christopher,
who have made it all worthwhile

Joseph C. Picken

To Carol Martin Gatton,
Dean Richard Furst,
and my colleagues
at the University of Kentucky

Gregory G. Dess

FOREWORD

Whenever I get the opportunity to get away from the pressure and complexity of today's competitive environment, I love to get out on the water to do some fishing. It's uncomplicated and relaxing—just the opposite of leadership today. People have been fishing for thousands of years, and although we've incorporated many technological advances, it's remained fundamentally the same. You have to be in the right waters, and you have to execute properly.

In the last decade or so, there has been an explosion of organizational concepts such as shifting paradigms, tornadoes, core competencies, virtual corporations, shamrock organizations, and so on. These concepts serve as an attempt to provide some insight to organizations during this period of unprecedented complexity and rapid change in business. Consultants and management experts carrying these newly discovered "answers" to improved global performance have deluged organizations with programmatic change to help us redesign and reengineer our companies. Some of these efforts succeed—at least for a while—and many fail. Sometimes the theories can't stand up to real-world ambiguities. Other times, our demand for quick results fails to bring the 'team' into the game with us, and instead of *executing* the plan, we have *executed* the plan.

Mission Critical is about the *timeless* management principles that are the foundation of many of their repackaged versions—TQM, continuous improvement, shared vision, empowerment, and others. It reminds us of those fundamental elements of leadership that got us this far. Most of us have encountered some form of the seven strategic traps outlined in this book—and many times have had to learn a lesson the hard way. In today's dynamic environment, leaders need to learn from every available source, not from just their own experience. This book also explodes the myth that the success of any company is dependent on people with rare qualities that can't be learned. Clearly, our challenge is to engage the leadership potential of *every* member in the organization.

Like fishing, avoiding pitfalls appears deceptively simple. It's not. Even if you get to the right waters, you still have to perform skillfully. Choosing the right application of technology, technique, and intuition is every bit as important as detecting opportunity. As Joseph Picken and Gregory Dess point out, avoiding these common errors does not guarantee success. But ignoring them is certainly a recipe for failure.

Les Alberthal
Chairman and CEO, EDS Corporation

TABLE OF CONTENTS

Preface   iii
Acknowledgments   v
Foreword   viii

Chapter 1

Mission Critical: The Strategic Challenge   1

Seven Strategic Traps   5
A Sound Strategy, Implemented Without Error   7

Chapter 2

Blind Spots in the Competitive Vision   9

Strategic Trap #1: Misreading the Environmental Tea Leaves   13
Focusing on the Environment—The Context of Strategy   13
Understanding the Environment—Scanning and Competitor Intelligence   15
Averting Disaster—Avoiding the Blind Spots   21
Spotting the Opportunity   27
Putting the Pieces Together   30
Strategic Inventory   32
Endnotes   34

Chapter 3

Flawed Assumptions: Right Strategy—Wrong Problem   37

Strategic Trap #2: Right Strategy—Wrong Problem   52
Assumptions, Premises, and Beliefs   53
The Dangers of the Dominant Logic   54
Build Your Strategy on a Sound Foundation   59
Strategic Inventory   62
Endnotes   64

Chapter 4

Creating Competitive (Dis)advantage   67

What Went Wrong at Food Lion?   69

Strategic Trap #3: Creating Competitive (Dis)advantage   71
Limitations of the Traditional Approach   76
Creating Competitive Advantage   78
Sustaining Competitive Advantage   91
Strategic Inventory   94
Endnotes   96

Chapter 5

Subtracting Value by Adding Businesses   101

Strategic Trap #4: Subtracting Value by Adding Businesses   105
Why Diversify? All the Wrong Reasons   107
Why Diversify? All the Right Reasons   111
Combining the Benefits from All Three Rationales   119
Is It Easy To Gain the Benefits of Strategic Diversification?   120
Making Diversification Work: Guidelines for Implementation   122
Strategic Inventory   127
Endnotes   127

Chapter 6

Tripping Over the Barriers   131

The Denver International Airport   131
What Went Wrong in Denver?   134
Strategic Trap #5: Tripping Over the Barriers   137
Limitations of the Traditional Model   138
A New Management Model: the "Boundaryless" Organization   142
Ensuring Effective Coordination and Integration   144
New Organizational Architectures   146
Management Tools and Techniques for Coordination and
Integration   155
Moving Toward the Boundaryless Organization   159
Strategic Inventory   159
Endnotes   161

Chapter 7

Out of [Strategic] Control   163

What Went Wrong at Bausch & Lomb?   167
Strategic Trap #6: Arbitrary Goals; Unbalanced Controls   168

Moving Toward Contemporary Control Systems   171
Building a Strong and Effective Culture   176
Motivating with Rewards and Incentives   183
Setting Boundaries and Constraints   185
Evolving from Boundaries to Rewards and Culture   187
Strategic Inventory   189
Endnotes   190

Chapter 8

[Mis]leading: Failures of Leadership   193

Defining Leadership   196
Strategic Trap #7: A Failure of Leadership   200
Principles of Effective Transformational Leadership   202
Move Quickly and Decisively—and Create a Sense of Urgency   203
Develop and Communicate a Vision and a Plan   208
Set Stretch Goals and Empower Others to Act   214
Institutionalizing Change   217
Strategic Inventory   220
Endnotes   221

Chapter 9

A Sound Strategy, Implemented without Error   225

Doing the Right Things . . . and Doing Them Right   226
Understanding the Strategic Context   227
Strategy Formulation—A Two-Step Process   230
Identifying the Potential Sources of Competitive Advantage   231
Crafting a Sound Strategy   233
Avoiding the Common Strategic Errors   236
Effective Implementation—Doing Things Right   238
Coordination, Integration, and Strategic Control   238
The Vital Role of Leadership   242
Avoiding the Dumb Mistakes   244
In the Final Analysis   245
Endnotes   246

INDEX   247

1

Mission Critical: The Strategic Challenge

You're at the starting line of the Olympic 400 meter hurdles—it's the finals! The roar of the crowd is tremendous, but it doesn't affect your concentration. You know who the competitors are—three on your right, four on your left—and you've been here before. The rules are the same—everyone stays in his lane—and the track and the hurdles are no different from the last hundred times you ran this race. Everything's set—it's a matter of execution now—get into your rhythm—don't trip over the hurdles—and get to the finish line first!

We're not all Olympic sprinters, but we're all in a race. As a manager, regardless of your level or the size of your organization, you're responsible. You're the one who must set the direction. You're the one who has to lead the charge and get your organization to the finish line first. In the venue of the corporate strategy arena, however, things are a lot tougher and more complex than they are on the track.

The rules are different, and always changing. The finish line is a moving target. You know who some of the competitors are, but as a few fall by the wayside, new entrants keep trying to crowd into your lane. The barriers in your path keep moving and changing— sometimes higher, sometimes lower, sometimes closer, sometimes farther away—so it's tough to get into a rhythm. You had a plan, but it fell apart when the first hurdle moved away from you and doubled in height. Now you're behind, and trying to catch up to that new guy who came out of the crowd and moved ahead into your lane.

You're a strategic manager. Your job is simple, right? Get ahead, stay ahead, avoid the obstacles, and keep from being blind-sided by the competitor who tries to muscle his way into your lane. And the stakes are higher—no silver medal for second in this race. *The mission is critical*—your company, your employees, probably your job, depend on your success in the arena. Your success depends on your ability to develop and implement a winning strategy—one that will put your organization ahead and keep you in the lead.

This book is about strategy, and about winning! And it's about some of the hurdles you'll have to get over along the way. A lot of things can happen between the starting point and the finish line and most of them, even if they don't knock you out of the race, can keep you from moving into the fast lane. Later on, we'll take a look at some of the firms that have stumbled badly midway through the race—considering, for example:

- How the A.T. Cross Company's pens were muscled out of the fast lane by a fat new competitor.
- How Microsoft missed a turn at the Internet signpost and is now scrambling to play catch up.
- How Murphy (of Murphy's Law fame) caught up with Raytheon and left the Beech Starship at the starting line.
- How Food Lion blew its lead—putting its head down, it drove hard for the finish—and failed to notice that the last hurdle was higher than all the rest.
- How the Dole Food Company tried to hedge its bets by entering another event—and ended up losing its track shirt.
- How Morrison Knudsen entered a promising draft choice in the race and watched him crash headlong into the grandstand.
- How Greyhound's dog almost died from an overdose of technology.

Each of these examples is a sobering reminder that the task of strategic management is not an easy one. Every situation is unique, but a common thread runs through them all. Each case involved one or more fundamental strategic errors, either in the formulation of strategy or in its implementation. Each CEO fell into a different strategic trap, but their mistakes were not unique (no consolation prize for creativity here!). Strategic traps are not confined to a particular industry or business environment, and they do not discriminate on the basis of the size or the age of the organization. As one sifts through the ashes of strategic failure, the same fundamental errors appear again and again, as if each CEO was blind to the lessons of history, seemingly unable to learn from the mistakes of those who had gone before.

As we noted earlier, this is a book about strategy: not about how to formulate it (dozens have already been written), not about how to implement it (probably a few hundred more), and not about how to manage or control it (sorry, we've run out of fingers and toes). This book is, very simply, about *how not to mess it up*—how to avoid the fatal strategic errors that have, again and again, caused the best laid of plans to go astray.

Over the years, we've observed that strategic management has a lot in common with sports. Sportscasters will tell you—it's a *bona fide* cliche—that the teams that win the big games are the ones that avoid the turnovers, those costly mistakes that make the difference between winning and losing. In Super Bowl XXX, Neil O'Donnell of the Pittsburgh Steelers had better numbers in almost every category than Troy Aikman of the Dallas Cowboys—he threw for more yards, had more completions, and passed for more touchdowns. In other words, he had a pretty good day! Oh, yes—he also threw two interceptions. More than anything he did right, those critical errors—the two interceptions—made the difference in the game.

In baseball they keep track of the errors, and the walks, and the wild pitches. In football, they count the fumbles and the interceptions. And in basketball, the number of turnovers is an important statistic. There must be a reason why. And there is! The team that makes the fewest errors, the pitcher who gives up the fewest walks, and the quarterback who avoids the critical interception usually comes out on top. And the same ought to be true in the competitive arena of any industry.

The focus in business, however, is often very different. Perhaps it has to do with the emphasis of the business press and their fascination with the bold strategic move, the exciting new technology, the mega-merger, or the colorful charisma of the high-profile business leader. Perhaps it has to do with the proliferation of management consultants and advisors with a seemingly endless parade of "one size fits all" solutions in search of a problem. But reengineering, TQM, strategic outsourcing, empowerment, and the like, are not strategies. Nor are they solutions. Rather, they are tools, to be used only when appropriate as one of several elements in the implementation of a well-crafted strategy.

Have we lost our focus? It seems so. How many times does last year's high-flyer come crashing down in a spectacular failure? Or a promising entrepreneurial startup fail to get off the ground? All too often. Frequently, the autopsy (with the benefit of hindsight) reports a familiar cause of death—one of the handful of common strategic errors that seem to be made over and over again. We've worked with hundreds of companies over the years and conducted more than a few autopsies. As we reflect on our experiences, we've reached what now appears to be a fairly obvious conclusion:

> The best of strategies, poorly implemented, is of little value. A flawed strategy—no matter how brilliant the leadership, no matter how effective the implementation—is doomed to failure. A sound strategy, implemented without error, wins every time.

In football, a well-designed game plan falls apart when a team fumbles on its own five-yard line. In baseball, a superbly pitched game ends up in the loss column when the reliever blows a lead in the ninth inning. In business, excellent strategies often fail when errors are made in implementation. And even the best of leaders can't win with a fundamentally flawed strategy.

We're convinced that avoiding the common strategic error, the mistake that torpedoes an otherwise valid strategy or implementation, is the surest way to success. The strategy need not be brilliant, just sound and well conceived. It doesn't take the world's greatest leader to succeed in implementation, just one who doesn't make any really dumb mistakes. And it's not all that hard to avoid the most common strategic traps—*if you know what to look for*. But somehow, the same fundamental mistakes keep cropping up, again and again. Why?

We all know that we learn from experience, but most often we learn from our own mistakes, not from the mistakes of others. Why can't business leaders learn from the mistakes of their peers and predecessors? We've got two theories. First, strategies are about the future, and most strategists are, by nature, optimists. There's a natural tendency to focus on the positive side of future events, to assume that things will go right and work out as planned, and little attention is typically paid to what might go wrong. Second, even when strategists acknowledge the possibility of failure, they tend to see every situation as unique and thus discount the patterns of failure that might be discerned from a careful analysis of the mistakes made by others before them.

SEVEN STRATEGIC TRAPS

We believe there is much to be gained from examining the strategic failures of others. As we've sifted through the ashes of numerous failures, we've observed that the root causes are often closely similar, with only minor variations on the theme appearing in each individual case. We have identified seven of the most common causes of strategic failure and labelled them as the *seven strategic traps*. Although our list of errors is far from exhaustive, it is clearly representative. All too frequently organizations, as they formulate and attempt to implement their strategies, end up entangled in one or more of the following strategic traps:

- *Strategic Trap #1: Blind spots: Misreading the environmental tea leaves*
  Failing to recognize and understand the implications of events and changing conditions in the competitive environment.

- *Strategic Trap #2: Flawed assumptions: Right strategy — wrong problem*
  Basing strategies on a flawed set of assumptions or premises, or failing to react when changing circumstances render the initial assumptions and premises invalid.

- *Strategic Trap #3: Creating competitive (dis)advantage*
  Pursuing a one-dimensional strategy that fails to create or sustain a long-term competitive advantage.

- *Strategic Trap #4: Subtracting value by adding businesses*
  Diversifying, for all the wrong reasons, into areas of
  activity that fail to add value for investors.

Even sound strategies can fail in implementation—especially
when leaders are snared in one or more of the following strategic
traps:

- *Strategic Trap #5: Tripping over the barriers*
  Failing to structure and implement mechanisms to ensure
  the coordination and integration of core processes and key
  functions across organizational boundaries.
- *Strategic Trap #6: Arbitrary goals; unbalanced controls*
  Setting arbitrary and inflexible goals and implementing a
  system of controls that fails to achieve a balance among
  culture, rewards and boundaries.
- *Strategic Trap #7: A failure of leadership*
  Ignoring basic principles and failing to provide the
  leadership essential to the successful implementation
  of strategic change.

While any one of these strategic traps may, by itself, be sufficient to trigger a strategic failure, the ultimate collapse of an organization is most often caused by a combination of several problems.
Frequently, these strategic traps are closely intertwined, and an organization exhibiting the symptoms of one malady will likely be
vulnerable to another in relatively short order, compounding its
problems and making it even more difficult to recover. Clearly the
safest and surest path to strategic success lies in avoiding these pitfalls altogether.

Our admonition to proceed with due caution should not be interpreted as a call to adopt a defensive posture and hold your
ground, lest you commit a fatal error. On the contrary, we believe
that strategy-making should be externally focused, positive, and
proactive. Growth, innovation and the pursuit of opportunities are
the essence of most successful competitive strategies. The identification of innovative products or service opportunities, and the aggressive pursuit of new and expanded markets generally offer the
potential for greater returns than alternative strategic postures. We
would argue, however, that the blind pursuit of opportunity, while

ignoring the most common sources of strategic failure, is a high risk course of action less likely to result in success than it is in failure.

A SOUND STRATEGY, IMPLEMENTED WITHOUT ERROR

Our central theme is that a sound strategy, implemented without error, is far more likely to come home a winner than the most brilliant and innovative of strategies, poorly implemented. And even the most competent of leaders will struggle to succeed in executing a fundamentally flawed strategy. A well-crafted strategy that avoids the obvious strategic errors, coupled with an effectively managed implementation that steers clear of the most common strategic traps, is generally a winner. The organization's accomplishments may not put its leaders on the cover of *Fortune* or *Forbes*, but it is a winner by any account, as the successful implementation of a sound strategy creates jobs, generates profits, and provides returns for its shareholders. Thousands of well-managed companies, most of which you've probably never heard of, make our point.

If the surest way to success is the avoidance of strategic errors, how does one begin? Sound strategies: (1) begin with a clear and unbiased interpretation of conditions in the competitive environment, (2) reflect an internally consistent set of assumptions about organizational purpose and capabilities, (3) emphasize the organizational competencies that can provide sustainable competitive advantage, and (4) avoid unwarranted diversification that dilutes shareholder values. Error-free implementation requires: (5) effective mechanisms for coordination and integration, (6) a balanced approach to strategic control, and (7) the guidance and inspiration of an effective leader. Each of these ingredients is essential for success. None is sufficient by itself.

Our seven strategic traps are the antithesis of these basic requirements. Organizations that fail to anticipate and provide effectively for each of these needs are, in effect, wandering through an unfamiliar jungle wearing a blindfold. Such an approach is foolhardy and usually results in an untimely plunge into one or more of the common strategic traps that lie along the intended path.

2

CHAPTER

Blind Spots in the Competitive Vision

It's a complex and uncertain world "out there." It's tough to sort the wheat from the chaff and really understand what it all means. For most managers, it's a lot easier to focus on the relatively stable and familiar surroundings of one's own organization and the traditional assumptions and beliefs about the "rules of the game" in the immediate competitive environment. And, by and large, that's what they do. Our research suggests that many executives are fumbling around in the dark when it comes to implementing their strategies in the competitive arena. In a recent series of in-depth interviews, we asked the CEOs and top executives of a group of mid-sized high-technology firms what they thought they needed to know about the competition, and then to tell us how much they really knew about each of their three closest competitors. Less than a third indicated they had a good understanding of their competitors' products and customers, objectives and strategies, and basic resources and capabilities. Only 6 percent felt they understood their rivals' competitive postures, weapons, and tactics—*how* they competed. Nearly half admitted that they knew very little about their competitors, and that their "understanding" was based more on rumor and reputation than on actual facts.[1] Research on larger organizations, even those with formal competitor intelligence activities, suggests a similar pattern.[2]

If managers typically know very little about their closest competitors, how well do they understand the broader context of the general environment and its impacts on their organizations and its strategies?

Not very well, based on the available evidence. Even though ignoring the environment is the organizational equivalent of an ostrich avoiding danger by burying its head in the sand, it's not hard to find examples of companies whose strategies have foundered because they failed to note or understand the changing circumstances in their environments. Consider, for example, what happened to the A.T. Cross Company:

For decades, the sleek gold-filled and sterling silver pens made by the A.T. Cross Company dominated the luxury pen market, both in the United States and abroad. Cross pens were the standard in the corporate recognition market and had a solid retail presence in upscale jewelry and department stores. In 1989, the company netted a robust 14.6 percent ($36 million) on sales of $247 million. Then the bottom dropped out. Four short years later, the Lincoln, R.I.–based company was struggling to survive. In 1993, sales plunged by a third, to only $165 million, and the company reported its first-ever loss. The company eked out a narrow operating profit only by draconian cost-cutting. The workforce was slashed by nearly 40 percent from 2,000 employees in 1990 to less than 1,250 by the end of 1993. And the end was apparently not in sight. Although international sales had picked up in the first quarter of 1994, domestic sales were 21.6 percent lower than in the same quarter of the prior year.

What happened? According to Samuel Zagoory, co-owner of Manhattan's fancy Rebecca Moss Ltd. pen boutique, "Cross had the market locked for so long they took it for granted." "Having a Cross in your pocket used to be a symbol of success," according to Zagoory, "but by the Eighties, it was a Montblanc." For years, Cross had dominated the market with its slender, elegant design that retailed, depending on the model, for $25 to $60. Beginning in the 1980s, however, Americans began to pay much higher prices for pens of different shapes and styles. Germany's Montblanc Simplo GmbH, for example, began to erode Cross's market position by aggressively marketing its fat, black Meisterstuck fountain pen with a gold nib for $360 and more. In 1987, Gillette Co. bought the French penmaker, Waterman S.A, and introduced its line of expensive pens into the U.S. market. By the late 1980s, Cross found itself repositioned as a mid-priced offering and squeezed by foreign competitors in its traditional channels. Broadening its distribution into the mass merchandising channels to maintain volume narrowed its margins and further eroded its image as a status symbol. Fighting back, Cross launched an upscale line in 1990. Introduced into an already crowded luxury market, just as a recession was taking hold, the Signature line failed miserably. In 1993, the company introduced a new line of "fat" pens in overseas markets. Encouraged by brisk sales in Europe, the line was introduced in the United States, with heavy advertising support, in 1994. By 1995, both sales and profits were trending up, but were still far below the levels achieved in the late 1980s.[3]

Did the management of the A.T. Cross Co. really take the market for granted? Was it complacency, or were they just not paying attention? Did they focus their attention too narrowly—attending only to competitors who, like themselves, produced ballpoint pens—and fail to heed the entry of a new competitor (with a substitute technology) into the arena? Whatever the cause, the result was devastating—for the management team (who were replaced), for the employees (who lost their jobs), and for the shareholders (who lost their shirts).

Its not just the competition that bears watching. Encyclopedia Britannica, Inc., a dominant player in reference book publishing, stumbled badly when they misread the impact of CD-ROM technology on their traditional business:

The bigger they are, the harder they fall! And so it was with *Encyclopedia Britannica*. First published in 1768 in Edinburgh, Scotland, the Encyclopedia Britannica is now the largest (44 million words) and arguably the most authoritative reference book in the Western world. It wasn't much of a business until 1943, when the master salesman, William Benton, took over. Benton cut a royalty deal with the University of Chicago to provide editorial support and built a North American sales force (2,300 strong in 1992) that sold the $1,500 set of books for a $300 commission. Most of the sales were on the installment plan, with high interest rates that padded profit margins. When Benton died in 1974, he left the business to a charitable foundation. The University of Chicago became the sole beneficiary. After a couple of acquisitions (*Merriam-Webster* dictionaries and the low-end *Compton's Encyclopedia*), the company's revenues topped $650 million in 1990. Then things started to fall apart.

Home computers equipped with CD-ROM drives first appeared in the mid-80s. Electronic versions of several popular encyclopedias were introduced shortly thereafter. Grolier's introduced a text-only version in 1986. Britannica was one of the first to offer a true multimedia version, introducing a CD-ROM of *Compton's Encyclopedia* in 1990. The nine-million word edition was an instant hit. In the same year, Microsoft introduced *Encarta*, based on *Funk and Wagnall's New Encyclopedia*, a low-end product previously sold through supermarkets. *Encarta* now sells for less than $100. In 1994, World Book, Inc., introduced its multimedia version for $395, about half the price of its hard copy volumes.

Not wanting to risk offending its sales force, Encyclopedia Britannica dragged its feet on the development of a multimedia version, which, even in the two-volume CD-ROM required to deliver the full product, could only command about a third the price of the printed version and would offer a much smaller sales commission. Meanwhile, sales of conventional encyclopedias plunged. With much cheaper CD-ROM versions available, an increasing number of Britannica's customers defaulted on their installment sales contracts. Close rival World Book, Inc.'s sales fell 28 percent from 1990 to 1992. Revenues for the privately held Britannica were not released, but earnings plunged from $40 million in 1990 to a loss of $12 million in 1991, and its sales force collapsed, shrinking to less than 1,100 active representatives by the end of 1993. Strapped for cash, Britannica sold *Compton's* to Chicago's Tribune Co. for $57 million in 1993. As part of the deal, Britannica agreed not to publish a competing version for at least two years, effectively locking it out of the fast-growing multimedia market. Belatedly, Britannica announced that its flagship product would be made available to libraries (on a subscription basis) over the Internet within two years. A CD-ROM version of the Encyclopedia Britannica was finally introduced in 1995.[4]

Britannica was clearly aware of the availability and the potential of CD-ROM technology–their subsidiary, *Compton's Encyclopedia,* was one of the first to market with a true multimedia product. But somehow they failed to understand the impact this technology would have on their flagship product. It's not hard to understand how they might have looked at the high-end *Britannica* and the low-end *Compton's* as competing in separate markets. *Britannica's* strengths were its depth of editorial content (lots of text and relatively few pictures) and its effective, but traditional independent sales organization. *Compton's*, on the other hand, was targeted to a different niche in the market (shallower editorial content, fewer words and more pictures) and was sold through different channels. Despite *Compton's* success in multimedia, it's fairly easy to understand management's reluctance to alter its traditional formula at the high end. The failure, however, to recognize the impact of this new technology on the business as a whole was disastrous. Not only did Britannica miss an opportunity, but in the end, management painted themselves into a corner with the contractual obligation not to compete in an emerging segment that could have significantly expanded the market for their entire product line.

STRATEGIC TRAP #1: MISREADING THE ENVIRONMENTAL TEA LEAVES

Both the A.T. Cross Company and Encyclopedia Britannica fell victim to Strategic Trap #1: *Failing to recognize and understand the implications of events and changing conditions in their competitive enviroment.* Somehow, despite their long traditions of industry leadership, they missed, or misread, the initial signs of change that led, ultimately, to a significant erosion of their competitive position.

> *OK—you've made your point. Lots of companies (maybe even mine) need to pay more attention to what's going on around them. But how do you go about it? What should we be focusing on?*

FOCUSING ON THE ENVIRONMENT—THE CONTEXT OF STRATEGY

Every strategy is conceived and implemented within the context of the organization's understanding of its strategic environment. Just as an understanding of the dimensions of the playing field and a knowledge of the rules of the game is fundamental to an appreciation of sport, an understanding of the context of the strategic environment is essential to the development and successful implementation of strategy—whether in business or on the battlefield. According to Michael Porter, "The essence of formulating competitive strategy is relating a company to its environment."[5]

One of the great debates of academia is the question of which of two environments really matters: the *objective environment* of the real world or the *subjective environment* that exists as a "mental model" only in the mind of the strategist. In the competitive arena, the debate about fact or perceptions doesn't really matter. The issue of practical importance is the degree to which the strategist's perceptions and interpretations are consistent with the conditions that actually prevail in the environment—how closely the manager's "mental model" approximates objective reality.

In describing an organization's strategic context, a somewhat artificial distinction is often made between the *general environment* and the *industry environment*. The industry environment consists primarily of the organization and its customers, suppliers, and competitors and the interrelationships among them that make up the industry structure. The general environment consists of all of the other entities, forces, and factors that make up the broader economic, political, and social context. The organization's key stakeholders, its owners, managers, employees, customers, suppliers, and the communities in which they live and work are also an important part of the strategic context—sometimes in the background of the general environment, at other times as key factors in the industry environment. The boundaries between the general and the industry environments tend to be fuzzy and in a continuous state of flux.

The tendency to focus primarily on competitive rivalries in the current industry environment often shifts attention away from conditions and events in the general environment, but none of the industry participants exists in a vacuum. Continuous interaction among the forces and events in the general environment, and the actions and reactions, moves and countermoves, of the players in the arena creates a complex and unpredictable background against which an organization's strategies must be developed and implemented. In our view, the artificial distinction between the general and the industry environments minimizes the importance of these interactions and often leads to an overly narrow definition of an organization's strategic context.

We prefer to conceptualize the relevant competitive environment somewhat differently, as illustrated in Figure 2–1. This figure emphasizes the key elements of the organization's competitive environment, the mutual interactions between the organization and the various sectors of the environment, and the complex linkages that exist among these sectors. The relevant environment includes not only the customers, suppliers, and competitors traditionally associated with the industry environment, but certain selected dimensions

FIGURE 2–1

The Competitive Environment: Key Elements and Inter-dependencies

of the general environment as well. While acknowledging the importance of monitoring each of the sectors of the general environment, practical considerations focus attention only on the political, legal, economic, social, and technological dimensions that have direct and significant impact on the organization, its customers, and its competitors.

UNDERSTANDING THE ENVIRONMENT—SCANNING AND COMPETITOR INTELLIGENCE

Comprehensive normative guidelines for the conduct of environmental scanning and competitor intelligence have been proposed by a number of authors.[6] Unfortunately, the strengths of these methodologies, their comprehensiveness, is also their major limitation. Only a few of the very largest companies have sufficient slack resources to be able to support and maintain an ongoing program of sophisticated environmental scanning and competitor intelligence. The vast majority of organizations, for better or worse, "make do" without a consistent or organized effort to learn about their environments or understand their competitors.

While most managers will acknowledge the need for a better understanding of their strategic context, many are unwilling to invest the organizational resources necessary to implement an ongoing program of sophisticated competitor intelligence. New approaches are clearly required. These must be less intimidating in their scope and comprehensiveness, less consuming in their demand for resources, and more clearly capable of demonstrating their value in the near-term competitive environment. Our research on competitor intelligence in small and midsized organizations provides a starting point for the development of a more practical approach to competitor intelligence. We have found that most small and midsized organizations tend to define their information needs narrowly and to focus on those things that will have the most immediate impact on performance in the competitive arena. The message is clear: *focus and prioritize!*

Narrow the Focus

The key first step in developing a practical understanding of the competitive environment is to narrow the focus—to define what *is* relevant and what *is not*. We begin with the assumption that both market boundaries and a relevant set of competitors can be defined in the same frame of reference. Researchers have argued that the definition of the boundaries of an organization's competitive space involves a progressively narrowed focus. "The definition of industry boundaries requires consideration of four interrelated issues: *domain* (where does the industry begin and end); *customer groups* (sectors to be served and their specific needs); *customer functions* (customer needs and purchasing patterns); and *critical technologies* (production, marketing and administrative systems). These factors should be considered simultaneously, otherwise the firm will err in selecting its competitive arena." Starting with the definition of an *industry domain*—a general class of product or service that satisfies a broad category of customers—the focus is progressively narrowed to a group of targeted customers, a more specific definition of the customer need to be met, and, finally, a particular way of meeting that need through a unique combination of product and delivery system technologies.[7]

In our research, we found that the top executives of product-oriented firms most often focused on product-market characteristics—defining their own organizations and their competitors narrowly in terms of the intersection of a set of products and a specific group of current and/or targeted customers. Service-oriented firms, on the other hand, tended to focus more on the production and delivery technologies—organizational resources and capabilities. There are no hard and fast rules—the important thing to keep in mind is that the definition of the business has significant implications:

> an underlying definition of the business acts as a cognitive reference point around which managers conceptualize an organization's competitive position. A business definition is a stable focusing device that orients the attention of managers toward some sectors of the environment and away from others.[8]

Different perspectives, based on different definitions of the boundaries of the industry, will frequently lead to very different understandings about what kinds of things are important in the competitive environment.

Identify the Key Players

The next logical step in sorting out what is relevant in the competitive environment is to identify the key players: current and potential customers, suppliers, strategic alliance partners, and competitors. In addition, it is important to identify an organization's stakeholders and understand their objectives and priorities. Research shows that managers rely heavily on "mental models" to organize and make sense of the complexity and diversity of organizational forms in their competitive environments.[9] These mental models take the form of hierarchical classification schemes (cognitive taxonomies) and are used to systematically organize and summarize the differences among organizations. A traditional organization chart that displays, in a hierarchical form, the functional breakdown of an organization into functional departments, geographic locations, and specific work groups is a taxonomy.

By grouping things (organizations) into categories, a strategist simplifies the process of understanding them and their various interrelationships. An industry taxonomy for the computer industry might define categories, at the first level, in terms of hardware, software, and services. The software category, at the next level, might be broken down into operating systems, utilities and applications software, and the like. Researchers have found that strategists tend to describe their own organizations using the label of a specific category within the industry taxonomy and to identify other firms within the same category as their closest competitors. Firms categorized into other branches of the taxonomy are generally considered not to be close competitors. While this "stereotyping" of organizations simplifies cognitive processing, it can also lead to problems, particularly when competitive circumstances change but the category labels applied to organizations do not.

Although research has established the existence of cognitive taxonomies and documented their use as a framework for understanding industries and identifying competitors, these structures tend to be implicit rather than explicit. We have found that developing explicit industry taxonomies and identifying the organizations competing at each branch and level of the structure is a useful exercise that helps managers to focus on both current and potential competitors. Considerable insight is gained by discussing why one organization is considered a competitor and another is not. Similarly, a better understanding of potential competitors can be achieved by asking what changes in strategy, market focus, or capability might cause a noncompetitor to be considered a competitor. There is no reason why a similar approach could not be productively used to focus on the important characteristics of an organization's customers or its network of suppliers and potential alliance partners.

Peter Drucker has provided another interesting perspective on identifying and understanding customers.[10] Making a distinction between being *customer-driven* and being *market-driven*, he argues that identifying and understanding current customers is only a first step. While it is important to understand a firm's customers, he suggests that it is even more important to understand an organization's *noncustomers:* "The first signs of fundamental change rarely appear within one's own organization or among one's own customers. Almost always they show up first among one's noncustomers. Noncustomers always outnumber customers. Wal-Mart, today's retail giant, has 14% of the U.S. consumer goods market. That means 86% of the market is noncustomers."

Define What Is Critical—Then Prioritize

Once the key players in the industry environment have been identified, the focus shifts to the kinds of information about them that must be gathered and analyzed. Again, the emphasis must be on *focus* and *prioritization.* The same rules apply to developing an understanding of the relevant technological, economic, social, cultural, government, legal, and regulatory factors in the general environment. Even an organization with unlimited resources will be quickly overwhelmed if it fails to decide what kinds of things are important and must be monitored closely, what is less important and can be observed more casually, and what is inconsequential and can safely be ignored.

As an example of this "sorting out" process, we will turn to our research on how managers identify and come to understand their competitors. We have found that strategists typically define their "competitive space" in terms of the intersection of their organization's product-service offering with a set of current and targeted customers. They identify an organization as a competitor only if it (*a*) enters or threatens to enter the "competitive space" claimed by the strategist's firm; and (*b*) represents a credible threat to the competitive position of the strategist's firm. In determining whether or not an organization represents a credible threat in the competitive arena, strategists rely most frequently on an assessment of its technology resources and delivery systems, its competitive posture (how it competes), and its reputation and legitimacy in the industry.

In sorting out what they need to know about their competitors, strategists tend to prioritize their information needs in terms of three criteria: (1) how important is the activity to overall success in the competitive arena? (2) what is the likely impact on near-term performance? and (3) how likely is it that things will change in the near term? Those factors that most directly affect the customer's decision to purchase were considered most important to competitive success. Thus the features, pricing, and price/performance characteristics of competitive product-service offerings and the effectiveness and competitive postures of their marketing and sales organizations were highest on the priority list. Technology resources and reputation-legitimacy in the industry were also important. The focus on near-term performance again directed their attention toward the product-customer interface, with less interest in the competitor's longer-term plans and underlying resource capabilities.

The strategists also tended to focus on those dimensions and characteristics that were subject to more frequent change, and to rely on the assumption that other dimensions will not change much in the short run. Products, pricing, marketing, sales and service tactics, and competitive postures are all subject to frequent change in response to conditions in the competitive environment. Basic objectives and strategies; engineering, operations, and manufacturing resources; organization and management; financial resources; ownership and reputation/legitimacy tend to remain stable over relatively longer time horizons. A similar approach can be applied to understanding product evolution. In the automobile industry, although frequent (annual) changes are made to highly visible components (colors, finishes, sheet metal panels, accessories, etc.), many of the basic components (frames, power trains, braking systems, heating and cooling systems, etc.) remain unchanged for years, and in some cases, decades. In personal computers, software and processor chips are upgraded every few months; more basic components like power supplies, disk drives, memory controllers, and the like are often stable for years.

Similar criteria should be developed within each organization to define and prioritize an organization's information needs about the technological, regulatory, economic, and other factors in the general environment. Retailers, for example, should be vitally interested in consumer credit and spending patterns; industrial finance companies in capital spending plans; military contractors in defense procurement reforms. None of these dimensions would, however, be of great interest or importance to the others.

AVERTING DISASTER—AVOIDING THE BLIND SPOTS

Researchers have identified a number of potential "blind spots" in environmental analysis—ways that firms either *miss* or *misinterpret* events or changes in their environments that may have significant performance implications. For example, similar organizations may define and understand their competitive environments very differently, leading to different strategies and different approaches to competition.

In early 1994, the market research firm, NPB Group, Inc., shocked the video game industry with its report that Sega Enterprises, Ltd. had captured a 63 percent share of the 16-bit game-player market during the 1993 Christmas season, as compared to 37 percent for Nintendo. Sega had gotten its 16-bit player to market earlier than Nintendo, had clearly won this round, and was expected to pass Nintendo as the industry leader in 1994.[11]

In reaction, Horoshi Yamauchi, president of the industry-leading video game maker, Nintendo Co., dismissed his critics as "naive" and "ignorant," and opined that the information highway and the coming "multimedia revolution" were mostly hype: "Multimedia is just a word, and that word is running ahead of the substance . . ." Nintendo was trimming costs and focusing its resources on the next generation of video-game players. Yamauchi emphasized that Nintendo would "concentrate on just one point—improving the quality of games in the current market."

Sega, meanwhile, was broadening its focus through a series of strategic alliances with AT&T, Yamaha, Hitachi, Matsushita, and JVC, and launching virtual reality theme parks, cable TV game channels, and interactive games to be played across the phone lines. Sega clearly held a very different view of the future. Sega's president Hayao Nakayama believed that multimedia and the information highway would lead to "a tectonic shift in society." Dismissing Nintendo's narrow perspective, Mr. Nakayama said, simply: "I don't consider Nintendo our competitor anymore."

These two companies clearly had a different understanding of the boundaries of the relevant competitive environment, different visions of where the industry was headed, and very different ideas about how to get there. By late 1995, Nintendo continued to lag in technology as new entrant Sony Computer Entertainment, Inc., mounted a strong challenge to Sega for market dominance.

Different perspectives will frequently lead to very different understandings about the kinds of things that are important in the competitive environment, and more importantly, may blind an organization to opportunity or prevent the early identification of potential competitors. Obviously, some firms just aren't paying attention. The story of the A.T. Cross Company suggests that complacency sometimes plays a role. Others seem to understand their core markets, but repeatedly stumble when they try to move into new segments, perhaps assuming similarities or synergies where none exist. In 1993, Apple Computer grossly overestimated the potential for the Newton personal digital assistant. Apparently, in the immortal words of Yogi Berra, it was "*deja vu* all over again" in 1995.

In early 1995, Apple Computer, with new management and on the rebound from the abortive introduction of the Newton handheld computer, announced a new strategy. In addition to upgrading and enhancing the high end of its Macintosh line, it would begin a major push into the burgeoning home computing market with the low-end Macintosh Performa. A year later, in January 1996, Apple announced a major restructuring with layoffs of up to 23 percent of the current work force in response to major operating losses in 1995's fourth quarter. Additional losses were projected for the first quarter of 1996. Although vague about the details, Apple indicated that the basic thrust of the restructuring would be to concentrate on the higher end of the education, home, and business markets, de-emphasizing less profitable markets such as the entry-level computers for consumers.

In reporting the story, *The Wall Street Journal* reporter observed that "Apple faces myriad problems besides bloated operations. Despite having some of the most elegant and versatile computers on the market, it has been incapable of properly forecasting how much customers want them, repeatedly undershooting or overshooting on demand . . . the company grossly underestimated demand of its higher-priced computers for much of last year while overestimating how many consumers would want entry-level ones . . . "[12]

Organizations often ignore or misinterpret environmental signals that are inconsistent with their assumptions about the "formula" for competitive success. There is a natural tendency for individuals and organizations, seemingly indifferent to changing market conditions, to stick with strategies that have succeeded in the past and avoid those that have been less successful. Consider the case of Bacardi Imports, Inc., a family-owned company whose strong traditions and beliefs, reinforced by years of commercial success, made it difficult to react to a changing environment.

Bacardi Imports, Inc., the U.S. distribution arm of Bahamas-based Bacardi Ltd., still boasts the top-selling liquor brand in the United States despite the worst sales decline in modern spirits history. After virtually uninterrupted growth for nearly three decades, U.S. sales of Bacardi light rum fell sharply from 8.7 million cases in 1991 to only 6.4 million in 1993. Higher wholesale prices were blamed at first, but sales have not rebounded since the increases were rolled back.

This staunchly conservative company is still run by descendants of Don Facundo Bacardi, who began selling rum from a tin shed in Santiago, Cuba, in 1962. "We've always tried to develop brands that would last 100 years," says Vice-President Thomas Valdes. In a rapidly changing market, however, Bacardi is falling behind the times.

Consumer tastes have changed, with vodka-and-juice-based drinks replacing the Cuba Libre (rum and coke) as the alcoholic beverage of choice among young drinkers. Stiffer competition has also emerged in the form of Captain Morgan Spiced Rum and new imported beverages, such as Jaegermeister, a bitter herb-flavored liqueur. These new brands typically do little advertising, but are aggressively promoted in college bars by teams of scantily clad young women called "Morganettes" and "Jaegerettes." The bars have an incentive as well, as liquor sales are considerably more profitable than beer. Bacardi has resisted change and been slow to respond. The company reluctantly introduced Bacardi Breezer, a spiced rum cooler, in 1990, after two years of test marketing. The launch was successful, but the brand stagnated as Bacardi was slow to adopt the aggressive promotional tactics of its competitors.[13]

Changing demographics often produce shifts in consumer buying habits. Frequently these changes occur over long periods, providing ample opportunity for organizations to identify these trends and make appropriate adjustments. Organizational inertia is powerful, however, and change often occurs only when it is forced. Organizations with substantial investments in or emotional ties to their existing product development resources, production systems, or channels of distribution often find it difficult to respond appropriately to new competitive realities, particularly when they have enjoyed years of success.

Hallmark, the world's largest greeting card company, had 1994 sales of $3.8 billion, more than twice those of its nearest rival, American Greetings. For most of the 20th century, Hallmark has sold its cards primarily through a network of over 10,000 specialty shops, 216 of which are company-owned, ensuring high margins and control over pricing. Yet, as industry sales and profits have soared, Hallmark's market share is slipping, profits have been flat or down since 1990, and return on equity has slipped from traditional levels of 15 to 20 percent to 8 percent in 1994.

Over the last 20 years, consumer buying patterns have shifted as more working women (who purchase 90 percent of all greeting cards) opted for the convenience of "one stop shopping." At one time, 65 percent of all greeting cards were sold through specialty shops; that figure is less than 30 percent today and shrinking rapidly, with drugstores, supermarkets, and discounters taking up the slack. As an initial response, Hallmark offered a discount line to these channels. The Ambassador line now accounts for 19 percent of the company's sales, but in the process, it has cannibalized the Hallmark brand and diluted the company's margins.

In 1990, Hallmark pioneered the personalized card, installing an employee-assisted in-store system to print personalized greetings for the consumer. These systems are now operational in 2,200 Hallmark shops. American Greetings has leapfrogged over Hallmark, however, with its more highly automated kiosks. Within 15 months after the October 1992 launch, American Greetings had more than 7,000 automated kiosks in place in a variety of retail outlets. Meanwhile, Hallmark was playing catch-up again. In reaction to American Greetings' success Hallmark began a rollout of automated kiosks in the second half of 1993.[14]

Just as the old adage "success begets success" doesn't always apply. Experience and success in one industry or market does not necessarily transfer to a different competitive environment. As we will see in the next example, Robert Goodfriend, the founder of Goody's Family Clothing, Inc., learned this lesson *twice* in the same encounter. In management, success in academia doesn't transfer easily to the real world; in merchandising, what works in the big city may well be a disaster in the country town.[15]

Robert Goodfriend was a success by almost any standard. Having built the family business, a chain of retail clothing outlets in small southern towns, to a profitable $273 million in sales in 1990, Goodfriend cashed in, selling 37 percent of the stock of Goody's Family Clothing, Inc., to the public. Shortly thereafter, he launched an aggressive expansion program, with the goal of $1 billion in sales by 1997. By 1993, Goodfriend concluded he needed professional management help to take the company to the next level. He hired Roger Jenkins, a professor of marketing and Dean of the University of Tennessee's business school, as the company's new president. To bolster his own lack of business experience, Jenkins hired George Rubin, merchandise manager of Lerner New York, to head merchandising. In the midst of the expansion program, Jenkins and Rubin decided to realign Goody's merchandising mix to narrow the assortment of styles and bring it more into line with national fashion trends.

Eighty percent of Goody's stores are in small southern towns with less than 75,000 people. In these small towns, without a wide range of shops, customers are more likely to do all of their shopping in one store. The new merchandise mix "might have worked in the New York suburbs," but it clearly wasn't a hit in the more conservative markets of central Kentucky. While revenues more than doubled from 1990 to 1994, comparable store sales growth declined and margins virtually disappeared. Goodfriend, seeing his net worth evaporate rapidly, tried to convince Jenkins to go back to the old formula. He refused. Things quickly got ugly as Goodfriend and Jenkins battled for control of the board. Jenkins won the first round and threw Goodfriend out. Goodfriend won the next round in the courts, and fired not only Jenkins, but the entire board as well. Back to the old formula with Goodfriend again running the show, sales were beginning to recover in 1995, but Goody's was still taking markdowns on some of the trendy "big city" merchandise.

Sometimes, the entry of a new competitor or a substitute technology will change the entire structure of an industry. Overnight, the accepted "formula" for success no longer applies. Such was the effect of the mini-mills on Big Steel and the impact of the open architectures of the personal computer on the traditional vertical structures of IBM, DEC, and other old-line computer manufacturers. When such a paradigm shift occurs, those that recognize the change and understand its implications are frequently able to adapt and survive. Those that fail to do so are vulnerable and often stumble badly. Home Depot effectively changed the rules and the formula for success in building products retailing with its huge self-service warehouse stores. The very different responses of two regional firms that dominated their markets prior to the entry of Home Depot illustrate this point.[16]

Atlanta-based Home Depot left a lot of competitors in the dust as it grew to revenues of more than $15 billion in less than 20 years, pioneering the concept of warehouse shopping for tools and building supplies. Until Home Depot began its national expansion in the early 1980s, the business was dominated by regional chains like Wickes Lumber in the West, Lowe's in the Southeast, and Grossman's in New England.

Grossman's, a family business around since 1895, virtually pioneered do-it-yourself home centers. In 1969, the family sold the business to Evans Products, a conglomerate that saw the business as a cash cow, rather than as a growth property worthy of further investment. The company eventually ended up in bankruptcy in 1985. In 1986, before Home Depot opened a single store in the Northeast, Grossman's emerged from bankruptcy with Mike Grossman, a descendent of the founder, at the helm. Grossman's regional dominance gave it a false sense of security, however, and it moved cautiously to modernize its chain of small, out-of-date stores. By 1989, Grossman's had built only one modern warehouse store, while Home Depot had entered the market with six mega-stores. Fading fast, Grossman's 1995 revenues are expected to be down more than 30 percent from their 1988 levels.

Lowe's almost met the same fate, initially underestimating the appeal of Home Depot's massive stores with their 50,000-item inventories. In 1989, the year Home Depot passed its regional competitor as the number one do-it-yourself retailer, Lowe's commissioned an exit survey of its customers. What they learned was unnerving, but they responded decisively and moved quickly to upgrade their stores to match the successful Home Depot formula. In addition, they added indoor-outdoor garden centers and special centers for the sale of high-margin power tools. In markets too small to support a full-scale superstore, they have augmented the product mix with appliances, televisions, and computers. The first new store opened in 1990. By late 1995, 68 percent of the stores had been modernized, Lowe's was growing, profitable, and holding its own against the competition.

Sometimes, the problem is bigger than the competition. Even Wal-Mart is not invincible.[17] Arguably the most successful retailer in history, over the past 25 years, Wal-Mart has successfully invaded the home turf of countless weaker rivals and dispatched each in turn. The undisputed heavyweight champ of the discount retailers, Wal-Mart had demonstrated its immunity to the vagaries of the business cycle by racking up 99 consecutive quarters of earnings growth as it gobbled up market share from its weaker competitors. In its 1994 annual report and at the 1995 annual meeting, it had proudly boasted of the impending arrival, in January 1996, of its 100th consecutive quarterly earnings gain. *So what happened on the way to the celebration?* Oops! Profits for the quarter ended January 31, 1996, were down 11 percent, the poorest showing in the company's 25-year history as a public company. The value of its shares dropped 9 percent in a single day. A Wal-Mart spokesman blamed the shortfall on sluggish Christmas spending and increasing consumer debt: "People have to pay off their debts before we'll see a significant increase in consumer spending."

Even the giant may have an Achilles' heel. Apparently, Wal-Mart has grown so large and pervasive that, although it may have out-run its competitors, it has become increasingly vulnerable to the ups and downs of the overall economy. And apparently, it was so accustomed to a never-ending stream of financial success that it failed to recognize, in its predictions and forecasts, the impact that increasing consumer debt and economic uncertainty would have on its retail sales during the 1995 Christmas season.

SPOTTING THE OPPORTUNITY

Environmental analysis isn't just about avoiding competitive disaster. Spotting opportunities is equally important. Those who successfully read the tea leaves are often rewarded handsomely, as the phenomenal success of Kinko's Graphics, Inc., will attest:[18]

Paul Orfalea has a sharp eye for an opportunity. The founder and owner of Kinko's Graphics, Inc., not only saw an opportunity and seized it, but has managed to stay well out in front of the competition in a simple business whose formula ought to be easy to imitate.

As a student at the University of Southern California in 1971, Paul Orfalea reckoned he could do just fine for himself by undercutting the university library's 10-cent per page charge for copy services. With a $5,000 bank loan, he rented a former hamburger stand near the campus of the University of California at Santa Barbara, leased a small Xerox copier, and set up shop in competition with the University. At only 4 cents per copy, the business took off. Taking in other students as partners, but always retaining control, he opened stores near most of the major university campuses up and down the West Coast. By 1990, he controlled 480 Kinko's outlets.

Competition was inevitable, but Orfalea always seems to be one step ahead. Recognizing an opportunity to provide more sophisticated graphics services to small businesses and the self-employed, Orfalea shifted his focus and began opening larger stores near business districts and in the suburbs. To get a leg up on local printers and franchised competitors like Sir Speedy and Pip Printing, Kinko's targets small business by advertising itself as "your branch office." They also offer better service—24 hour-a-day, seven day-a-week access to self-service copiers and computers with word processing and graphics software, high-speed and color copying services, and a wide range of value-added services.

There were probably hundreds, maybe even thousands, of students who interpreted the library's inflated pricing for Xerox copies as a "ripoff," but only one who saw the opportunity. What made Paul Orfalea different? Sure, he was an entrepreneur, willing to take risks, willing to work hard. Lots of people are willing to work hard, lots of people are willing to take risks (at least with other people's money). But only a few are really good at spotting an opportunity. Paul Orfalea obviously has a knack—and the ability to keep his formula fresh as the market matures and a shift in focus is required. The difference, perhaps, is not so mysterious. We suspect it is more a matter of orientation than any unique skill. People who spot opportunities are externally aware and curious about the world about them. And this curiosity is broadly focused. Bill Gates, describing his first meeting with Warren Buffet, described the encounter this way, "He asked good questions and told educational stories. There's nothing I like so much as learning, and I had never met anyone who thought about business in such a clear way."[19] We have observed that most successful entrepreneurs have a broad range of interests—they are committed to their business, but at the same time are fascinated by technology, interested in the arts, obsessive golfers, fanatic sports fans, and so on. When they see something interesting they invariably ask why or how. This natural curiosity leads them to observe, to learn, and to recognize patterns and discontinuities in their environments.

By contrast, many managers are literally "wrapped up in their work," with blinders so tight that they see or pay attention to very little beyond the narrowly defined boundaries of their own organization and its immediate competitive environment. Recall the earlier example of Nintendo and Sega. Which organization is more likely to spot the next opportunity in electronic amusement?

In small entrepreneurial organizations, one externally aware visionary is probably enough. In larger organizations, however, the CEO can't do it all by himself. He can, however, create and reinforce a culture that is sensitive to and aware of its environment, curious about its surroundings, and responsive to the early signals of change. One individual within an organization who recognizes a potential opportunity or sees the first signs of impending danger is not enough. The organization must also be capable of responding in an appropriate fashion. Internal processes and procedures must be developed to ensure that the pieces of the puzzle are assembled and brought to management's attention. The organization must also be prepared to act, as the story of Chrysler's successful introduction of the front-wheel-drive minivan, and Ford and GM's failures, will attest.[20]

Chrysler's minivan is one of the most profitable consumer products ever built. First to market with a front-wheel-drive vehicle, Chrysler has virtually owned this segment of the market, and the minivan has kept the struggling automaker afloat during some of its darkest hours. In the first quarter of 1994, its 47 percent market share accounted for more than 25 percent of Chrysler's revenues and nearly two-thirds of its record $918 million in profits.

Chrysler's smashing success in producing the most profitable model line in Detroit (average gross profit of $6,100 per vehicle), has been a source of embarrassment for both Ford and General Motors. Each had a chance to get to the showroom before Chrysler, but failed to seize the opportunity. In the late 1970s all three U.S. automakers began to look for ways to modernize their existing vans, shrink them, improve fuel economy, and broaden their appeal. All three converged on the same technical solution—a front-wheel-drive minivan with creature comforts more often associated with station wagons than with the trucks upon which the existing vans were based.

Both GM and Ford had market research that supported the viability of the product in the late 1970s, but funding constraints and personalities blocked further development. At Ford, Lee Iacocca and Hal Sperlich actually came up with a prototype in 1974 and proposed it to Henry Ford II, who rejected the idea as too expensive and too risky. Sperlich continued to press the issue and eventually, in 1977, was fired by Ford and moved on to Chrysler. A year later Iacocca also fell out of favor and departed. When he left, Iacocca (with Ford's permission) took the customer research on the minivan with him. Reunited with Sperlich when he took the reins at Chrysler in late 1978, Iacocca made the minivan a top priority, and the product was introduced in the fall of 1983. GM and Ford have been playing catch-up ever since.

Just spotting the opportunity is not enough. Ford and GM saw the same trends, had access to similar market research (in Ford's case, the same), and had greater resources than Chrysler, but missed the opportunity because internal barriers such as priorities, cultures, and organizational politics got in the way. This example highlights the problem of the internal barriers that impede the free flow of information within the organization (more about this in Chapter 6). Often, early signals of environmental change may be detected at various points of interface with the environment, but they are not recognized as important because they have arrived in piecemeal fashion, from multiple sources, and at different points in time. No one individual ever has enough pieces early enough in the process to begin to assemble the puzzle. Even worse, vital information may be obtained but not acted upon because "it's not my job," or "I didn't think it was important."

PUTTING THE PIECES TOGETHER

Successful organizations got that way because they spotted an opportunity and made the most of it. Those that remain successful are also good at identifying threats and positioning themselves to counter them. Too often, however, companies forget or "unlearn" the skills of environmental awareness and competitor intelligence and find themselves missing opportunities, stagnating in the marketplace, and strategically vulnerable to the entry of new competitors or adverse events and changes in the external environment. Companies that want to be successful, or those that are successful and want to stay that way, must avoid blind spots in their competitive vision. We recommend four key areas on which to focus your efforts.

Understand the Strategic Context

Competitive strategy must be based on the solid foundation of a clear and complete understanding of the strategic context. The framework outlined earlier in this chapter will provide a useful starting point for any organization. The key steps include: (1) defining the boundaries of the organization's "competitive space"; (2) identifying the key players, both current and potential: customers, suppliers, competitors, and alliance partners; (3) defining what is critical and prioritizing information needs; (4) gathering and interpreting the necessary information; and, (5) sharing it widely within the organization.

Create a Culture of Environmental Awareness

Hundreds of pairs of eyes and ears will clearly be more effective than one or two in detecting the early signals of environmental change. "Boundary-spanners" at both ends of the value chain are important sources of environmental intelligence. In most organizations the sales force and distribution network is closer to the customer and sees a lot more of the competition than the top management team. Engineers and purchasing agents have more contact with suppliers and alliance partners. Yet, in most organizations, these resources are rarely asked about their knowledge of the environment and the competition. In order to tap this valuable resource, the CEO must do at least three things: (1) create a culture of environmental awareness by sharing her understanding of the strategic context and making the organization aware of what kinds of trends and events in the environment are important to the organization; (2) ask for their help; and, (3) create internal processes and incentives to ensure that important environmental and competitor information is captured and communicated in a timely fashion.

Ensure the Free Flow of Information

Barriers to effectively sharing environmental information and competitor intelligence cannot be allowed to blind the organization. Intelligence is useful only if it gets to the right place in a timely fashion and is interpreted correctly, so that appropriate action may be taken. Effective leadership actions must be taken to ensure that information is shared freely within the organization.

Provide Structure and Focus to the Intelligence Process

Very few organizations can afford to structure and staff dedicated environmental scanning and competitor intelligence operations. Those that have tried have struggled with numerous problems and achieved, at best, mixed results. Most organizations, particularly smaller and midsized companies, do nothing at all, and in return, know very little about their competitive environments. There is a middle ground. Most organizations, by clearly focusing on a limited set of priorities and providing a little structure and direction, can significantly improve their internal environmental awareness and competitor intelligence processes. Key ingredients include: (1) clear definition of information needs and priorities; (2) a designated focal point for gathering and disseminating competitor information; (3) a straightforward process to get important information to the focal point in a timely manner; (4) effective analysis and interpretation of the information; and (5) regular feedback to the organization to share important insights, encourage continued support, and provide examples of the kind of information that is of value. How these activities are accomplished will vary depending on the size and resources available to the organization. It is important to recognize, however, that even a modest amount of structure and focus will provide significantly better results than none at all.

STRATEGIC INVENTORY

Does your organization understand its strategic context?

- Who are your customers? Who are your noncustomers? Why?

- Who are your competitors? What are their strengths and weaknesses? How do they stack up against yours?

- Who are your key suppliers? How dependent are you on their skills and expertise? What would happen if a competitor acquired one of them? What alternatives are available?

- What are your organization's strengths and weaknesses? What would your competitors say? Are you vulnerable? Could a competitor exploit your weakness?
- What are the key technologies that make a difference in your industry? How are they likely to change over the next few years? How would these changes impact your organization?
- How important to your strategy is stability in the political/legal/regulatory environment? What changes are anticipated? What difference would it make?
- How important to your strategy is stability in the economic/social/cultural environment? What changes are anticipated? What difference would it make?
- How are your relations with organizational stakeholders? Are they partners or adversaries? Does it make a difference? How could these relationships be managed to strengthen your organization?

Is your organization environmentally aware?

- Does a culture of environmental awareness exist in your organization?
- Do key boundary-spanners know what to look for? Who to watch? What your intelligence priorities are?
- Do key boundary-spanners know you want their help? Are there incentives for them to do this critical job?
- Are the processes and procedures in place to ensure that intelligence gets to the right place in a timely fashion?

Does important information flow freely within the organization?

- Are effective communications a priority within the organization?
- Are mechanisms in place to ensure that environmental information and competitor intelligence gets to the right place in a timely fashion?

Does the intelligence process have structure and focus?

- Are information needs and priorities clearly defined?
- Is there a designated focal point for the collection and interpretation of environmental intelligence and competitor information?
- Is there an effective process for the expeditious handling of important intelligence data?
- Is the information analyzed and interpreted effectively?
- Is environmental intelligence and competitor information shared, as appropriate, throughout the organization?

ENDNOTES

1. Picken, Joseph C. December 1995. *Organizational Attributes in Competitor Identification and Competitor Intelligence.* Unpublished doctoral dissertation, University of Texas at Arlington.
2. See, for example, Prescott, John E. and Daniel C. Smith. May-June 1989. The largest survey of "leading edge" competitor intelligence managers, *Planning Review*: 6–13; and Lenz, R.T. and Jack L. Engledow, 1986. Environmental analysis units and strategic decision-making: A field study of selected "leading edge" corporations. *Strategic Management Journal* 7: 68–89.
3. Schuman, Michael. May 9, 1994. Thin is out, fat is in: A.T. Cross Co. missed the move to $300 luxury pens. Can Russell Boss recoup? *Forbes*: 92–94; Demaio, Don. April 29, 1994. Cross points to new line of pens for turnaround. *Providence Business News*, May 9, 1994; Tooher, Nora. Cross sees recovery in sales, earnings. *Providence Business News*; Mook, Bradley L. January 26, 1996. A.T. Cross Company. *Value Line*: 1119.
4. Samuels, Gary. February 28, 1994. CD-ROM's first big victim, *Forbes*: 42–44; Reid, Calvin and Maureen O'Brien. April 13, 1992. Donnelly, Compton Join in Electronic Publishing Push, *Publisher's Weekly*: 9; Miller, James P. July 7, 1993. Tribune to Acquire Compton's Group from Britannica, *The Wall Street Journal*: B7, B8; Gardner, Elizabeth. April 18, 1994. Encyclopedia goes on-line with Internet. *Crain's Chicago Business*; Anonymous, October 1995. Britannica upgrades CD Encyclopedia. *Information Today* 12(9): 30
5. One of the most comprehensive treatments of the problem of environmental analysis is found in Michael Porter's *Competitive Strategy: Techniques for analyzing industries and competitors*, published by The Free Press, New York, 1980. Porter's focus is primarily on the industry

environment, arguing that "the key aspect of the firm's environment is the industry . . . in which it competes".

6. Comprehensive guidelines and methodologies have been developed and recommended by Porter, M.E. 1980. *Competitive Strategy: Techniques for analyzing industries and competitors.* The Free Press, New York; Fuld, Leonard M. 1985. *Competitor Intelligence: How to get it; how to use it.* John Wiley & Sons, New York; Fuld, Leonard M. 1988. *Monitoring the Competition.* John Wiley & Sons, New York; and Gilad, Benjamin and Tamar Gilad, *The Business Intelligence System: A new tool for competitive advantage.* American Management Association, New York. These treatments are the most comprehensive; numerous other articles have appeared in *Long Range Planning, the Planning Review, Academy of Management Review, Strategic Management Journal* and similar journals.

7. Zahra, Shaker A. and Sherry S. Chaples. 1993. Blind spots in competitive analysis. *Academy of Management Review* 7(2): 7–27; Abell, Derek E. 1980. *Defining the Business.* Englewood Cliffs, NJ. Prentice-Hall.

8. Porac, Joseph F. and Howard Thomas. 1994. Cognitive categorization and subjective rivalry among retailers in a small city, *Journal of Applied Psychology* 79(1): 54–66.

9. Research by Porac and Thomas and their associates at the University of Illinois have developed a theory of competitor identification based on cognitive categorization theory that is solidly grounded in a substantial body of psychological research. The theory is outlined in: Porac, Joseph F. and Howard Thomas. 1990. Taxonomic mental models in competitor definition. *Academy of Management Review* 15(2): 224–240 and has been supported by a number of empirical studies, including a recent study by Dr. Picken.

10. Drucker, Peter F. 1994. The theory of the business. *Harvard Business Review.* Sept-Oct: 95–104.

11. This example draws on a number of diverse sources, including: Hamilton, David P. February 14, 1994. Video-Game Leaders Diverge on Multimedia's Future, *The Wall Street Journal*: A1, A6; Carlton, Jim. February 14, 1994. Sega Gains, Nintendo Slips in Segment, *The Wall Street Journal*: A1, A6; Levenson, A. February 21, 1994. SEGA! *Business Week*: 66–70; Williams, Scott. March 10, 1994. Nintendo, Sega marketing duel intensifies with rating debate. *Seattle Times*; McGann, Michael E. October 1995. Crossing Swords. *Dealerscope Merchandising* 37(10): 63, 65.

12. Carlton, Jim. January 18, 1996. Apple's Losses to Stretch into 2nd Period. *The Wall Street Journal*: B3.

13. Hwang, Suein L. May 13, 1994. Young Drinkers Do Shots in Potent New Flavors. *The Wall Street Journal*: B1; Hwang, Suein L. July 6, 1994. As Rivals Innovate, Old-Line Bacardi Becomes a Chaser. *The*

Wall Street Journal; Benady, David. November 17, 1995. Morgan's Spiced Rum goes nationwide. *Marketing Week* 18(35): 10; Briceno, Carlos. April 30, 1995. Bacardi shows sunny disposition as it enters the flavored tropics. *Beverage World* 14: 18.

14. Stern, William M. March 14, 1994. Loyal to a fault. *Forbes*: 58–59; Fitzgerald, Kate. February 21, 1994. Happy Birthday, (Name Here). Advertising Age; Anonymous. June 19, 1995. Can Hallmark get well soon? *Business Week*: 62–63.

15. Moukheiber, Zina. December 18, 1995. Know thy customer. *Forbes*: 147.

16. Schifrin, Matthew. December 18, 1995. Goofus and Gallant. *Forbes*: 115–117.

17. Helliker, Kevin and Bob Ortega. January 18, 1996. Falling profit marks end of era at Wal-Mart. *The Wall Street Journal*: B1, B11.

18. Moukheiber, Zina. July 17, 1995. I'm just a peddler. *Forbes*: 42–43.

19. Gates, William. Jan-Feb 1996. What I learned from Warren Buffett. *Harvard Business Review*: 148–152.

20. Taylor, A. May 30, 1994. Iacocca's Minivan. *Fortune*: 56–66; Mitchell, J. November 3, 1993. Ford Plans to Take Another Shot at the Booming Minivan Market. *The Wall Street Journal: B1, B7*.

3

CHAPTER

Flawed Assumptions: Right Strategy—Wrong Problem

We built a great mousetrap—but there were no mice.[1]

Gary W. Weber, PPG Industries, Inc.

In Chapter 2, we emphasized the importance of understanding the organization's *external* environmental context. This chapter will focus on another dimension: the strategist's assumptions, premises, and beliefs—the *internal* frame of reference within which strategies are devised and evaluated. It is important to understand this frame of reference because it serves both as a road map and as a set of constraints on the thought processes of the strategist. Peter Drucker calls this assumption set the "theory of the business." He argues that the theory of the business consists of a set of interrelated assumptions about the organization's environment (society and its structure, the market, the customer, and the competition), its mission, and the core competencies needed to accomplish that mission. The assumptions about the environment "define what an organization gets paid for"; the assumptions about mission "define what an organization considers to be meaningful results"; and the assumptions about core competencies "define where an organization must excel in order to maintain leadership."[2]

Hamel and Prahalad, in *Competing for the Future*, maintain that "every manager carries around in his or her head a set of biases, assumptions and presuppositions about the structure of the relevant 'industry,' about how one makes money in the industry, about who the competition is and isn't, about who the customers are and aren't, about which technologies are viable and which aren't, and so on." They call this assumption set a "managerial frame of reference" that "also encompasses beliefs, values and norms about how best to motivate people; the right balance of internal cooperation and competition; the relative ranking of shareholder, customer and employee interests; and what behaviors to encourage and discourage."[3]

Strategies frequently go awry when management's internal frame of reference is out of sync with the realities of the business situation—when one or more of management's assumptions, premises, or beliefs are incorrect, or when internal inconsistencies among them render the overall "theory of the business" no longer valid. The powerful influence of top management's perspective, orientation, and fundamental assumptions about an organization and its industry are clearly apparent in the wild ride the Dallas-based Greyhound Lines, Inc., has given its investors.[4]

In the 1960s, nearly 30 percent of all interstate travel was by bus. Dozens of bus companies operated across the country, but Greyhound Lines, Inc., was by far the largest, and it was the only company with a truly nationwide route system. The interstate bus industry's primary competition was the private automobile—hence Greyhound's familiar advertising slogan, "Leave the driving to us." Even in the early days of airline deregulation in the late 70s, private automobile travel was considered the industry's only real competitive threat. By the 1980s, however, market conditions had changed dramatically. The interstate highway system had been completed and almost every family owned at least one automobile; the two- (or even three-) car family had become commonplace. Airfares had come down sharply with deregulation, and the rapid growth of the commuter airlines in the mid-80s (annual increases in passenger traffic in excess of 35 percent) extended the reach of the air transportation network into many smaller communities where the bus had previously been the only source of public transport. By the early 90s less than 6 percent of all interstate travel was by bus.

Both Greyhound Lines, Inc., and Trailways, Inc., the number two carrier, had grown through the acquisition of smaller regional carriers during the 50s and 60s, when the market was expanding. But in the late 70s, passenger traffic began a steady decline (that has continued into the 90s) and the industry entered a period of consolidation and retrenchment. Dallas-based Trailways, Inc., was acquired in a 1979 leveraged buyout by a group of former Greyhound executives. Phoenix-based Greyhound was purchased in March 1987 in a leveraged buyout by an investor group headed by Fred Currey (formerly CEO of Trailways, Inc.) and a group of experienced bus-industry executives. In July of the same year, Currey's group acquired the failing Trailways, Inc., and the operations of the two companies were combined in Dallas. The new management team aggressively downsized, shedding workers and assets, consolidating operations, and reducing schedules. By 1989, the combined fleets had shrunk from more than 6,000 to less than 3,900 buses, and employment had been cut sharply. In 1990, management took an aggressive stand against the unions and their antiquated work rules. A bitter labor battle ensued, with the striking drivers firing shots at the buses as nonunion replacements kept them rolling down the interstates. As the turmoil continued, ridership declined and losses mounted. Both sides dug in and held their ground. Crippled by the impasse, the company filed for Chapter 11 bankruptcy in early 1991.

By October 1991, Greyhound emerged from Chapter 11 in the hands of new management, CEO Frank Schmeider, formerly an investment banker, and CFO J. Michael Doyle, a financial executive with a background in the oil business. The problem with Greyhound, in their view, was clear: ridership was declining, costs were too high, and asset utilization was poor. Fighting the unions was a no-win battle. Times had changed and they were convinced that the old bus industry business model no longer worked. Reengineering was in vogue, and the solution appeared obvious: adopt a new business model and reengineer—what else?

The business model they chose was that of the airline industry. The similarities were obvious. Both airlines and buses were in the people-moving business, both were asset-intensive, substantial portions of their operating costs were fixed, revenue was both cyclical and seasonal, and asset utilization was the key to profitability. The airlines had addressed these problems, in part, through the development of hub-and-spoke route structures and sophisticated computerized reservations and yield-management systems. Hub-and-spoke routing facilitated scale economies through the consolidation of ground-based maintenance and terminal operations. Reservation systems were a convenience for passengers, but more importantly, they were a source of management information to improve the scheduling and utilization of equipment and personnel. In addition, yield management systems made it possible to manage complex discounted and promotional fare structures to squeeze maximum revenue out of the system.

The turnaround plan they devised in late 1991 was well received on Wall Street. It began with downsizing—the number of buses was slashed by 35 percent, maintenance facilities by half, and employees and ticket sales outlets by 25 percent and 20 percent respectively by the end of 1992. Many old-line bus company executives and terminal employees were sacked; part-timers and low-paid "customer-service associates" replaced some of them. The route structure was revamped, cutting capacity 25 percent by eliminating small-town stops and trimming unprofitable routes. Between 1991 and 1993, the only thing that went up consistently was executive compensation. Revenues continued to decline, but an aggressive new marketing plan was in the works to reverse the trends.

Greyhound's typical rider earned less than $17,000 per year and walked up to the terminal and bought a ticket a few hours before the trip. The plan was to retain this core group and attract additional passengers with guaranteed reservations, discounted advance purchase fares, local promotions, and "frequent rider" plans, all of which mimicked airline marketing techniques. The plan's cornerstone was a new $6 million computerized reservation system (TRIPS) under development by a contract programming house. Scheduled for national rollout in mid-1993, TRIPS would permit the company to better utilize its assets, increase load factors and improve revenue yields. Things were looking up by the end of 1992— ridership continued to trend down, but load factors and yields had steadied and the aggressive cost cutting was beginning to show on the bottom line. For the full year 1992, Greyhound eked out a narrow profit—its first since 1989—and Wall Street rewarded them. The company's stock soared—from about $12 to over $21 per share by May 1993. The company completed a successful $100 million stock offering and moved ahead with the implementation of the new reservations system.

Let's explore Schmeider and Doyle's key assumptions. The first was that the bus business was closely similar to the airline business. Having accepted that premise, a whole series of additional assumptions logically followed: (2) the airline business model would work in the bus industry; (3) the major difference between the airlines and Greyhound was in marketing—the way the airlines priced their product and managed revenue with computerized reservations and yield management systems; (4) if the bus company had a computerized reservations system, it could be managed more efficiently and marketed to attract a broader range of customers; (5) it would be simple and inexpensive to develop a reservations system for Greyhound, based on the airline model; and, (6) even though revenues were declining, costs could be cut even faster without impacting operations or the core customer base, thus buying time to implement the new marketing strategy.

Unfortunately, almost every assumption they made was incorrect. The differences between the airline and bus industries were greater than they appeared on the surface. While even large airlines typically have only a few hundred aircraft and serve less than 200 cities, Greyhound operated 2,400 buses and over 2,600 terminal locations. Average one-way bus fares of $33 were about a tenth of the typical airline fare. The demographics and purchasing habits of the customer base were markedly different. Airline-style pricing and promotional efforts failed to attract new riders. Ruthless cost-cutting alienated the remaining employees, who, in turn, alienated more customers. The development of the reservations system was far more difficult and took longer than originally anticipated. When initially tested, it failed miserably. Management, unwilling to admit that the system wasn't ready, pushed ahead with the scheduled July 1993 launch.

The results were disastrous. The system was overwhelmed. The new toll-free reservations number was swamped—on average, customers had to try a dozen times before they got through to make a reservation. It frequently took five minutes or more to print a ticket. The lines at the terminals got longer. Even worse, according to Jack Haugsland, Greyhound's current chief operating officer, "over 80 percent of those who made reservations were no-shows." With a nearly empty bus waiting outside, people were standing in line with cash in hand waiting to buy a ticket, but "the system wouldn't let you sell [them] a ticket." "Pretty soon . . . people get discouraged and quit coming down to the terminal," Haugsland observed. Greyhound was hemorrhaging cash—losses totaled $72 million in the first nine months of 1994—and losing passengers to its regional competitors. In the first half of 1994, its revenues were down 12.6 percent, while its nine largest regional rivals posted a combined gain of 2.2 percent. By the third quarter of 1994, Schmeider and Doyle were out, an interim management was in place, and the company was preparing another Chapter 11 filing.

Schmeider was ultimately replaced by Craig Lentzsch, a bus industry veteran who had been part of the original 1987 buyout team, in November 1994. Bankruptcy was averted through a financial restructuring. The problems with the phone system have been fixed—customers now get through on the first try. Former bus industry executives have been rehired. By late 1995, Lentzsch was well on the way to turning things around, with a third quarter profit of $15.3 million, after six consecutive losing quarters.

What was his secret? Run it like a bus company! Lentzsch's first step was to dismantle the airline business model and scrap the reservation system. He replaced the concept with a much simpler one: "If you want to travel by bus, you show up at the terminal and within a reasonable time you get a seat on the bus at an affordable price." "If we fill up the bus that is supposed to leave at 10 AM, we will keep rolling out buses until everyone has a seat," Mr. Lentzsch explains. The second step was to change the pricing structure—gone are the discounts for advance purchase reservations—to an "everyday low price" structure. Frequencies have been increased on popular routes. Greyhound now runs hourly shuttles between Boston and New York, with every half-hour service on the weekends. It appears to be working. The traditional bus riders are coming back. Revenues are up. Costs are under control and Lentzsch is currently projecting a profit for the full year in 1996.

The jury is still out on the turnaround at Greyhound. The traditional "old bus" business model of the 70s and 80s clearly had its problems, as the failure of Trailways, Inc., in 1987 and the bankruptcy of Greyhound in 1991 will attest. Schmeider and Doyle thought they had the answer in a new business model, based on the airline industry. It, too, failed miserably. Now, bus industry veterans are back in the driver's seat and attempting to restore the company to profitability. The revolving door in the executive suite, with each revolution bringing a new strategic approach reminds us of the observations of Petronius Arbiter, a Roman soldier who, sometime during the first century AD observed:

> We trained hard—but it seemed that every time we were beginning to form up into teams, we would be reorganized. I was to learn later in life that we tend to meet any new situation by reorganization, and a wonderful method it can be for creating the illusion of progress while producing confusion, inefficiency and demoralization.

It is clear from the reaction of Wall Street that, for a time, Schmeider and Doyle produced an "illusion of progress." It didn't last, however, and a seemingly valid strategy based on an unsupportable premise produced little, in the end, but "confusion, inefficiency and demoralization." Pondering the words of Petronius, it sometimes seems that little has changed in 2,000 years.

The example of Greyhound Lines, Inc., represents an extreme. Rarely does one encounter a situation in which a new management team attempts to change the entire paradigm. More frequently, strategies fail either because (*a*) they are based on overly optimistic or unrealistic assumptions about future conditions and events that are ultimately proven wrong; or, (b) perfectly reasonable and valid assumptions are overtaken by events that were not, and perhaps could not have been, foreseen at the time. Optimistic assumptions are not uncommon—new managers frequently believe that they have a better idea and they are willing to bet significant sums that their instincts are correct. Raytheon clearly thought they had it figured out after they acquired Beech Aircraft. The story of the Beech Starship is a classic tale of a great idea, based on a set of premises that, in the end, didn't pan out.

In the early 1980s, Raytheon Co., eager to reduce its dependence on the highly cyclical defense business, acquired Wichita-based Beech Aircraft. Beech's traditional core business—light aircraft—had virtually collapsed over the previous decade as aggressive trial lawyers chased the deep pockets and won mega-judgments for the victims of private aviation mishaps. Aviation product liability premiums soared, and the manufacturers headed for their foxholes. All the major domestic manufacturers of single-engine light aircraft exited the business. The other remaining Wichita-based aircraft manufacturers, Cessna and Learjet, were market leaders in small corporate jets. Beech, a family-owned company, continued to hang on with the King-Air, the leading corporate turboprop aircraft, but had not launched a new product in a decade.

Raytheon installed its own management team after the 1980 takeover. Determined to jump-start Beech's business, but unwilling to risk a head-on challenge to Cessna and Learjet, they conceived a bold plan—an advanced turboprop design based on the latest materials technology that would provide performance competitive with low-end business jets at a fraction of the cost. Originally conceived as a 10-passenger aircraft capable of 400 knot speed (versus 450 kts for a jet and 315 kts for a conventional turboprop), the all-composite aircraft would be more fuel efficient than a jet, require only a single pilot, and sell for only about $3 million (versus $4.5 to $6 million for a comparable business jet). Not only did the design, dubbed the Starship, look great on paper, but an 85 percent scale model, demonstrated in 1983, drew rave reviews. Inundated with orders, Beech committed to an initial production run of 53 aircraft and announced that the plane would be ready for shipment in late 1985—only two years later.

Let's take a look at Beech's key assumptions. First the design—Beech assumed, as it announced in 1983, that it could complete the design and achieve FAA certification for the all-composite aircraft in two years. The key to the design lay in the anticipated weight savings: carbon fiber composites are 350 percent stronger than aluminum, but 15 to 20 percent lighter. By building the plane from these stronger and lighter materials, the aircraft could carry more payload farther and faster than a conventional turboprop, with significantly better fuel economy than a jet. Second, the FAA—although existing regulations did not address the new carbon-fiber technology, Beech's new managers must have assumed that the regulators would work within the spirit, rather than the letter, of the regulations. Third, the market—Beech had every reason to believe, based on the enthusiastic response and initial flurry of orders, that a significant number of aircraft would be built, justifying the investment in a new factory. Finally—and this is only speculation—they assumed that Murphy's Law, *which says that if anything can go wrong, it will*, would be temporarily suspended for the duration of this endeavor.

What happened? Murphy showed up, wearing the badge of an FAA inspector. The FAA had never certified an all-composite aircraft and, according to *Fortune*, "no bureaucrat wanted to be remembered as the guy who had signed off too quickly on . . . a plastic airplane." The 1983 prototype was classified as experimental and did not have to comply with the FAA's requirements for production aircraft. As the design progressed, the bureaucrats began to insist on compliance with certain existing standards (such as the thickness of structural members) for metal aircraft. Composite fiber parts had to be redesigned to comply with the design rules formerly applied to aluminum parts, resulting in an incredibly strong composite fiber aircraft that, in the end, weighed about as much as a metal one. As the weight increased, bigger engines were required, and bigger engines meant more fuel, which meant more weight, requiring a redesign of the structure, and so on. As the weight spiraled upward, the Starship outgrew the "light aircraft" category and moved into the "commuter aircraft" weight class and now required not one, but two pilots (a requirement since waived). Murphy showed up again: the FAA was in the middle of a rewrite of the commuter aircraft standards, a moving target of regulatory chaos and obfuscation.

The Starship finally made it to market in 1989—four years late. While pilots give it high marks for comfort and stability, in the end, the design didn't come close to meeting its original performance expectations. The latest version carries six passengers (versus 10) at a cruising speed of 335 knots (versus a target of 400 kts.) and costs almost $5 million (versus an estimated $3 million). Not surprisingly, the anticipated market never materialized. The sleek, but unconventional, design turned out to be a liability rather than an asset, as Raytheon discovered that the conservative, older-generation CEO "doesn't want people pointing at him as he lands."

Through 1994, Beech had sold only 19 airplanes and leased an additional 10. More than 20 additional aircraft (a $100 million inventory) were completed and gathering dust in Wichita. The production line was shut down shortly thereafter and Raytheon announced its plans to discontinue marketing efforts. By contrast, Beech's neighbor down the road, Cessna, delivered nearly 400 comparably priced Citation II and Citation V jets during the same period. Beech's conventional turboprop, the King-Air 350, also continued to sell well.[5]

In this case, Beech's business model was the same as those of its major competitors. Beech, Cessna, and Learjet each saw the same market opportunities, the same technologies, and the same channels of distribution. Beech's current product offering, the King Air turboprop, competed with the low end of the Cessna and Learjet lines, but at a significant performance disadvantage. Raytheon's strategy for Beech was bold, but appeared to make good sense—as the dominant producer of business turboprops, Beech could move up in performance with an advanced-design turboprop based on the latest defense-industry technologies that would compete effectively and win market share from its competitors at the low end of the business jet market. The strategy was, however, based on a number of key assumptions, none of which panned out. When the FAA refused to bend in its interpretation of a set of regulations based on an older technology, the failure of the design—in hindsight—became inevitable.

Greyhound's Schmeider and Doyle based a strategy on one key premise—that the bus industry was not that different from the airline business. The executives at Raytheon and Beech based a bold strategy on carbon fiber composites—proven in the defense industry—but made the erroneous assumption that the regulators at the FAA shared their enthusiasm for advanced technologies. Both strategies failed because their basic premises were proven wrong and the "product" fell short of the market's expectations. In our next example, management based their strategy on the assumption that the aura of success enjoyed by a product in one environment would be carried forward and translated into a similar success in another.

In 1983, AM General Corporation was awarded an Army contract to develop a replacement for the venerable WWII-vintage Jeep. The High Mobility Multipurpose Wheeled Vehicle (HMMWV) was called the Humvee. A total of 100,000 Humvees were sold to the U.S. Army and foreign governments. Noting the popularity of four-wheel-drive sport utility vehicles such as the Jeep Cherokee, Land Rover, and Ford Explorer, AM General decided to offer a civilian version, the Hummer, to the general public in 1990. After the high-profile success of the Humvee in the 1991 Desert Storm campaign, and a one-two finish in the 1993 Baja 1000 off-road race, the company expected nonmilitary sales to take off.

Let's explore the implicit assumptions: (1) four-wheel-drive sport utility vehicles are a hot market segment; (2) the Hummer is the ultimate off-road vehicle; (3) the pricing is not out of line with the high end of the market; (4) the Hummer's high profile showing in Desert Storm and the Baja 1000 will provide the publicity needed to jump-start sales; and, (5) all we need is a dealer network. Convincing themselves they had a market, AM General moved ahead to set up a dealer network and offer the Hummer to the general public. The results have been a major disappointment, with sales averaging less than 1,000 Hummers a year.

Why didn't the Hummer sell? First of all, availability was limited and much of the public was unaware the product was being offered to consumers. Only 25 dealers were set up initially, and, according to some reports, they were not well supported. In an industry that spends billions to create consumer brand awareness and loyalty, AM General's advertising and promotional efforts were so limited as to be nonexistent. Second, the product lacked many of the creature comforts offered by the competition's high-end products. Off the road, it was unbeatable. On the street, it rode and handled more like a tank than a sport utility vehicle. Overengineered and overpriced for the civilian market, the limited dealer network found it hard to sell against the more sophisticated competition. Despite its seven-foot width, three-ton weight, and two-ton carrying capacity, it only had room for four passengers. Reluctantly, management has made some changes to accommodate the con-

sumer, but these appear to be too little, too late. Four years after its introduction, although the new models now come equipped with better heating
and air conditioning, a glove box, arm rests, power steering, power windows, reclining seats, and the like, sales are still below expectations.[6]

The Hummer, a product that was a great success in the government market, was an apparent bust with consumers, and management's assumption that success in one environment would
carry over to the next was clearly a pipe dream. The errors in this
case were, first, the assumption that no significant changes would
be required to appeal to consumers in a different market; and second, the assumption that the aura of success in Desert Storm would
create a consumer demand without the expenditure of millions in
advertising and promotion.

In other cases, strategies fall short of achieving sustainable
competitive advantage not because their initial premises were
wrong, but because these perfectly reasonable and valid assumptions were overtaken by events that could not have been reasonably
foreseen at the time. Two examples, one focusing on the basis of
competition, the other on the timing of events, will help illustrate
this point. Consider, first, the case of General Motors and its drive
to achieve parity, in cost and quality, with its Japanese competitors:

In the early 80s, it was widely believed that outdated manufacturing techniques and processes were the number one competitive problem for the
Detroit automakers. The "lean production" techniques incorporated by
the Japanese automakers were responsible for an almost insurmountable
cost and quality advantage. General Motors, still the world's largest automaker, responded with a number of initiatives. Although the Saturn
project has received more publicity, GM and the rest of the domestic automobile industry have also learned a great deal from the 1983 joint venture
with Toyota known as New United Motor Manufacturing, Inc. (NUMMI).
The sprawling NUMMI facility in Fremont, California, produces a line of
nearly identical vehicles—the Toyota Corolla and GM's Geo Prism—sold
in the United States through two separate distribution channels.

In the beginning, it was assumed that NUMMI would provide a
number of advantages for General Motors: (1) by building the cars on a
common assembly line, GM would achieve manufacturing cost and
quality parity with Toyota; (2) both GM and Toyota would benefit from

the economies of scale associated with a larger production volume; and, (3) GM would learn how to build automobiles the "Japanese way," and would be able to lever this knowledge into an improved competitive position for its other product lines. Toyota, on the other hand, would reduce the threat of punitive import duties on one of its most popular models and also benefit from the scale economies.

NUMMI appears to have been a success for both companies, in that the initial objectives clearly have been achieved. As U.S. auto manufacturers have focused on quality and adopted the same lean production techniques, the Japanese competitive advantage in product cost and quality has largely evaporated. But, unfortunately for GM, the rules have changed, and U.S. automakers still are lagging behind. The sources of competitive advantage have shifted to design, marketing, and supply chain management. While GM and the rest of Detroit focused on cost and quality, the Japanese seized the high ground on the new competitive battlefield.

An example from a study by John Lindquist of the Boston Consulting Group makes this point. In 1990 to 1994, the Toyota Corolla and the Geo Prism both came off the same assembly line and cost the same to produce—an average of $10,300. Toyota, based on the strength of its reputation and brand image, sold 200,000 vehicles annually at an average dealer price of $11,100. GM, on the other hand, sold an average of 80,000 vehicles at a price of $10,700. Over the period, Toyota made $128 million more in operating profits from NUMMI than did GM; downstream, its dealers made an estimated $107 million more from higher retail prices. Once sold, the superior service provided by the Toyota dealer network sustained and amplified the initial edge. Depreciating more slowly, a five-year-old Corolla now sells for 18 percent more than a similar Geo Prism on the used car lot.[7]

GM has clearly benefited in a number of ways from its experience with NUMMI. This example points out, however, that the competitive arena is built on shifting sands— things never remain stable for very long—and as conditions change, so must the premises and the focus of an organization's strategy. GM has made great strides in addressing the cost issue and has put the brakes on development spending. While GM is now profitable, this strategy is not without risks. As its competitors are spending heavily to introduce new models and new technologies, some industry observers suggest that GM's strategy of aggressive cost reduction and "value pricing" of older technologies may result in short-run benefits, but create long-run competitive problems. Opinions differ. GM's marketing czar, Ronald Zarella, maintains that "aesthetics is not the most important thing to consumers, but terrific value is." Other industry observers note that GM is "making a virtue of necessity, considering that it doesn't have any exciting product to sell . . . more than any other company, GM is selling yesterday's sheet metal."[8]

The current turmoil over the Internet and the World Wide Web provides numerous examples of how rapidly shifting market and technology environments can play havoc with the best-laid plans and strategies. You can't be a player in the software business without being aware of the Internet, but many were surprised by the rate at which the World Wide Web grabbed the interest and imagination of the mass market.

Since the early 80s, when Microsoft's MS-DOS became the industry standard for personal computer operating systems, the company has increasingly dominated the PC software business, first in operating systems, then in applications. Over the last couple of years, Microsoft's Windows NT has mounted a strong challenge in network operating systems, and with the launch of the Microsoft Network in the fall of 1995, the company entered the market for on-line services. It was almost inconceivable that Microsoft, seemingly unstoppable, with the ability to eventually dominate every market it entered, would be taken by surprise in the heart of its market, but it happened!

According to *Business Week*, "Gates has been caught remarkably flat-footed by the birth of the raucous World Wide Web. He acknowledged as much last May [1995] when he fired off a widely leaked internal memo urging every employee to make the Internet a top priority." Netscape Communications Corp. and Sun Microsystems have seized the initiative and are now setting the agenda. In early December 1995, more than 30 companies—including IBM, Oracle, Apple Computer, and Silicon Graphics—committed to the development of Internet software around Sun's Java programming language and standards developed by Sun and Netscape. It's not that Microsoft was blind to the existence or potential of the World Wide Web—its proprietary products to access the Web were under development— rather, it appears to have been caught off guard by the timing. Gates acknowledges that "Java is the language that is the darling of the industry right now. It's a good example of how, in this industry, people are always looking for the next thing that will unseat the giants." Netscape's chairman and founder, James A. Clark, commented "The Internet basically blew apart [Microsoft's] whole strategy."[9]

While it's far from clear that Microsoft's whole strategy is now in tatters, the company does appear to be scrambling to catch up, and doing it in a rather uncharacteristic way. Rather than pursue the in-house development of proprietary technology so that it could control both the product and the pace of its evolution, Microsoft appears to be in a hurry to piece together a response based on technologies developed by others. Microsoft has recently announced that it will license and support the Java language from Sun Microsystems and incorporate elements of Sun's technology into its own Internet offerings. In addition, Microsoft recently acquired Vermeer Technologies, Inc., the developer of FrontPage, an applications software package used to develop Web pages.[10]

Microsoft was not the only major industry player taken by surprise by the rapid acceptance of Web technologies. IBM paid $3.5 billion in July 1995 to acquire Lotus Development Corporation, primarily to gain access to Lotus's market-leading Notes software package, which lets organizations publish and share information for groups of workers across a private network. Three months later, Compaq Computer Corp, a high-profile Notes customer, announced its plans to drop Notes in favor of a Web-based system for sharing information with its suppliers and distributors. In the marketplace, Lotus is slashing prices and aggressively pursuing market share before the Web-based systems establish a beachhead. In the back room, developers are scrambling to update the proprietary Notes software to ensure its compatibility with the new de facto standard—Sun's Java technology.[11]

The popular on-line services—Prodigy, Compuserve, and America OnLine—have also been thrown into turmoil. For the last several years, the proprietary on-line services have mainly battled among themselves, focusing on their industry rivals and trying to establish the largest possible subscriber base before Microsoft entered the arena in the fall of 1995. While their attention was focused primarily on market share, the World Wide Web has emerged as a substitute technology that threatens to obsolete the entire industry. To many subscribers, the Web does all the on-line services can do—and much more—at a significantly lower price. Internet direct-access providers are growing by leaps and bounds, offering an opportunity to bypass the on-line services (who charge by the hour) at fixed monthly rates. According to Scott Kurnit, formerly second in command at Prodigy, the rise of the Internet "turns the model of the on-line services industry upside down." Forrester Research analyst William Bluestein agrees: "Their whole proprietary model has been shattered . . . [they're about to be] blown out of the water." With the apple cart upset, Prodigy's owners, IBM and Sears, are looking for a buyer; America Online has formed strategic alliances with AT&T, Netscape, Sun Microsystems, and Microsoft; AT&T has dropped its plans for a proprietary on-line service in favor of an Internet-based model; and Sprint and MCI have countered AT&T by aligning with Sun Microsystems and Microsoft, respectively. Meanwhile, it's not entirely clear that the Web will live up to the hype, as *The Wall Street Journal* notes: "legions of computer users are finding the Web less of an electronic wonder than an electronic bore . . . access is slow . . . sites are difficult to find . . . and the content of many offerings [is] frivolous or outdated."[12]

In each of these examples, one significant event—the rapid emergence of the user-friendly World Wide Web on the Internet—has shattered the assumption base and turned strategic models inside-out. Many companies are scrambling in reaction, either toward a perceived opportunity or away from a potential disaster. It certainly appears that Microsoft, IBM, and the on-line service providers initially drew the short straw, and Netscape and Sun Microsystems emerged as the winners. But, as in baseball, a home run in the first inning is a great start, but one long ball rarely determines the final outcome. Within the emerging pattern of alliances, it appears that no one company will dominate, but that each will share, with its partners, in a piece of the pie. If the patterns of technology evolution run true to form, today's assumption base may be out of date before the ashes of the last discredited version are yet cool.

I understand the examples, but where's the common thread? How do these all tie together? Clearly Greyhound made some major mistakes, but that industry was in trouble anyway. It might have gone under regardless of the strategy. Raytheon's a different story, but government bureaucrats

*have done similar things to lots of companies—look at the savings and
loan industry. AM General should have known better—there's no excuse
for misreading a market that badly! And the Internet took everyone (almost) by surprise—how does one defend against that?*

STRATEGIC TRAP #2: RIGHT STRATEGY—WRONG PROBLEM

In each of the first three examples, Greyhound, Raytheon, and AM
General—the products and strategies appeared to be sound and
well thought out—given the initial assumptions and premises. In
each case, however, these organizations fell into the trap of *basing a
strategy on a flawed set of assumptions that, in hindsight, proved to be
false.* In the end, what worked for the airlines didn't apply to the
bus industry; the bureaucratic regulators of the FAA didn't share
Raytheon's enthusiasm for new materials technologies; and the
product features and characteristics that made the Hummer an un-
qualified success in the military environment didn't translate effectively to the consumer marketplace. Misled by the fundamental
assumptions and biases of their individual and collective assumption sets, the managers of each of these companies embarked upon,
and then persisted in, a failing strategy long after outsiders recognized the folly of their endeavors.

In the last two examples, the issues are more subtle, but are
still closely related. For GM and for the established players in the
computer business, the initial premises upon which their strategies
were based were, for the most part, correct. But as their markets
evolved, in GM's case over a matter of years, in the computer industry in a matter of months, the key players also fell into the
strategic trap as they *failed to react when changing circumstances ren-
dered their initial assumptions and premises invalid.* As the rules of the
game have changed, GM, Microsoft, and the others have been
placed on the defensive and forced to play catch-up. It's a familiar
position for General Motors, but totally new for Microsoft. It's too
early to tell, at this point, how successful GM, Microsoft, and the
other organizations caught in this trap will be in shifting their focus
and priorities to adjust to the changing realities of the marketplace.

*I guess that makes sense. If the basic assumptions are wrong, the strategy
isn't likely to work too well—and if circumstances change and your assumptions are no longer valid, you've got to change the strategy. But how*

do you test your premises in the beginning? How do you ensure that they're still valid? How do you guard against this kind of strategic error?

ASSUMPTIONS, PREMISES, AND BELIEFS

Let's begin by looking at the sources of a manager's knowledge and beliefs about business in general, and about the environment, the industry, and his organization in particular. Most managers learn about business from a number of sources: formal and informal education, observation, and personal experience. College and business school courses, seminars, and company-sponsored training courses are all sources of formal education. Informal education may come from reading—both business-related books and magazines and other, less directly related sources—and from personal contact and interaction with mentors, consultants, and other management gurus. Much can be learned by direct observation of the successes and failures of others, and from personal experience—learning what works and what doesn't by trial and error.

Managers learn about their specific industry environments from a variety of sources—trade journals and the general business press, associates within their own organizations, and interaction with customers, suppliers, peers, and competitors within the industry. In addition to business and industry knowledge, each individual also has his own set of moral and societal values and beliefs about what is right and what is wrong, about what kind of conduct is appropriate and what is not, and about the roles of individuals and groups and how they ought to interact with each other. Many of these core values and beliefs have their roots in family, culture, and religion, and they often have a greater influence in shaping an individual's perceptions and values than is consciously acknowledged.

Although each individual may see the world a little differently, the natural process of socialization and accommodation within an organization tends to produce, over time, a set of broadly shared assumptions and beliefs about the organization and the industry in which it competes that may become more important in guiding management decisions than the objective reality it mirrors.[13] Many organizations seek out and hire individuals with similar educational backgrounds, put them through the same indoctrination and training programs, and teach them the same rules of survival in the corporate culture. The more an organization promotes from within and the longer the tenure of the senior management team, the more they come to share a common view of the organization and its environment. Over time, this common view becomes so pervasive that it has been given a label—the *dominant logic* of the organization.[14] Researchers have found that this process of social reinforcement also extends beyond the boundaries of the firm, as customers, suppliers, and competitors also become involved in a process of social interaction and reinforcement of a commonly shared set of "rules" for conduct and competition within an industry.[15] This commonly accepted understanding of the organization, its competitors, and "how things work" in the organization's industry and environment corresponds to Drucker's "theory of the business" and has a powerful influence on the way an organization formulates its strategies and conducts its affairs in the competitive arena.

Over time, these commonly held beliefs about the firm and its industry become institutionalized as part of the firm's organizational fabric. They reinforce certain perspectives and exclude others in the definition of business unit boundaries and the identification of competitors, in accounting and reporting systems, in decision-making processes, and in other organizational practices, policies, and procedures. The more deeply these commonly shared beliefs, practices, and procedures are entrenched, the less likely they are to be questioned, even when external circumstances change. Over time, as Hamel and Prahalad observe, "These premises bound or 'frame' a firm's perspective on what it means to be 'strategic,' the available repertoire of competitive stratagems, the interests that senior management serves, the choice of tools for policy deployment, ideal organizational types, and . . . [they] limit management's perception to a particular slice of reality. Managers live inside their frames and, to a very great extent, don't know what lies outside"[16]

THE DANGERS OF THE DOMINANT LOGIC

The dominant logic is like a two-edged sword. On the positive side, a cohesive management team with common goals and a common perspective on the business and its competitive environment is more likely to make decisions and implement strategies with a minimum of delay and disruption due to internal disagreements or political infighting. If, however, a management team's set of assumptions and beliefs, its "theory of the business," is inconsistent with actual conditions in the ever-changing environment, blindly following the conventional wisdom may result in significant strategic errors. Formulating strategy on erroneous assumptions is like building a mansion on a foundation of quicksand—no matter how elegant the design, the structure will not stand the test of time.

Drucker argues that, in order for an organization's theory of the business to be valid, it must meet four criteria: (1) the assumptions about environment, mission, and core competencies must fit reality; (2) the assumptions in all three areas must be consistent with each other; (3) the theory of the business must be known and understood throughout the organization; and (4) the theory of the business must be tested constantly. As a hypothesis about things that are in constant flux—society, markets, customers, technology— the theory of the business must be continually tested and revised to reflect new information, or it will, over time, become invalid.[17]

Testing the validity of a set of assumptions is not always easy. Managers often become so locked into a particular view of the world that they lose sight of *why* they believe *what* they believe. Our research on managers' understanding of their competitors suggests that they are often unable to differentiate between fact and assumption or to identify the original source of specific items of "knowledge" about competing organizations. In addition, strategists frequently become so focused on a narrow segment of the environment that they come to believe that what lies beyond—what they don't know—is not really worth knowing.

When the dominant logic is built on false premises or blinds a management team to the realities of the situation, it can prove to be the undoing of an organization. In early 1993, one of the authors was involved in a turnaround management consulting assignment. Shortly before he took control of the parent company, it had made a working capital loan to AMT International Industries, Inc., and was in negotiations to acquire the smaller, privately held organization.

AMT International Industries, Inc., a small private company that designed and built modems for the computer OEM market, was run by a husband and wife team, Jerry and Jean, whose entire life revolved around the company they had built over a period of seven years. A year earlier, the company had lost its largest OEM customer and was in deep financial trouble. Jerry, AMT's CEO, was an enthusiastic and likeable promoter who truly believed that, despite its current financial condition, his company was "world class" in every other respect—products, customers, management team, and internal systems and controls. During the course of the negotiations, we also met the "industry-leading" engineering team, viewed test results that clearly made his products the "best in class," and enjoyed "world class" lasagna and the "world's best" burgers at his favorite local dining establishments. Jean reinforced Jerry's view of the world at every turn. The only thing that wasn't "world class" about this company was its operating and financial performance—sales were declining, inventories were bloated, and the company was in a cash crisis. In Jerry's eyes, however, that was only temporary—within a matter of weeks, even days, a major order would be received from Dell Computer, AST, or Compaq that would put things back on track. No matter that Jerry had not made a sales call in a year and his sales manager had not called on these accounts in months—he had told the story so many times he had come to believe it, and the rest of the management team was caught up in it too. Negotiations were impossible—our views of "reality" were totally different. Not surprisingly, the big order never arrived. In the end, AMT defaulted on the working capital loan and we were forced to take over the remaining assets and restructure the company. Jerry was retained for a few weeks as a consultant, but his fairy tale view of reality kept throwing up roadblocks that got in the way of the restructuring efforts and his services were terminated.

The dominant logic is also dysfunctional when it limits an organization's vision to the narrow confines of its currently served markets. As Hamel and Prahalad observe, "Any company that defines itself in terms of a specific set of end product-markets ties its fate to the fate of those particular markets."[18] A company that defines itself solely in terms of its current industry may well miss opportunities created by technologies or market forces that ultimately will replace or redefine the current segment. The example of Nintendo and Sega, cited in Chapter 2, illustrates these different perspectives. In 1994, Nintendo's president Yamauchi was clearly focused on the market he currently served, and discounted multimedia as overblown hype as he vowed to "concentrate on just one point—improving the quality of games in the current market." Sega's president Nakayama viewed the world very differently, and he prepared for competitive battles on multiple fronts as he projected that the multimedia revolution would produce "a tectonic shift in society." Which one is right? Only time will tell.

One of the critical limitations of an organization's dominant logic is that it is invariably linked more to the past than to the future. Researchers have demonstrated that managers' mental representations of the world are based, predominantly, on historical information, rather than on expectations about the future, and that individuals tend to discount or ignore new information that is inconsistent with their current frame of reference.[19] The tendency to view the world in the context of familiar industry surroundings and to discount new information is not at all uncommon. The example of Reed Elsevier provides an illustration.

Reed Elsevier is the world's largest publisher of academic journals. The $5.5 billion company publishes over 1,100 separate academic journals. It's a unique business—the editorial content is contributed free by academic scholars who must publish to get tenure. Academic libraries are a captive market—faculties insist that the libraries subscribe to their favorite journals—and prices are high. A one year subscription to *Neuroscience*, published 24 times a year, costs $3,775; a subscription to *Brain Research*, at 114 issues a year, costs $14,000. The pretax margin on Reed Elsevier's academic publishing operations is about 40 percent.

Competition from electronic publishing is looming on the horizon. Over 140 peer-reviewed electronic journals are now being published. Reed Elsevier also offers electronic subscriptions to their journals for 110 percent of the price of a paper copy but has only a handful of subscribers. Perhaps the price is not right. An experiment in electronic publishing on the Internet at Los Alamos National Laboratory now has over 35,000 users and processes up to 70,000 transactions a day. UnCover Co., a Denver-based article retrieval company, places the tables of contents from a wide range of academic journals on the Internet and delivers copies of the articles to its customers within 24 hours. Two years ago, Louisiana State University's library subscribed to UnCover's service and cancelled subscriptions to 1,569 scholarly journals that cost $446,000 annually, but guaranteed copies of articles to its faculty and graduate students within two days. In its first year of operation, the library was able to obtain all the articles requested for only $25,000 in copyright and delivery fees.

Is the market shifting? Will the new technology obsolete the traditional marketplace? Reed Elsevier is apparently unconcerned. Herman Bruggnik, its co-chairman, insists that "The market we serve is perfectly happy with the product we deliver." *Forbes* asks, provocatively, will Reed Elsevier be "the Internet's first victim"? [20]

An understanding of competitors and their likely actions and reactions is an important element in the formulation of successful strategies. In competitive situations, managers often lay out strategies without fully considering the likely reactions of their competitors. If strategists do consider a competitor's reactions, they often implicitly simplify the situation by assuming either that (*a*) the reactions will be consistent with the competitor's historical patterns of behavior, or (*b*) the competitor shares a common view of the world and, therefore, will behave rationally in accordance with that perspective. When competitive reactions are ignored or inappropriate simplifying assumptions are substituted for a clear understanding, a variety of strategic errors may arise, including the so-called "winner's curse," which leads to overbidding in the acquisition marketplace; nonrational escalations of commitment, in which decision makers tend to make inappropriate decisions primarily because they justify prior actions; and overconfidence in judgment, in which decision makers tend to believe that a rational third party would support their perspective— losing sight of the fact that the competitor is also subject to the same biased view. [21]

Management researchers have pointed out a number of common blind spots in competitor analysis, noting that organizations frequently misjudge the boundaries of their industries, do a poor job of identifying their competitors, and make erroneous assumptions about them.[22] By focusing narrowly on their served markets, executives tend to pay less attention to other parts of the industry and may fail to notice or understand the importance of events that will change or redefine the boundaries of the industry. When strategists misjudge the boundaries of an industry, they also tend to do a poor job of identifying competitors, focusing primarily on a small set of other organizations that are most like their own. A short-term perspective often causes managers to focus primarily on the existing resources and capabilities of current competitors and to miss or misread the presence or actions of others. By focusing primarily on the most visible aspects of a competitor's operations, strategists often end up with an incomplete assessment of the capabilities of their competitors. A common error results when strategists anticipate the moves of competitors on the basis of extrapolation of past behavior, rather than on a more insightful interpretation of the competitor's true strategic intent. By categorizing and stereotyping competitors, managers tend to overgeneralize and perpetuate inaccurate perceptions and understandings.

It should be clear by now that successful strategies depend to a great extent on the validity of the initial assumptions and premises upon which they are based. They also depend on an ongoing review and analysis of this foundation to ensure that the key premises remain valid over the full period of strategy implementation.

BUILD YOUR STRATEGY ON A SOUND FOUNDATION

Every strategy is built on a foundation of assumptions and premises—an *internal* frame of reference that recreates, in the mind of the strategist, a model of the *external* competitive environment. The extent to which the internal model adequately represents the external realities is a major determinant of strategic success. Strategies that succeed are built on the foundation of an internal frame of reference that meets two tests of consistency. First, the assumptions and premises must be consistent with the external realities of the competitive environment. Second, they must be internally consistent with each other. The causes of strategic failure often can be traced to errors or inconsistencies in the initial set of assumptions and premises. Because the key elements of the competitive environment are in a state of constant flux, ensuring the validity of the initial assumptions and premises is not enough; the assumption set must be continuously tested and evaluated and then updated as required to conform to changes in the environment.

Building a solid foundation of assumptions and premises involves both developing an initial assessment, understanding, and validating the assumption base and making an ongoing effort to monitor changes in the environment and evaluate their impact on the continuing validity of the assumption base.

Understanding the Assumption Base

Developing a clear understanding of an organization's assumption base is not an easy thing to do. The first step is the most difficult—making the (usually implicit) assumptions explicit. For many reasons, as described earlier, an organization's assumptions and premises are embedded in a complex and tangled web of understanding, in which it is often difficult to distinguish assumption from fact. Often, it is easier to ask a series of questions, beginning broadly with asking what we know (or assume) about our environment, our industry, our organization, and so on. Once the collective knowledge base has been articulated, the next question—"how do we know this?"—will help to distinguish between fact and assumption.

It is usually helpful to begin at a midrange level of analysis, starting with a definition of the boundaries of "our industry." An industry taxonomy as described in Chapter 2, is a useful starting point and helps to define and make explicit the boundaries of the industry. It is critically important, at this point, to consider the "industry" in the broadest possible context, taking into account the organization's core competencies and looking beyond current products and current customers to consider both new products and potential new customers.[23] The focus can be sharpened progressively by asking why firm A is included in the industry, but firm B is not, and continuing the process with other firms. With the industry boundaries defined, it is appropriate to move on to a more detailed level of analysis, identifying the organization's key assumptions, one category at a time. Figure 2–1 may be used as a guide to identify the important categories. Key assumptions about the general environment, including economic, social, cultural, technological, and regulatory factors, often can be more easily described in the context of their influence on the overall industry than on an individual firm. Assumptions about customers, current and potential competitors, partners, suppliers, and stakeholders are usually more firm-specific. Within the organization, in addition to understanding the served market, it is important to understand the assumptions implicit in the value chain, cost structures, production technologies, key vendors and sources of supply, and organizational structures. It will often be productive to explore key assumptions about the relationships between customers and suppliers and a firm's competitors as well. Again, separately addressing "what do we know?" and "how do we know it?" is useful in distinguishing between fact and assumptions.

Validation

Once the key assumptions have been identified, each should be tested for its "fit" with the realities of the external environment. In some cases, this is relatively straightforward; in others some digging and analysis will be required. Similarly, the internal consistency of the assumption set must be evaluated. This is often the most interesting and stimulating part of the process. Key assumptions are compared to each other, one pair at a time, by asking "if this assumption is true, does this one logically follow?" Invariably, inconsistencies will surface, raising questions about the validity of the initial set of assumptions, and so on. The process should be continued, in an iterative fashion, until a reasonable consensus has been achieved.

Prioritization

The final step in the process is assessment and prioritization. Some assumptions are clearly more important than others; some are made with greater confidence; some are more likely to change. It is important to identify the key assumptions and monitor them closely, and to weed out those that are relatively inconsequential. At least four criteria must be considered in evaluating each assumption: (1) how important it is to operating performance; (2) how important it is to strategic direction; (3) how confident we are that the assumption is correct; and (4) how likely it is to change. If the most important criterion is organizational performance—and it often is—the development of a business model and the use of sensitivity analysis is a good way to test the performance implications of key assumptions. A word of caution must be offered at this point. Financial sensitivity analysis tends to focus on near-term performance, rather than on longer-term strategic positioning. Care should be taken to ensure that short-term performance is balanced against other strategic criteria in determining which assumptions should be monitored most closely.

Communication

Once the prioritized assumption base has been defined, it should be documented and shared among the key members of the management organization. Key boundary-spanners—the sales force, purchasing agents, and engineers—who have the most frequent contact with suppliers, customers, competitors, and industry peers should be included as well. Everyone involved should know and understand the key premises underlying the organization's strategy and be alert to changes in the environment that might call one or more assumptions into question.

Ongoing Monitoring and Control

Key assumptions and premises should be monitored on an ongoing basis. Many different approaches are possible, depending on the nature of the environment and the organization. Periodic formal reviews of the assumption base may be appropriate and are often the best way to ensure the internal consistency of the entire set. In other situations, functional executives may be assigned to monitor only those assumptions that pertain to their areas of expertise and to alert the rest of the team, on an ad hoc basis, to trends and events that may impact the validity of the assumption base. At a minimum, each organization should devote a few hours, at least annually, to a collective review and discussion of the assumption base. This is often an excellent way to kick off the annual planning cycle.

STRATEGIC INVENTORY

Defining the boundaries of the competitive environment

- What are the boundaries of our industry? What is our served market? What products/services do we provide?
- Who are the customers? Who are the noncustomers? What is the difference between them?
- Who are our competitors? Who are the noncompetitors? What makes one firm a competitor and the other not?
- What are the key competencies required to compete in this industry? Where is the value added?

Defining the key assumptions

- Who is our customer? What kinds of things are important to him? How does he perceive us? What kind of relationships do we have?
- Who is the ultimate end user? What kinds of things are important to her? How does she perceive us? What kind of relationship do we have?
- Who are our competitors? What are their strengths and weaknesses? How do they perceive us? What can we learn from them?
- Who are the potential competitors? New entrants? What changes in the environment or their behavior would make them competitors?
- What is the industry's value chain? Where is value added? What is the cost structure? How does our firm compare? How about our competitors?
- What technologies are important in our industry? Product technologies? Production technologies? Delivery and service technologies? How does our firm compare? How about our competitors?
- What are the key factors of production? Who are the suppliers? Are we dependent on a limited number of sources? How critical are these relationships? How solid?
- What are the bases for competition in our industry? What are the key success factors? How do we measure up? How about our competitors?
- What trends and factors in the external environment are important to our industry? How are they likely to change? Over what time horizon?
- Are we able, in assessing our knowledge and assumptions, to clearly separate fact from assumption?

Is our assumption set internally consistent?

- For each pair of assumptions, can we answer "yes" to the question: "If assumption A is true, does assumption B logically follow?"

Do we understand the relative importance of our assumptions?

- In terms of its potential impact on performance?
- In terms of our level of confidence in its validity?
- In terms of the likelihood and expectation of near term change?
- In terms of its strategic impact?

Are our key assumptions broadly understood?

- Have we documented and communicated our key assumptions? To our key managers? To the boundary-spanners? To other key employees?

Do we have a process for reviewing and validating our key assumptions and premises?

- Is there a process in place? Are responsibilities assigned? Are periodic reviews planned and scheduled?

ENDNOTES

1. Gary W. Weber, Vice president for science and technology, PPG Industries, Inc., commenting on PPG's development of blue windshield glass, as quoted in "A New Paint Job at PPG". *Business Week*. November 13, 1995: 74–75.
2. Peter F. Drucker used the term "Theory of the Business" in his article of the same title in the Sept-Oct 1994 *Harvard Business Review*: 95–104. Hamel and Prahalad use the term "managerial frames" to refer to the same phenomena in *Competing for the Future* (see Note 3). The others have used the terms "strategic frame" and "managerial frame of reference." All refer to the same basic sets of assumptions, premises, beliefs, and values. Portions of this chapter rely on insights attributable to each of these sources.
3. Hamel, Gary and C.K. Prahalad. 1994. *Competing for the Future*. Boston: Harvard Business School Press: 50.
4. Some of the perspectives are from personal experience—one of the authors was a senior financial executive for Trailways, Inc., the num-

ber two interstate bus line, in the late 1970s. More current sources include: Tomsho, Robert. December 2, 1993. New Software Drives Greyhound's Modernization. *The Wall Street Journal*: B2; Wendy Zellner. August 22, 1994. Greyhound is Limping Badly. *Business Week*: 32; Tomsho, Robert. October 20, 1994. Real Dog: How Greyhound Lines Re-Engineered Itself Right into a Deep Hole. *The Wall Street Journal*: A1; Rampey, Jennifer. November 11, 1994. Investor Suits Dog Greyhound. *Dallas Business Journal*: 1; Tomsho, Robert. November 4, 1994. Debtholders Move to Drive Greyhound into Chapter 11; Stock Slumps 25%. *The Wall Street Journal*: A4; Anonymous. January 16, 1995. Dog-tired in Dallas. *Fortune*: 94; Myerson, Allen R. January 17, 1995. Greyhound, the Airline of the Road. *New York Times*: D4, D5; Deener, Bill. January 14,1996. The Greyhound Turnaround. *The Dallas Morning News*: H1.

5. McClellan, J. Mac. June 1993. On a New Voyage. *Flying*: 71–80; Wilke, John R. September 29, 1993. Beech's Sleekly Styled Starship Fails to Take Off with Corporate Customers. *The Wall Street Journal*: B1, B8; Farnham, A. May 2, 1994. It's a Bird! It's a Plane! It's a Flop! *Fortune*: 108–110; Phillips, Edward H. December 12, 1994, Poor sales kill Beech Starship. *Aviation Week and Space Technology* 141(24): 47-49.

6. Wattenberg, Daniel. 1994. Humvee! *Forbes FYI*: 116–120; Berber, Ben. January 24, 1994. Military's Hummer Shifts to Civilian Market. *The Christian Science Monitor*: 6; O'Reilly, Brian. October 2, 1995. What in the world is that thing? *Fortune* 132(7): 146–152.

7. Anonymous. January 6, 1996. What's in a name? *The Economist*: 53.

8. Stern, Gabriella and Rebecca Blumenstein. January 15, 1996. Out of Reverse: The frills are gone in GM's showrooms, but profits are back. *The Wall Street Journal*: A1, A5.

9. Cortese, Amy, K. Rebello, R. Hof & C. Yang. December 18, 1995. Win 95, Lose 96? *Business Week*: 34–35.

10. Clark, Don. January 16, 1996. Microsoft to Buy Maker of FrontPage, Software to Create Internet Web Pages. *The Wall Street Journal*: B8.

11. Judge, Paul C. January 29, 1996. Lotus is Learning to Live With the Net. *Business Week*: 70–71.

12. Sandberg, Jared and Bart Ziegler. January 18, 1996. Web Trap: Internet's Popularity Threatens to Swamp The On-Line Services, *The Wall Street Journal*: A1; Ziegler, Bart and Jared Sandberg. January 15,1996. IBM, Sears Explore Selling Prodigy On-Line Service. *The Wall Street Journal*: A3, A4; Sandberg, Jared. January 22, 1996. AOL, Netscape Are Discussing An Alliance. *The Wall Street Journal*: A3, A4; Rigdon,

Joan E. January 26, 1996. For Some, the Web is Just a Slow Crawl to a Splattered Cat. *The Wall Street Journal:* A1, A8.

13. See, for example, Smirchich, Linda and Charles Stubbart. 1985. Strategic management in an enacted world. *Academy of Management Review* 10(4): 724–736.

14. See Prahalad, C.K. and Richard Bettis. 1986. The dominant logic: A new linkage between diversity and performance. *Strategic Management Journal* 7: 485–501 for a discussion of the processes by which organizations develop a common view of the world around them.

15. See Porac, Joseph F., Howard Thomas & Charles Baden-Fuller. 1989. Competitive groups as cognitive communities: The case of Scottish knitwear manufacturers. *Journal of Management Studies* 26(4): 397–416 and Spender, J.C. 1989. *Industry recipes: An enquiry into the nature and sources of managerial judgement.* Cambridge, MA. Basil Blackwell, Inc. for a discussion of the development of common perspectives at the industry level.

16. Hamel and Prahalad, op. cit.: 50.

17. Peter F. Drucker. Sept-Oct 1994. Theory of the Business. *Harvard Business Review*: 100–101.

18. Hamel and Prahalad, op.cit.: 83.

19. See Keisler, J. and L. Sproull. 1982. Managerial response to changing environments: perspectives and problem sensing from social cognition. *Administrative Science Quarterly* 37: 548–570 for a discussion of the historical basis of managerial assumptions, and Schwenk, Charles R. 1984. Cognitive simplification processes in strategic decision-making *Strategic Management Journal* 5: 11–128 for a description of the cognitive processes that tend to discount discrepant information.

20. Hayes, John R. December 18, 1995. The Internet's First Victim? *Forbes*: 200.

21. Zajac, Edward J. and Max H. Bazerman. 1991. Blind Spots in Industry and Competitor Analysis: Implications of Interfirm (Mis)Perceptions for Strategic Decisions. *Academy of Management Review* 16(1): 37–56.

22. This paragraph draws upon the observations of Shaker A. Zahra and Sherry S. Chaples in Blind Spots in Competitive Analysis. May 1993. *The Academy of Management Executive* 7(2): 7–28.

23. Hamel and Prahalad, in Chapter 4 of *Competing for the Future,* op cit., offer some useful guidelines for broadening the organization's horizons and identifying new opportunities in the organization's competitive environment.

4

C H A P T E R

Creating Competitive (Dis)advantage

Success doesn't beget success. Success begets failure because the more that you know a thing works, the less likely you are to think that it won't work. When you've had a long string of victories, it's harder to foresee your own vulnerabilities.

Leslie Wexner, CEO, The Limited, Inc.[1]

In the early 1990s few firms were ridiculed as much as Food Lion. Starting with the expose on ABC's *"PrimeTime Live,"* with its charges of employee exploitation, false package dating, and unsanitary meat handling practices, Food Lion faced an avalanche of bad press. The result: not only a blow to their reputation, but also sharp declines in sales and earnings. What makes the Food Lion story so fascinating is the company's astonishing change in fortune. Few corporations have rewarded their initial investors as richly. Food Lion's original 100 plus investors have been treated royally: a single share of stock bought for $10 in 1957 would have split into more than 12,000 shares by 1991 with a value of over $200,000![2] Food Lion's employees have not fared nearly so well, however, and their discontent is a major source—but certainly not the only cause—of Food Lion's problems. Let's take a closer look at Food Lion's predicament.

Food Lion was formed in 1957 in Salisbury, North Carolina by three former Winn-Dixie employees, Wilson Smith and two brothers, Ralph and Brown Ketner. Stock was peddled at $10 per share to any takers in Salisbury. Tom Smith, one of the store's first employees, is presently chairman and CEO. Food Lion was hardly an overnight success. It struggled during its first 10 years of operation. Nothing seemed to work—trading stamps, contests, and drawings all failed to draw customers. However, 1967 marked the turning point.

That year, Ralph Ketner pored over six months of receipts and determined that if Food Lion lowered its price on all 3,000 items and sales increased 50 percent, the company would survive. The strategy paid off, the company was reborn as a resolute cost cutter, and the slogan LFPINC (Lowest Food Prices in North Carolina) soon appeared on bumper stickers. By 1983 sales topped $1 billion. Over the next nine years, sales and net income grew at over a 22 percent annual clip, to $7.2 billion and $178 million, respectively. Buoyed by its market success in the Southeast, Food Lion boldly opened over 100 stores in Texas, Louisiana, and Oklahoma in the early 1990s. Then disaster struck, and the downside of Food Lion's fervent quest for cost control became strikingly evident.

The first blow against Food Lion came on November 5, 1992, when ABC's "PrimeTime Live" uncovered charges of unsanitary meat handling practices and false package dating. Jean Bull, a meat wrapper who had worked in 12 different Food Lion stores over a 13 year period, charged:

> I have seen my supervisor take chicken back out of the bone can, make us wash it and put it back out, and it was rotten. It's just unreal what they'll do to save a dime. They take that pork that's already starting to get a slime to it, it gets what they call a halo to it, a kind of green tinge to it, and they take and put that into a grinder with sausage mixture, and they put it back out for anywhere from 7—10 days as fresh, home-made sausage. And it's rotten.[3]

Throughout its history, Food Lion's nonunion status and labor practices have hardly endeared the firm to its employees or the United Food and Commercial Workers (UFCW) Union. In its efforts to organize Food Lion's employees, the UFCW has applied pressure by bringing violations to the attention of the Department of Labor and allegedly mailing more than a million brochures to consumers to remind them of the "PrimeTime Live" expose. Shortly after the "PrimeTime Live" broadcast, the Labor Department began investigating violations of child safety laws and pressures by management to work "off the clock," that is, work after quitting time without pay. In August 1993, the firm agreed to pay $16.2 million to settle charges of more than 1,000 violations in the largest settlement ever by a private employer over wage and hour violations.

Unfortunately, timing is everything. These problems surfaced shortly after Food Lion had begun its major expansion into the Southwest, where it faced strong entrenched competition. In Dallas-Fort Worth, where the company planned to open 54 new stores, Kroger, Albertson's, and Winn-Dixie were well-established national players with excellent locations. Strong regional competitors included Tom Thumb, Minyard's, IGA, Simon David's, and Danal's. These competitors had fine-tuned their market analysis to the point where they offered a product mix tailored to the economics and demographics of local neighborhoods. Into this foray, Food Lion's stringent cost control strategy dictated smaller stores (33,000 square feet versus the 45,000 to 70,000 square foot stores of competitors), limited product selection, and fewer employees. Store managers, operating within the confines of stringent cost controls, lacked the resources and flexibility to respond to the highly competitive and focused market environment. Whatever competitive position Food Lion had hoped to build quickly eroded with the *"PrimeTime Live"* expose and surrounding controversy.

In 1993, the year after the expose, Food Lion earned $108 million, less than 1.6 percent on sales, compared to $205.2 million in 1991. Food Lion's credibility and reputation in the marketplace have suffered greatly and its stock has fallen from a split-adjusted $18 per share in 1992 to about $6 per share, where it continues to languish as of early 1996.

What went wrong at Food Lion? Was it worker exploitation? A management team out of touch with operations? A failure to adapt to new markets? Too much focus on the bottom line—or on the top line, for that matter?

WHAT WENT WRONG AT FOOD LION?

Food Lion was extraordinarily successful for many years. Founded in 1957, its performance soared after it adopted an across-the-board cost cutter strategy in 1967. By 1983, sales had reached $1 billion; by 1992, they passed $7 billion. With such extraordinary performance, it's little wonder that management continued to pursue and reinforce its proven success formula, based on stringent cost controls, in every new store. Food Lion's "everyday low price" strategy required that store workers perform multiple tasks to exacting time standards—company rules and procedures dictated the time to be used for unloading delivery trucks, trimming produce for display, and a variety of other operational tasks. Labor was budgeted based on a store's sales volume. If sales were down, a manager was forced

FIGURE 4–1

Retail Grocery Distribution Model and Value Chain

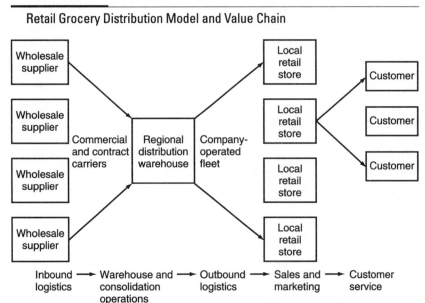

to accomplish the same tasks and provide the same service level with fewer employees, which contributed to pressures for employees to work "off the clock." As Food Lion expanded into the Southwest, however, it entered a different competitive environment—a more sophisticated market where cost control alone was insufficient to ensure success. We will use Figure 4–1, which illustrates a typical retail grocery distribution model and compares it to the primary activities of the grocery distribution value chain, to describe Food Lion's competitive problem.

As illustrated in Figure 4–1, the value chain of the retail grocery distribution model includes three "upstream" activities and two "downstream" activities. The upstream activities—inbound logistics, warehouse and consolidation operations, and outbound logistics—are concerned with purchasing, inventory management, and trucking operations and in most companies are highly centralized and tightly controlled. The downstream activities—sales and marketing and customer service—are focused on the local market (with the possible exception of certain regional advertising and promotional functions) and are primarily the responsibility of local store managers. The upstream activities of most grocery chains look pretty much the same; they differ considerably, however, in the way they manage their downstream operations and in the amount of autonomy and discretion they allow local store managers.

Food Lion was very effective in driving down costs in their upstream activities—inbound logistics, operations, and outbound logistics. Here, the powerful chain was able to establish strong bargaining positions with suppliers of products (e.g., grocery items, produce, meat) and services (e.g., transportation). Their strong cost culture and rigid control systems had traditionally served them well in creating a competitive advantage. This same approach was equally effective in squeezing out costs when applied to the downstream activities of sales, marketing, and service. It is here—store operations—where the giant chains interact with individual customers. In the Dallas-Fort Worth market, Food Lion's competitors also focused on cost control upstream, but worked hard to differentiate their stores by focusing on product selection and customer service downstream. In these markets, the public had come to expect a wider variety of product offerings, excellent customer service, and a pleasant ambience.

In this case, Food Lion's ruthless cost-cutting backfired. Its small stores, limited selection, and rigid cost and manpower control procedures contributed to a rather spartan atmosphere—long on efficiency but short on customer service amenities—an approach that fell flat in its new markets. Rather than attracting customers, Food Lion's single-minded focus on stringent cost control throughout the value chain, reinforced by an untimely run of bad publicity, led to a competitive failure. The company has subsequently closed many of the stores it had opened only a few years earlier.

STRATEGIC TRAP #3: CREATING COMPETITIVE (DIS)ADVANTAGE

Food Lion fell victim to Strategic Trap #3: *pursuing a one-dimensional strategy that fails to create or sustain a long term competitive advantage.* By relying on its principal strength—its ability to drive down costs—Food Lion came to dominate its Southeastern markets. As the company expanded into the Southwest, however, its narrowly focused generic strategy of cost leadership fell apart. Differences in the competitive environment dictated a different approach. By continuing to blindly pursue its traditional cost-cutter approach, Food Lion apparently missed the message: competition in the Dallas-Fort Worth market called for greater product variety and a higher level of customer service in their store operations. Even in Food Lion's traditional markets, its high-pressure management tactics and hard-nosed employee practices came home to roost when *"Prime-Time Live"* offered employees a chance to vent their frustrations by blowing the whistle.

The Food Lion debacle is not unique. Many organizations base their strategies on organizational strengths that do not create competitive advantages, or rely so heavily on a single source of competitive advantage that they fail to recognize the need for a different approach when environmental conditions change. The Japanese automakers have made a similar error in recent years. Their traditional strengths have been their ability to differentiate through high-quality manufacturing, excellent R&D, and impressive technological innovations. These strengths were important in helping Toyota, Honda, and Nissan develop strong market positions in the U.S. market. When over-emphasized, however, the same strengths led to excesses that have eroded their competitive position.[4]

By the first quarter of 1993, Japan's market share in the U.S. car and light truck market had dropped from its 1991 peak of 25.8 percent to 23.3 percent, with a decline to 22 percent projected by 1995. With the average Japanese nameplate costing between $2,000 and $3,000 more than comparable U.S. models, the challenge appears formidable. There are several reasons for the erosion of Japan's market share: the exceptionally strong yen; the improved quality, stiff price competition and impressive strength of domestic manufacturers in popular market segments such as minivans and sport utility vehicles; and some increased "Buy American" sentiment in reaction to Japan's huge trade surplus with the United States. In addition to these largely uncontrollable factors, the Japanese automakers have contributed to their own demise by "goldplating"—adding costly features and gimmicks that consumers simply don't value. *Let's look at a few examples:*

- The compact Toyota Corolla uses sophisticated and costly soundproofing technology borrowed from the Lexus.
- The goldplated sensors on the air bag systems are too thick— literally a case of "goldplating!"
- Even subcompacts include gadgets such as vibrating side mirrors to shake off the rain.
- Excessively narrow seams between body panels that buyers don't seem to notice. This has prompted Takayasa Honda, Corolla's

chief engineer to ask: "If the market accepts lower standards, is it really a good idea to keep standards at our level?"

Such expensive gadgetry and overengineering have driven up costs and made many models less competitive. The Toyota Corolla, which once appealed to economy car buyers, recently sported a not-very-economical sticker price of $18,670. Takahio Fujimost, an auto expert at the University of Tokyo, echoes the sentiment of many both inside and outside the industry: "Japanese automakers overused their strengths. They must now develop a keen sense of priority."

Of course, the Japanese manufacturers don't have a monopoly on automobiles with too many "bells and whistles." Mercedes' new CEO, Helmut Werner, who joined the company in May 1993, suggested that Mercedes "was guilty of overengineering cars and maybe overpricing them as well."[5] A prime example may be the 12-cylinder 600 SEC model, which sported a pricey $122,200 sticker price in the United States in 1993. The good news is that the annual price increases have averaged less than 2.5%. The 1996 Mercedes S600 (a roughly equivalent model) carries a sticker price of only $131,195!

A strategy of differentiation, in order to create a competitive advantage, must not just "be different." Rather, the concept of differentiation implies meaningful differences that are *valued by the customer*. Some of the Japanese automakers have gotten the message. Honda, for example, has found ways to cut costs without eliminating product features that customers would notice. The 1996 Civic model will replace the rear disk brakes with cheaper drums, integrate the dashboard clock into the radio display, replace the trunk hinge with a simpler design, use 30 percent fewer threads in rear seat materials and have the factory—rather than the dealer—install air conditioning systems. The cost savings have enabled Honda to add many features *that customers value*, including a more powerful 1.6 liter engine, electronic controls for automatic transmissions that ensure a smoother ride, and a higher roof with an improved design that creates a more spacious car with extra rear leg room.

Food Lion based an entire strategy on cost leadership; the Japanese automakers carried differentiation to excess. Other firms have fallen into the trap of pushing too hard for innovation. Apple

Computer's disastrous experience with the Newton is an example of what happens when an organization bets its future and launches a new product before either the product or the market is ready.

Apple Computer has always prided itself on being a "different" kind of computer company, and until very recently it was.[6] Although a minority player in the hotly competitive U.S. personal computer market, the company's innovative designs and fanatically loyal customer base resulted in industry-leading margins. In the first quarter of 1994, Apple's gross profit margin was 38 percent, admittedly a slide from the 1990 margin of 54 percent but still far better than competitors like Dell Computer, which operated on a much slimmer 23 percent.

Apple has historically competed on the basis of differentiation and quick response: the firm emphasizes R&D and innovation and strives to bring new products to market well ahead of competitors. Some of their "firsts" include:

- 1977: Apple II, the first successful personal computer.
- 1983: Lisa, the first PC with a graphic user interface (GUI).
- 1984: The Macintosh PC with its numerous technological innovations.
- 1985: LaserWriter printer—with Macintosh, it set the standard for desktop publishing.
- 1991: PowerBook Notebook, the first notebook computer to reach $1 billion in annual sales.

Given this string of innovation, the media eagerly bought into CEO John Sculley's bold new vision of the future. In early 1993, Sculley predicted that by the turn of the century, Apple would be giving away hardware and reaping vast profits through software and information brokering! The first step on this journey was the Newton, which was, in Sculley-ese, a "personal digital assistant." The Newton was a high-tech alternative to a Day Runner or Franklin Planner with built-in E-mail, fax capability, and much, much more! Sculley described the Newton (a full year before it was even released) as "the most important product that Apple has ever done," and predicted that Newton would spawn a $3.5 billion industry.

In the first month, Apple sold 50,000 Newtons—not too bad for an embryonic industry! However, subsequent sales quickly dropped to about 7,500 units per month. These sales represented just 1 percent of Apple revenues, well below the 25 percent predicted for the product's first year. Given this weak return on a $100 million R&D investment,

Apple eliminated about one-fifth of its workforce dedicated to this "growth" industry—including CEO John Sculley.

What went wrong? In its rush to enter the market, Apple made several critical mistakes. First, Sculley was too concerned with being a visionary—one analyst suggested that Sculley "had lost touch with the present because he was so caught up in the future." Second, with all the internally generated publicity, management felt compelled to release the Newton before it was ready. Sculley's successor as CEO, Michael Spindler, said that he tried to slow the Newton juggernaut until the software was ready, but "I lost that discourse internally at the time." Consequently, the Newton hit the streets with numerous software bugs and failed to live up to the expectations created by a year of hype and publicity.

Most of the new model's glitches were related to the lack of its promised ability to decipher handwriting, but the Newton fell short in other areas as well. It was useless as a communications device—Newton was ready, the fax modems were available, but the portion of the operating system responsible for linking Newton's CPU to the modem had not yet been designed. Although the Newton could connect with other Newtons using infrared beams, the device could not efficiently transfer data to or from the user's office network or personal computer. Later releases addressed these issues with improved handwriting recognition and a complete communications package, but sales have been disappointing.

So, is there a future for Newton? The reviews are mixed. In late 1995, CEO Spindler reportedly filed a recent proposal for a "new and improved" Newton with a larger screen in the "electronic ashtray" category along with other questionable products. With Spindler's ouster in January 1996, more layoffs underway, and the entire company on the auction block, it seems unlikely that Newton will, like the Phoenix, rise again from its smoldering ashes.

Thus far, we've described several organizations with impressive strengths in a wide variety of functional areas such as manufacturing, outbound logistics, operations, R&D, and so on. None was able to convert its primary strength into a sustainable competitive advantage. Rather, in each case, the organization's dominant strength contributed to a significant strategic failure. The root of the problem lies in a myopic vision of what the organization was trying to accomplish—a vision that carried a strategy of cost-cutting to a dysfunctional extreme, led to value-less attempts at differentiation, or pushed ahead with an innovation that the market neither wanted nor appreciated. Danny Miller describes the phenomenon in his book *Icarus Paradox,* in which he describes how an organization's success often sows the seeds of its ultimate failure. He illustrates his point with the legend of Icarus, from Greek mythology:

> The fabled Icarus of Greek mythology is said to have flown so high, so close to the sun, that his artificial wax wings melted and he plunged to his death in the Aegean Sea. The power of Icarus' wings gave rise to the abandon that so doomed him. The paradox, of course, is that his greatest asset led to his demise. And that same paradox applies to many outstanding companies today: their victories and their strengths often seduce them into the excesses that cause their downfall.[7]

Food Lion, Toyota, and Apple are not isolated examples. Miller provides a number of others—including Gulf & Western, A&P, Wang, and ITT. Somehow, perhaps blinded by their strengths, each made similar strategic errors. What did they miss? Where did they go wrong? Part of the answer may lie in the way their top strategists understood, interpreted, and applied traditional tools and guidelines for strategy formulation.

LIMITATIONS OF THE TRADITIONAL APPROACH

The traditional approaches to the analysis and formulation of strategy—SWOT analysis, industry analysis, Porter's five forces model, and the related notion of generic strategies—all require an initial analysis and assessment of the organization and its competitive environment.[8] The so-called SWOT analysis, an examination of the firm's internal Strengths and Weaknesses, and an assessment of the Opportunities and Threats posed by the competitive environment, is probably the best known and most widely used. Industry analysis adopts a similar perspective. Each examines the organization and its relationships and interactions with the other entities in its competitive environment. There's nothing wrong with these approaches—they have much to contribute—but these analyses, by themselves, rarely point the way to the development of sustainable competitive advantage. Let's look at some of the limitations.

Strengths May Not Lead to Advantage

A firm's strengths and capabilities, no matter how unique or impressive, may not enable the organization to achieve a competitive advantage in the marketplace. It's a little like having a concert pianist in a gang of hoodlums. Few would argue that such a skill is unique in the environment, but it hardly helps to attain the organization's "goals"! Similarly, the skills of a highly creative product designer offer little competitive advantage in a firm that produces low-cost commodity products—where little differentiation is encouraged or essential to be competitive. Building a strategy on the foundation of an organizational strength or capability that cannot, by itself, create or sustain a competitive advantage is a wasted effort.

Too Narrow a Focus

Strategists who rely on "traditional" definitions of their industry and competitive environment frequently focus their sights too narrowly on current customers, technologies, and competitors. By so doing, they fail to notice important changes on the periphery that may trigger the need to redefine industry boundaries and identify a whole new set of competitive relationships.

A One-Shot View of a Moving Target

A major weakness of both the SWOT and industry analysis techniques is that they are static analyses—they focus much of their attention on a snapshot in time. Static analysis is a little like studying a single frame of a motion picture—you may be able to identify the principal actors and learn something about the characters and the setting, but it's real tough to get much insight into the plot! Competition among organizations is played out over time, as circumstances, capabilities, and strategies change, and a static analysis falls short of understanding the dynamics of the competitive environment.

Overemphasizing a Single Dimension of Strategy

The misunderstanding of a related concept—generic strategies—may also contribute to an inappropriate emphasis on a single dimension of competitive advantage. In 1980, Michael Porter introduced the notion that there were three potentially successful generic strategies—cost leadership, differentiation, and focus—that could, if consistently implemented, enable firms to outperform their rivals.[9] Quick response has been offered as a fourth option.[10] Generic strategies were originally presented as mutually exclusive alternatives—an organization that attempted to hedge its bets by pursuing more than one generic strategy at a time would invariably end up "stuck in the middle" and worse off than they were before. For many, the concept of a generic strategy—for example,"Low cost becomes the theme running through the entire strategy" was so simple and appealing that many managers forgot Porter's admonition that "quality, service and other areas cannot be ignored." It is important to understand, as we will discuss later, that Porter's generic strategies are more appropriately used as building blocks for the development of a strategy, rather than as complete strategies by themselves. Excessive reliance on a single dimension of strategy frequently leads to difficulties.

> *The examples clearly show that a one-dimensional focus on an organization's greatest strengths may lead to disaster. The limitations of the traditional approaches to analysis are also apparent, and the connection between misreading the competitive environment and problems in strategy formulation is obvious. It's far from clear, however, where this all leads. Just how does an organization go about creating competitive advantage?*

CREATING COMPETITIVE ADVANTAGE

Our examples clearly demonstrate that the single-minded pursuit of a narrowly-defined source of competitive advantage is often insufficient to guarantee success. Organizations that have created sustainable competitive advantages typically do not rely on a single strength, but strive to identify and pursue multiple strategies and approaches. Earlier, we described Porter's three generic strategies—cost leadership, differentiation, and focus—and added a fourth, quick response, to the list. Each of these can contribute to competitive advantage, if used appropriately. The key is to identify where and how to apply these strategic approaches.

In the preceding section, we argued that traditional approaches to strategic analysis have limitations that may lead to strategic errors. How do strategists avoid making the unfortunate strategic errors that, rather than leading to competitive advantage, lead to disadvantage? What approach should be pursued? In our experience, there is no single, easy answer that applies across the board. Most organizations that have created significant competitive advantages and sustained them over time tend, however, to rely on several approaches and guidelines:

- Understand the business as a process—focus on the value chain.
- Expand the boundaries to include customers and suppliers.
- Identify strengths and weaknesses at each link in the chain.
- Add value in multiple activities and in multiple ways.
- Achieve close integration of value-creating activities.
- Focus on the dynamics of the competitive environment.
- Innovate by adding value in new and unique ways.
- Focus on strengths by outsourcing noncritical functions

Understand the Business as a Process

We briefly introduced the concept of the value chain—looking at the organization as a sequential process of value-creating activities—in our analysis of Food Lion. Understanding an organization in terms of its value-creating activities is a powerful conceptual tool for understanding the building blocks of competitive advantage. In 1985, Michael Porter popularized the notion of the value chain in *Competitive Advantage*.[11] He argued that five primary activities—inbound logistics, operations, outbound logistics, marketing and sales, and service—contributed to the physical creation of a product or service, its sale and transfer to the buyer, and customer service after the sale. Support activities—purchasing, human resource management, information systems, research and development, and organizational infrastructure—either add value by themselves or contribute indirectly by supporting primary activities. Although these generic value chain activities are useful for illustrating the basic concepts, we have found them awkward in practical application. The categories apply to manufacturing organizations, but are difficult to apply to other kinds of businesses. In addition, the generic value chain de-emphasizes the important interdependencies between the firm and other organizations in a broader value chain, and the ways in which these linkages can be used to add value for the ultimate end user.

We strongly advocate the development of a process-oriented view of the firm as an essential first step in understanding the organization and its position in the competitive environment. In our experience, the development of a *unique and specific value chain* tailored to represent the strategic situation and including all key

service and support activities is preferable to an attempt to force-fit
the generic value chain, which consists of predetermined primary
and support activities, to all situations.[12] It is important to conceptualize the value chain in its broadest context, without regard to organizational boundaries, and to explicitly place the organization
into the context of the broader value chain that involves suppliers
and intermediate customers, as well as the ultimate end user. We
prefer to define the value chain as: *(a) a sequential arrangement of
(b) processes or activities that (c) operate on inputs, (d) add value, and
(e) collectively produce outputs such as a product or service (f) created for
and delivered to an end-user.*

This definition facilitates the conceptualization of an organization's role as an integral part of a larger value chain that may include upstream suppliers and intermediate customers in the firm's
downstream channels of distribution. In addition to a thorough understanding of the activities that create and add value *within the organization,* managers must also understand how value is created for
the end user through interactions with other organizations *in the
larger value chain.* Strategists who use the value chain to conceptualize their organizations *as part of a larger process* frequently gain valuable insights that are hidden from those who tend to view the
organization as a self-contained entity with clearly-defined boundaries that isolate it from its environment.

Expand the Boundaries to Include Suppliers and Customers

Strengthening the competitive position of a business in an industry
often requires managers to look beyond their organizational
boundaries. They must ask: How can we enhance the value chains
of our suppliers and customers? That is, managers must view their
firm's value chain *as a part of a system* of value chains. The hotly con-
tested automobile industry provides an example of the way manufacturers, by working closely with their suppliers, can improve
quality and reduce costs and cycle time—with the benefits shared
by both parties.

Honda has developed a mini-reengineering program aimed at
strengthening its suppliers.[13] Early in its partnership with Donnelly
Corporation of Holland, Michigan, a mirror producer, Honda sent
engineers to study two of the supplier's plants. "The goal," contends Jim Wehrman, a Honda purchasing manager "is to give al-

most a consultant's outside view of the operation." Overall, Honda hopes Donnelly will reduce costs about 2 percent a year, with both companies sharing the savings. Additionally, Donnelly built an entirely new plant to make Honda's mirrors, a plant that puts Donnelly in competition for business from other customers. Not only does Honda get low-cost, high-quality components, but Donnelly's payoff is impressive: From $5 million in sales the first year (1986), the partnership will grow to $60 million by 1997. In this case Honda has integrated its value chain with that of a supplier to the mutual benefit of both organizations.

Motorola is another example of how excellent customer-supplier relationships add value in the electronics industry.[14] Motorola sharpens its suppliers' skills by teaching them its own total quality management techniques, including requiring them to take courses in cycle time reduction, customer satisfaction, and other skills at Motorola University, the firm's extensive in-house educational program. According to Motorola procurement chief Tom Slavinka: "We're teaching and coaching and pushing them in a direction that's been successful for us, towards a culture and a mindset that show that quality and cycle times have a direct relation to the cost of the product." By encouraging suppliers to analyze how much defects add to their costs, many have found that 12 percent to 20 percent cost-reduction opportunities are feasible. By helping to strengthen their suppliers' value chain activities, everybody's competitive advantage is enhanced.

The establishment of tight linkages between the value chains of a firm and its customers can also create competitive advantage. Robin Transports provides an example of how a firm can improve its customer's inbound logistics. Robin's trailers were designed with fabric walls to enable them to be unloaded from both sides as well as from the rear. These trailers can load closer to General Motors' assembly lines since they can load and unload in places where standard trailers cannot go. Additionally, Robin unloads the trailers in sequence for ease of handling and delivers at specified times when GM is ready to receive shipments. GM has realized productivity improvements because just-in-time (JIT) delivery promotes more efficient materials handling and inventory reduction. To justify its investment in special handling equipment for trailers, Robin obtained status from GM as a preferred supplier with a premium rate. The lesson: Robin Transport's competitive position was strengthened by directing its efforts at one of its customer's critical value chain activities—inbound logistics.

Identify Strengths and Weaknesses at Each Link in the Chain

Once one begins to view the business as a process (or series of parallel processes), it becomes only natural to assess the organization's strengths and weaknesses in the context of the value chain and to identify potential sources of competitive advantage and areas of relative weakness at this level of analysis. Managers must identify, sequence, and prioritize activities that add value for the customer or end user. Effective managers strive to strengthen value chain activities and relationships that add value and eliminate activities that erode or don't contribute to customer value.

The processes and techniques of SWOT analysis are appropriate and useful at this level. Industry analysis also becomes more meaningful when addressed in the context of the value chain. The ways in which individual value activities combine to create unique organizational capabilities become apparent from an understanding of their interrelationships and interdependencies. Benchmarking is often used to compare an organization's performance at the level of individual primary or support value activities with "best in class" performers, regardless of industry, and is useful in identifying ways to enhance organizational performance. Throughout this chapter we will provide examples that illustrate how value chain analysis can provide insights into the factors that contribute to an organization's success or failure.

Add Value in Multiple Activities and in Multiple Ways

Managers should strive to determine (1) what activities add customer value, (2) what relationships are important among value activities, and (3) what forms of competitive advantage can be successfully exploited at each stage in the value chain. Successful firms with enduring sources of competitive advantage not only identify activities that add value, but also recognize the important interrelationships among value activities. These organizations seek to add value at multiple points along the value chain and in a variety of different ways, each of which complements and reinforces other value-creating activities. Businesses pursuing a competitive advantage of differentiation succeed by creating unique bundles of products and/or services that customers value highly. Attributes that businesses use to differentiate their products and services include desirable product features, favorable image and reputation, competent and convenient after-sales service, manufacturing consistency and reliability, technological innovation, and status symbols. Lexus has established itself as a premier nameplate by selling cars of exceptional quality with superior customer service. Let's look at how they create competitive advantage at multiple points in their value chain.

Lexus, a division of Toyota, appears to have mastered the nexus among profits, customer loyalty, and employee turnover.[16] Despite a sticker price in the mid-fifties for a top-of-the-line LS400 sedan and the newness of its five-year-old nameplate, a remarkable two-thirds of the Lexus buyers are repeat customers. This represents the highest repeat purchase rate in the luxury car segment. Their approach to differentiation has paid off handsomely. While some of their product features and service practices may be viewed as "goldplating" in the lower and midprice segments, the more affluent Lexus customers typically value these attributes as an integral part of the luxury package.

For the past three consecutive years, Lexus has been rated number one in product quality and dealer service among all cars sold in the United States, according to J.D. Power and Associates. States Lexus's general manager George Borst: "We try to make it very hard for you to leave us. When you buy a Lexus, you don't buy a product. You buy a luxury package."

Toyota endeavors to put the same level of crafted precision in its service that it does in the automobile itself. Among other things, dealers are honor bound to give every new car a two hour check-up—including a test drive—before placing it on the selling floor. And all buyers receive four years of free roadside service, anytime, anywhere in the United States. Claims Borst: "Our challenge was to get people to buy a Japanese luxury car. The quality of the product wasn't the issue. Everybody knew that Toyota could make a top quality product. The issue was creating a sense of prestige. And where we saw a hole in the market was in the way dealers treated their customer."

To get a closer look at the Lexus experience, let's look at a typical dealer. At South Bay Lexus, close to Toyota's Torrance, California, headquarters, many people are surprised by what does *not* happen when they enter the showroom. Even though salespeople are paid on commission, they don't hover, pry, or solicit. Instead they are, in essence, out of sight until the customers tell the receptionist they are ready for a consultation. According to

John Lane, South Bay's service manager, "Customers won't stand for the hustle effect."

If you want to buy a car—and most customers make two or three visits before they are ready—the sales consultant leads you into a product presentation room, an alcove with no doors, no clutter, a semicircular marble-top table, and three leather chairs that are exactly the same height. This setting provides the implicit message that there are no traps and no surprises.

All employees at Lexus dealerships regularly attend national and regional training courses to learn about cars—including competitor offerings—and customers. Lane contends that he received more training during his first month at Lexus than his entire 18-year tenure at Cadillac.

Lexus customers are truly pampered. The first two regularly scheduled maintenances are free. While waiting for work to be completed, customers can either use an office with a phone or stand in the customer viewing area and watch the service technician repair their car in an immaculate, brightly lit garage. Customers who need to be somewhere are either lent a car or given a ride. When repairs are completed, all cars are washed and vacuumed by a valet detail specialist whose compensation, like everyone else's at South Bay, is linked to customer satisfaction. Like the customers, the employees love Lexus. South Bay's annual turnover rate since it opened in 1989 is a low 7 percent.

This example shows how strong relationships among value activities help to reinforce and strengthen the total perception of value by the customer. In addition, it illustrates the benefits of integrating key value activities with those of the immediate customers—the dealer—to create value for the end user. Clearly, Lexus must establish and maintain close ties with its dealers, providing resources such as advertising materials, parts supplies, and, of course, automobile inventories. One could easily imagine the futility of Lexus's superb marketing, sales, and service efforts if the company could not maintain tight tolerances to product specifications in the manufacturing operations, or if procurement were unable to acquire high-quality components. Clearly, superb marketing and service—by itself—would be inadequate to support Lexus's differentiation strategy.

Spartan Motors is an example of a business that achieves competitive advantage in different ways at different points in its value chain. A business that strives for a low-cost competitive advantage must achieve an absolute cost advantage relative to its competition. This is typically accomplished by offering a no-frills product or service to a broad target market, accompanied by long production runs and standardization to derive the greatest benefits from economies of scale and experience effects. Such an approach is usually inconsistent with a quick response strategy. Spartan Motors achieves both by emphasizing different strengths at different points in its value chain.

Spartan Motors, of Charlotte, Michigan, is a cost leader in its semicustom business of manufacturing custom chassis for fire trucks and motor homes. Its effective low-cost strategy has made it the producer of choice in its narrow markets, enabling its sales and earnings to soar between 40 and 58 percent annually over a recent five-year period. Many aspects of the firm's infrastructure, including top management and its budgeting and control systems, have played key roles. Qualities of thrift, discipline, and flexibility are central to this firm's success. Spartan's rigid cost control permeates the entire company. For example, CEO George W. Sztykiel has never permitted any budgets; expenditures must be approved on a case-by-case basis. "People spend what's in a budget, whether they need to or not. Plus that budget tends to increase each year. . . " claims Sztykiel. There are no expensive perks and no secretaries. According to Sztykiel: "Got rid of mine years ago. She separated me from the troops."

The unique configuration of its value chain also contributes to an industry-leading cycle time for the design and introduction of new products. Spartan slashes costs and inventories using common parts across the various models of its diverse product line, and saves development time by emphasizing the use of standard components readily available from suppliers. When combined, these tactics allowed its Metrostar fire truck chassis to go from the drawing board to prototype in less than three months. In contrast, a Big Three automaker may need three to five years to design a new product!

Additional insights into the reasons for Spartan's success can be gleaned by viewing its overall operation in the context of its value chain. Although their products are often highly customized to meet the unique needs of each customer, Spartan's design process, based on standard components and modular assemblies that can be built from off-the-shelf parts, shortens the design cycle considerably. Starting with a standard chassis design, Spartan is able to quickly specify the additional components required, integrate them within a modular design, and procure and assemble the necessary parts, thus providing maximum customization while maintaining highly competitive lead times. Unlike Food Lion, Spartan doesn't focus *solely* on cost leadership throughout all of its value activities. Cost leadership is of paramount importance, but differentiative and quick response are also important sources of competitive advantage.

An example of how one key element of strategy can enhance all three forms of competitive advantage is Southwest Airlines' well-known 15-minute turnaround time between flights.[18] It has been estimated that this quick turnaround (versus a standard 40-minute turn) saves Southwest approximately $175 million (seven airplanes at $25 million each) in capital expenditures alone through more efficient utilization of their aircraft. Also, greater aircraft utilization enables the airline to offer more flights—a source of differentiation because it provides their customers with a more frequent arrival and departure times at each destination serviced. Ensuring such tight turnarounds requires superb coordination among several value chain activities including ticketing, catering, baggage handling, fueling, maintenance, weight and balance calculations, and flight plans and local clearances.

Achieve Close Integration of Value-Creating Activities

Atlas Door successfully exploits all three forms of competitive advantage and achieves its unique position through the close integration of all of its value-creating activities.[19] This firm manufactures industrial doors in a virtually infinite variety of sizes, materials, and constructions. Atlas Door entered the industry determined to beat the time that competitors typically required to complete an order—about four months. How did they do this? Atlas invested in information systems and related processes to set up a just-in-time (JIT) factory that vastly exceeded industry norms for delivery logistics. They developed computer-aided design (CAD) capabilities so that customers could describe a door to an Atlas engineer over the phone. During the conversation, the engineer could draw up the order while the customer answered questions. Figure 4–2 highlights some of the important relationships among value chain activities at Atlas Door.

Computer-aided design enables Atlas to provide better customer service and improve sales and marketing efforts through tighter customer interfaces and quicker response time to orders and

FIGURE 4–2

Support Activities Enable Close Integration of Value Chain Activities.

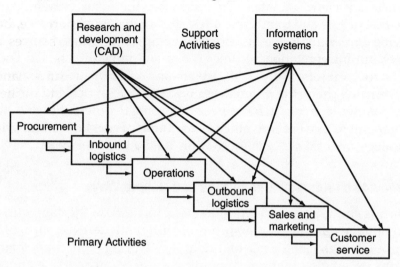

changes. In addition, the CAD system permits Atlas to develop more accurate raw material requirements. The added precision improves product quality and lowers defect rates and scrappage. The CAD system also reduces design time, thus lowering labor costs. The information systems and related processes and procedures that support the JIT inventory system also provide many sources of competitive advantage. Customer orders are handled more efficiently, improving customer service, lowering costs, and enabling more efficient throughput from procurement through outbound logistics. Not only are orders filled quicker, but less warehousing space, lighting, and staffing are required. And, since no product improves with age—with the exception of cheese and wine—losses due to damage and theft are reduced.

Focus on the Dynamics of the Competitive Environment

The competitive environment is in a continual state of flux, as customers, suppliers, and competitors enter and depart, as technologies evolve, and as competitive initiatives are launched and countered in the arena. It is essential to avoid the pitfalls of static analysis and to focus on the ongoing dynamics of the competitive marketplace. This extraordinarily difficult task becomes considerably more manageable when viewed in the context of an organization's key value activities. By narrowing the focus only to those market factors and trends that affect the organization's key value activities, not only is the bewildering complexity reduced considerably, but interpretation becomes easier and more direct. Had Food Lion focused separately on the upstream and downstream activities in its value chain, the differences between its approach and those of its competitors might have been interpreted differently, and the competitive moves its rivals used to counter Food Lion's low-price strategy might have been more easily seen and understood.

Innovate by Adding Value in New and Unique Ways

During the 1980s, much attention was focused on the competitive advantages of cost leadership and differentiation (in particular, through high standards of quality).[20] During that time, many firms became so adept at combining these two forms of competitive advantage that the Japanese began referring to the situation as *atarimae hinshitsu*, which means "value is taken for granted." When a particular form of competitive advantage becomes so common and widespread that it is accepted, in effect, as the minimum standard for industry participation, firms must find new forms of competitive advantage in order to sustain above-normal levels of profitability. During the early 1990s, many firms have discovered that they could regain competitive advantage by shifting their focus to speed or response time. Many academics, consultants, and executives have extolled the virtues of speed and quick response:

> Ultimately, speed is the only weapon we have.
>
> *Andrew S. Grove, Intel Corporation.*[21]

> Strategy making has changed . . . The premium now is on moving fast and keeping pace . . . The best strategies are irrelevant if they take too long to formulate.
>
> *Kathleen M. Eisenhardt, Stanford University*[22]

> Speed kills the competition.
>
> *Richard D. Stewart, CEO, Computer Corporation of America*[23]

As a strategic weapon, time is the equivalent of money, productivity, quality, even innovation.

George Stalk, Jr., Boston Consulting Group[24]

Speed can be a particularly strong source of competitive advantage when a supplier provides a critical element of its customer's product or production process. Here, if downtime is extremely costly, reliability and quick response become paramount concerns. Many readers will be familiar with Caterpillar's capabilities in rapidly supplying parts for its large and costly earth-moving equipment. Caterpillar's support logistics system has one objective: minimizing costly downtime for its customers.[25] Another firm that consistently makes *Fortune's* annual Most Admired list provides some rather interesting insights into how quick response strategies are implemented:

Dynatec (a unit of Illinois Tool Works with 1995 sales of $4.2 billion) routinely exceeds its customers' expectations for reliability and quick response.[26] The unit specializes in hot-melt adhesive applications typically used in high-volume, continuous operations, such as diaper manufacturing, case sealing, and carton packaging. In February 1994, Dynatec (located in Hendersonville, Tennessee) began offering a 24-hour emergency telephone hotline. The hotline is linked to a pager and beeper system that ensures that technical experts are always available to solve problems and keep equipment operating properly in customer plants. So, at closing time, a designated staff member takes home a beeper and a briefcase packed with after-hours shipping instructions, airline schedules, home telephone numbers of technical personnel, and other emergency resources. Three examples illustrate the effectiveness of Dynatec's "quick response" strategy:

One evening a Dynatec customer called to report equipment problems. The service technician diagnosed the problem over the phone, collected the replacement parts, and hand-delivered the package to the airport for immediate shipment. By midmorning the next day, the repair parts had been installed and the customer's operation was running smoothly.

Another customer, facing a Monday deadline, called Saturday at 10 AM. A Dynatec technician delivered the necessary parts to the customer's plant and repaired the equipment. Later that day, by 2 PM, the line was operating, allowing the customer to meet the deadline.

On another Saturday, a customer in Indianapolis called for help in operating Dynatec equipment. The technician on call provided assistance and shipped the required parts for same-day delivery. That evening, Dynatec's engineering manager visited the customer's plant to ensure smooth operations and customer satisfaction.

Some people may view quick response as just another form of differentiation. However, Dynatec helps to show why speed can form a powerful source of competitive advantage in and of itself. Dynatec's customers report that the hotline has helped to reduce both their downtime and service call expenses. Clearly, when customers are dependent on suppliers (such as Dynatec or Caterpillar) for quick response to minimize downtime, rapid availability of replacement parts or services becomes of paramount importance.

Focus on Strengths by Outsourcing Noncritical Functions

Competitive advantage can be enhanced, in some cases, by focusing organizational attention primarily on those activities that are critical to the development of a competitive advantage and outsourcing those noncritical functions that can be performed more effectively or more efficiently by others.[27] Strategic outsourcing is not just about reducing costs; in many cases the resulting reconfiguration of the value chain can redefine the terms of engagement in the competitive arena. One recent example is Pepsi's cost leadership strategy at its Taco Bell unit. CEO John Martin introduced the K-minus concept (the K stands for kitchen) in 1989 to drive down costs and improve the focus on service.[28] Under this plan, many food production activities such as crushing beans, dicing cheese, and preparing beef were removed from the restaurants and centralized in contractor-run commissaries. The cost savings enabled Taco Bell to slash prices. Equally important, however, the company was able to reduce the average size of its kitchens by 40 percent, freeing up more space—and employees—to serve customers. Outsourcing will be addressed in further detail in Chapter 6, where we discuss the concept of the modular organization.

You've talked about a number of ways to create competitive advantage—but how do you stay ahead of the competition over the long haul? Just what do you mean by sustainable competitive advantage—and how do you achieve it?

SUSTAINING COMPETITIVE ADVANTAGE

One way to gain insight into the sustainability of a firm's competitive advantage is to view the business in terms of the specialized assets, resources, and skills that it possesses.[29] The resources may be in the form of tangible assets such as advanced technological processes or efficient distribution centers, or such intangible assets as a reputation for outstanding customer service, a culture exemplified by a strong work ethic, or a cadre of loyal and dedicated employees. Four criteria that a resource must satisfy to provide a firm with a sustainable competitive advantage are

- Is the resource valuable?
- Is the resource rare?
- Is the resource extremely difficult to imitate?
- Are there few substitutes?[30]

Two examples will help to illustrate the concept of sustainability. One of the authors recently interviewed the CEO of a medium-sized specialty publishing firm that had implemented a sophisticated digital processing technology to integrate the key activities of its production cycle. The implementation had been successful and had enabled the firm to reduce costs, improve image quality, and shorten delivery times from 11 to 9 weeks. The improved turnaround time was strategically important given the highly seasonal nature of the industry—high school and college yearbooks (where, of course, students want to receive the books at the end of the spring term, but before the summer recess begins). The new technology clearly enhanced several forms of competitive advantage: the firm's cost position, its ability to differentiate through higher quality, and its ability to provide quick response in the marketplace.

Were these advantages sustainable? Probably not on the basis of the technology alone. The system was not proprietary. Competitors could easily adopt the same (or even better) technology. If, however, the firm's implementation—the integration of the technology with other systems in the organization, the development of more effective work group processes, unique skills, and so on—was particularly valuable and would be difficult to imitate, the organization's competitive advantage might be sustained. Other key questions also must be addressed. For example, are competitors also implementing the same or better technologies? Do other approaches represent viable substitutes with better cost/benefit trade-offs? If the answers to these questions are in the affirmative, it is unlikely that the competitive advantage will be sustained for an extended period.

Our second example is Wal-Mart, the world's largest retailer.[31]

Ostensibly, Wal-Mart is in the business of selling moderately priced goods to the public. However, Wal-Mart took a closer look at its industry's value chain and decided to reframe the competitive challenge. The business they felt they were really in was not retailing at all, but transportation logistics and communications. That was the battleground on which they chose to compete. By redefining the rules of competitive engagement in a way that played to their strengths, they were able to achieve sustainable competitive advantages that dominate their industry.

The logistics technique known as cross-docking was a key element of their strategy. Goods are continuously delivered to Wal-Mart's warehouses where they are selected, repacked, and then dispatched to stores—often without sitting in inventory. Thus, instead of spending valuable time in the warehouse, merchandise just crosses from one loading dock to another in 48 hours or less. This enables Wal-Mart to achieve economies that are associated with purchasing full truckloads of goods while avoiding the usual inventory and handling costs. This reduces Wal-Mart's costs of sales by 2 percent to 3 percent relative to its competitors. The benefits to Wal-Mart (and their customers) "multiply." The lower costs help make possible the everyday low prices, which in turn means that Wal-Mart will save even more by eliminating frequent promotions. Stable prices also lead to more predictable sales, thus reducing stockouts and excess inventory. Finally, everyday low prices bring in more customer traffic, which translates into higher sales per retail square foot. In aggregate, these economies make the greeters and profit sharing easier to afford.

Although cross-docking would seem to be rare, valuable, and relatively immune to substitutes, why isn't this practice easily imitated and diffused throughout the industry? If imitation were easy, competitive advantage would only be temporary. However, this practice is extremely difficult to manage. To make it work, Wal-Mart had to make strategic investments in a variety of interlocking support systems. These systems, perhaps individually but certainly collectively, would be extremely difficult to imitate, thus making Wal-Mart's competitive advantage sustainable:

- Continuous contact among Wal-Mart's distribution centers, suppliers, and every point of sale in every store to ensure that orders can flow in and be consolidated and executed within a matter of hours.

- The company's fast and responsive transportation system, which includes 19 distribution centers serviced by nearly 2,000 company-owned trucks.

- Fundamental changes in managerial control that allow the stores to "pull" products when and where they need them (instead of the supplier "pushing" products into the system). Such an approach places a premium on frequent, informed cooperation among stores, distribution centers, and suppliers—with far less centralized control.

- Information systems that provide store managers with detailed data about customer behavior, while a fleet of airplanes regularly ferries store managers to the Bentonville, Arkansas, headquarters for meetings on market trends and merchandising.

- A video link connecting each store to corporate headquarters and every other store.

- Programs like stock ownership and profit sharing geared to making personnel responsive to customers.

The sustainability of competitive advantages over time varies rather dramatically across organizations—different tactics are used in different industries—and some firms are clearly more successful, over the long haul, than their competitors.[32] Companies such as USAir in Pittsburgh and Bristol-Myers Squibb have traditionally blocked imitation through the strong isolating effects of one-of-a-kind resources, such as geography, patents, and close customer relationships. At the other end of the continuum, companies such as Motorola and Sony produce products that are easily and quickly duplicated by competitors. Idea-driven products such as Motorola's palm-size cellular telephones and Sony's personal stereo are rather easily reverse-engineered by competitors. Motorola and Sony are formidable competitors, however. Sony's depth of capability in research and product design is a competitive advantage that is significant and difficult to imitate and that keeps Sony one step ahead of the competition in consumer electronics. Motorola's quality-driven culture places the company at the head of the pack in the low-cost, high-reliability manufacture of cellular telephones and similar consumer products. While the product designs are relatively easily cloned, very few competitors can compete with Motorola's excellence in manufacturing.

Often, the inherent sustainability of an organization's resources is not readily apparent or visible to the competition. The Bain & Company management consulting firm, which competes on knowledge and brainpower, earns substantial profits year after year without inviting strong competition. On the other hand, Wall Street's "rocket scientists" create innovative products using knowledge and brainpower but incur much quicker imitation—typically within months. What explains the difference in sustainability of competitive advantage(s)? The answer can be partly found in what might be termed "hidden" core capabilities or assets—assets that sustain competitive advantages indirectly. Some examples of these hidden assets would include proprietary knowledge, specialized equipment, company reputation, a strong company culture, or, as in the case of Microsoft's MS-DOS operating system, the emergence of a de facto standard that enables the production of ancillary products.

The answer also lies in what has been termed *complementary assets*, that is, resources that permit an organization to capture profits for innovation. Mazda, for example, had the repair facilities needed to support the introduction of the rotary engine. Finally, the power of organizational learning processes, unique management styles, and culture can sustain advantage. Examples include Jack Welch's dynamic leadership style at General Electric as well as Southwest Airlines' pervasive company culture.

STRATEGIC INVENTORY

1. Where in the organization's value chain do we create value for the ultimate customer? (Value chain activities may vary for each organization.)

Value Chain Activity	Yes/No	How Do We Create Value for the Cusomter
Inbound logistics		
Operations		
Outbound logistics		
Marketing and sales		
Service		
Procurement		
Research and development		
Information systems		
Management and administration		

2. What are the important relationships among the value activities? What are the important interdependencies? For each activity, identify internal customer/supplier relationships and interdependencies.

	Inbound Logistics	Operations	Outbound Logistics	Marketing and Sales	Service	Procurement	R & D	Information Systems
Inbound logistics	▓							
Operations		▓						
Outbound logistics		X	▓					
Marketing and sales			X	▓			X	
Service			X		▓			
Procurement		X				▓		
R&D				X			▓	
Information systems	X	X	X	X	X	X		▓

3. For each of the value-creating activities identified above, what form(s) of competitive advantage are emphasized? What activities and/or relationships among activities need to be strengthened to improve the organization's competitive advantage(s)?

- Do we add value in multiple activities and in multiple ways?
- Are our key value activities closely integrated?
- Will our competitive advantage survive in a changing environment?
- Can we innovate by adding value in new and unique ways?
- Can we add value by expanding the boundaries to include our suppliers?
- Can we add value by expanding the boundaries to include our customers?
- Can we add value by focusing on a few key activities and outsourcing the rest?

4. What forms of competitive advantage are emphasized by our competitors? What opportunities/risks does this suggest?

5. What resources, activities, and relationships will enable our organization to achieve a sustainable competitive advantage?

Resource/Activity	Is It Valuable?	Is It Rare?	Are there Few Substitutes?	Is It Difficult to Imitate?
Inbound logistics				
Operations				
Outbound logistics				
Marketing and sales				
Service				
Procurement				
Research and Development				
Information Systems				

ENDNOTES

1. Leslie Wexner, CEO of The Limited, quoted in Davis, J.E. October 17, 1994. Can The Limited fix itself? *Fortune*: 161–172.

2. Sources for the Food Lion example include: Swoboda, F. March 1, 1993. Labor's food fight: Food Lion tests strength of supermarket union. *The Washington Post:* C1. Southerland, D. August 4, 1993. Food Lion to settle claims it violated U.S. labor laws. *The Washington Post:* A1. Swoboda, F. February 4, 1994. Food Lion accused of selling outdated infant formula. *The Washington Post:* B2. Royce, M. November 18, 1994. Food Lion Inc. 'B'. *Value Line:* 1500. Ketelsen, J. January 17, 1994. Lionized no more. *Forbes:* 16. Salwen, K.G. August 3, 1993. Food Lion to pay big settlement in labor case. *Wall Street Journal:* A3–A4.

3. Wolfe, J. Food Lion comes to Tulsa . . . "Hello, I'm Diane Sawyer" in Hitt, M.A., Ireland, R.D. & Hoskisson, R.E. 1995. *Strategic Management: Competitiveness and Globalization*, Minneapolis/St. Paul: West Publishing Company: 584.

4. Templin, N. October 17, 1994. Why Japan will endure in the U.S. car market. *The Wall Street Journal:* A1. Armstrong, L., and Miller, K.L. April 26, 1993. While Toyota loses its hold . . . *Business Week:* 28-29. Miller, K.L. May 3, 1993. Japan's new credo: Average can be good enough. *Business Week:* 124. Updike, E.H., Woodruff, D. & Armstrong, L. September 18, 1995. Honda's Civic Lesson. *Business Week:* 71–76.

5. Hitt, M.A., Ireland, R.D. & Hoskisson, R.E., 1995. *Strategic Management: Competitiveness and Globalization*, Minneapolis/St. Paul: West Publishing Company: 76

6. Halfhill, T.R. December, 1994. Apple's high-tech gamble. *Byte*: 50–70. Anonymous. August 28, 1993. Apple Computer: Falling to Earth. *The Economist*: 61–62. Rebello, K. July 11, 1994. Newton: Will what fell down go up? *Business Week:* 41. Hill, C. February 3, 1994. First handheld data communicators are losers, but makers won't give up. *The Wall Street Journal:* B1, B6. Johnson, B. February 26, 1994. Sculley the 'brand' comes undone. *Advertising Age:* 31. Rebello, K. October 3, 1994. Spindler's Apple. *Fortune:* 42–56. In 1993, one of the authors was CEO of a supplier of communications hardware for Casio/Tandy's competing entry into the PDA market and was involved in numerous discussions with key personnel involved with the Newton project. We'd also like to thank Professor Brian Boyd of Arizona State University for his input on this example.

7. Miller, D. 1990. *Icarus Paradox*. New York. HarperBusiness.

8. See, for example, Ansoff, Igor. 1965. *Strategy,* New York: McGraw-Hill; Abell, Derek F., 1980. *Defining the Business, the Starting Point of Planning.* Englewood Cliffs, NJ: Prentice-Hall; Porter, M.E.1980. *Competitive Strategy,* New York: The Free Press; Porter, M.E. 1985. *Competitive Advantage,* New York: The Free Press; and Andrews, Kenneth R. 1987. *The Concept of Corporate Strategy* (3rd ed.) Homewood, IL: Irwin, for representative examples.

9. Porter, Michael E. 1980. *Competitive Strategy,* New York: The Free Press: 34–46.

10. Stalk, G., Jr. July-August 1989. Time: The next source of competitive advantage. *Harvard Business Review* 66: 41-51.

11. Michael E. Porter in his 1985 book *Competitive Advantage,* New York: The Free Press, has made many important contributions to value chain analysis.

12. J.B. Quinn, in *Intelligent Enterprise,* New York, The Free Press, 1992: 37, recommends that "all nonproduction elements in the value chain, and at corporate staff levels need to be redefined as 'services' which can either be produced internally or potentially outsourced to external firms."

13. Magnet, M. February 21, 1994. The new golden rules of business. *Fortune:* 60–64.

14. Bowersox, D.J. 1990. The strategic benefits of logistic alliances. *Harvard Business Review,* 68(4): 35–45.

15. A seminal contribution to the outsourcing literature is Quinn, J.B. 1992. *Intelligent Enterprise: A Knowledge and Service-based Paradigm for Industry.* New York: The Free Press.

16. Henkoff, R. June 27, 1994. Service is everybody's business. *Fortune:* 52, and Sellers, P. May 31, 1993. Companies that serve you best. *Fortune:* 74–78.

17. Tertelbaum, R.S. December 28, 1992. Spartan Motors. *Fortune:* 55.

18. The Southwest Story. December 13, 1993. *Southwest Airlines News.* Internal company publication: 10.

19. Miller, A., and Dess, G.G. 1996. *Strategic Management,* 2nd ed. New York: McGraw Hill: 162.

20. Miller, A., and Dess, G.G. 1996. op. cit.: 158.

21. Vinton, D.E. 1992. A new look at time, speed, and the manager. *Academy of Management Executive,* 6(4): 7.

22. Eisenhardt, K.M. Fall 1990. Speed and strategic choice: How managers accelerate decision making. *California Management Review,* 32: 1–16.

23. Stewart, R.D. November-December, 1989. Speed kills the competition. *Chief Executive*: 46–49.
24. Stalk, G. Jr., op. cit.
25. 1994 Caterpillar Annual Report.
26. Dynatec and Signode offer customers round-the-clock assistance. July 1994. *ITW Update* (Company publication), and *Illinois Tool Works 1994 Annual Report*; John D. Nichols, CEO of Illinois Tool Works, *Illinois Tool Works* personal communication with the authors; Leach, Mark. January 5, 1996. Illinois Tool Works, Inc. *Value Line*: 590.
27. See Chapters 2 and 3 of Quinn, J.B., *Intelligent Enterprise*. 1992. New York, The Free Press: 31–97 for a comprehensive discussion of the approach and rationale for strategic outsourcing.
28. Henkoff, R. June 27, 1994. Service is everybody's business. *Fortune*: 48–60.
29. For a detailed review of the resource based model, refer to: Mahoney, J.T. 1992. Organizational economics within the conversation of strategic management. In, P. Shrivastava, A. Huff & J. Dutton (eds.) *Advances in Strategic Management*. Greenwich, CT: JAI Press. 8: 39–61.
30. Barney, J. 1991. Firm resources and sustained competitive advantage. *Journal of Management*: 17: 99–119.
31. The Wal-Mart example draws on Stalk, G., Evans, P., and Shulman, L.E. March-April 1992. Competing on capabilities: The new rules of corporate strategy. *Harvard Business Review* 70: 140–147, and Kiernan, M.J. February, 1993. The new strategic architecture: Learning to compete in the twenty-first century. *The Executive*, 4: 7–21.
32. Williams, Jeffrey, and R. Spring: 29–51. 1992. How sustainable is your competitive advantage? *California Management Review*, 34: 29–51.

5
CHAPTER

Subtracting Value By Adding Businesses

Studies show that 33% to 50% of acquisitions are later divested, giving corporate marriages a divorce rate roughly comparable with that of men and women.[1]

T. P. Pare, Fortune

With odds like that, the chances for success in a strategy of growth through acquisition appear about as good as we'd expect on a roulette wheel in Las Vegas. Rather than view diversification as a crapshoot, however, the focus of this chapter is on the factors that need to be considered—and the mistakes that must be avoided—in order to tip the odds in your favor. The stakes, of course, can be huge. Witness Disney's acquisition of Capital Cities/ABC ($19 billion), Time's acquisition of Warner Communications ($13.9 billion), Viacom's acquisition of Paramount Communications ($9.7 billion) *and* Blockbuster Entertainment ($7.7 billion), and so on.

Although there are many examples of misguided diversification to choose from, we'll start with one of France's most recognizable firms—Lyonnaise des Eaux. It is the world's second largest distributor of water and much more—or less—depending on your perspective. Until about a decade ago, their only businesses were wastewater treatment and environmental services. But, my how times have changed:

Today, Lyonnaise des Eaux is a $19 billion industrial group with a presence in over 80 countries; its businesses include water, waste management, energy technologies, cable and broadcast TV, health care, building construction and civil engineering, road building, management and operation of toll roads, carparks, off-shore works, and much more.[2] Lyonnaise can offer true "cradle to grave" services to their customers—PFG, a Lyonnaise subsidiary, is the largest funeral services provider in France. Think of the synergies: a mausoleum with long-term parking, or a funeral channel on one of their cable TV operations!

The firm is led by an autocrat, Jerome Monod. A former civil servant, Monod has run Lyonnaise since 1980 and has only recently shared power with his deputy chairman, Guy de Panafiew. Lyonnaise des Eaux's performance has been decidedly lackluster. For 1993, net earnings were $135.8 million on sales of $15.8 billion.[3] That might seem pretty bad, but it's even worse when one notes that the core water services business contributed $213 million to net earnings!

Is there a method behind the madness of Lyonnaise's extensive diversification? Some have argued that the company's activities grew logically from a particularly French understanding of its businesses and the special skills they have developed. In France—unlike most Western countries—public infrastructure is handled by private companies that act as "concessionaires." These firms raise the capital, design the projects, build the infrastructure, manage the assets, bear the risks, and keep the profits. Concessionaires describe their distinctive expertise as *amenageur des villes*, roughly translated as "urban systems designer and outfitter." Thus, Lyonnaise sees its business as "entire systems of services, and their core competence in terms of the financial, social, legal, managerial, and technical engineering that ensures the smooth operation of public infrastructure." Sounds reasonable. The firm's defenders claim that this strategy should help Lyonnaise diversify out of the water business, and that earnings from its multimedia empires will eventually match those from its utility businesses. *OK, but at what price?*

As it turns out, the price is pretty steep. Between 1987 and 1993, Lyonnaise's debt soared from $304 million to $1.9 billion; it claims to have made investments of $4.7 billion since the troubled 1990 merger with construction firm Dumez. The construction industry has been hammered by a slump in French property values, forcing Lyonnaise to make provisions of $338 million since 1991 and to pump an unspecified sum into Dumez.

Although 1994 earnings improved slightly, the company's return on equity was still less than 8 percent.

Clearly, the grandiose vision of their role as "urban systems designer and outfitter" does not appear to be working. Some critics have argued that Lyonnaise would have been much better off had it focused on exporting its expertise in water and environmental services, an area where it has had great success. In Britain, the first large European country outside of France to deregulate its water business, Lyonnaise serves close to 3 million homes. Last year, a joint venture between Lyonnaise and James Montgomery, an engineering specialty firm from Los Angeles, won a landmark deal to manage Indianapolis' water service. Lyonnaise also has been successful in providing water services outside the United States and Europe. During the past two years, the firm has won contracts to provide drinking water for a large part of Mexico City and for Guangzhou, China. In 1993, it won the largest drinking water contract ever awarded—a $300 million-a-year, 30-year deal to supply Buenos Aires' population of 9 million.

Lyonnaise has so much to offer the water market—broadly defined—that it is difficult to see what skills the firm brings to operations such as multimedia, other than the ability to dig up roads, lay cable, and patronize politicians. Here, we have a firm that defined its source of synergy far too broadly as "urban system designer and outfitter." It takes quite a bit of imagination to see how the skills learned over time in the core water business can be applied to its many, newer lines of business.

Another firm that suffered performance declines for a similar reason is Dole. Dole's specialty is growing and processing fruit. The company ran into a lot of problems when it tried to develop some of its vast real estate holdings. Perhaps we have even a more extreme case of moving outside of one's area of expertise than Lyonnaise. Here, we have a pineapple processor tackling island management!

Pineapples and bananas come to mind when most people think of the Dole Food Company.[4] Dole's brand awareness is strong and its food business accounts for about 90 percent of the firm's revenues. However, Wall Street has long viewed Dole's real estate holdings as the firm's hidden gem. Dole's failure to convert these assets into profits demonstrates the problems that firms encounter when they move beyond their traditional lines of business.

One of the largest produce companies in the world, Dole has been battered in recent years by softening prices for bananas and pineapples. This helps explain some disappointing financial results. In 1993, Dole's operating income fell 8 percent to $170 million as its revenues rose less than 1 percent to $3.4 billion. From September 1991 through late 1994, Dole's stock lost over a third of its value. Not a lot of return for the shareholders!

Unfortunately, Dole's real estate ventures have not been much help—but it is not for want of assets. Founded in 1851, Dole and its predecessors acquired enormous tracts of farmland over the decades, including 150,000 acres in California and Hawaii and 80,000 acres abroad, estimated by one of Dole's big shareholders to be worth up to $1 billion.

To exploit these large holdings, Dole appeared to put the right person at the helm when billionaire David Murdoch became CEO in 1985. Murdoch had spent much of his career on expansive and exclusive real estate projects. His plan for Dole seemed sound: Sell off the properties that were immediately marketable, develop the rest to improve their appeal, and then sell them, too. Unfortunately, things didn't work out that easily.

One of Murdoch's first moves strayed from the plan. Rather than sell existing properties, he purchased more than 9,000 acres to build single-family homes and apartment complexes in Bakersfield, California. Unfortunately, a 1989 real estate bust dried up financing for ambitious development and narrowed the pool of potential buyers for the properties.

His most grandiose venture has been a lavish resort development dubbed "The Private Island." Formerly a pineapple-growing outpost, Lanai is located eight miles off Maui. Dole owns 98 percent of this 141-square mile island, which it purchased in 1922. Dole began planning the Lanai resorts in the mid 1970s, when high local labor costs made it difficult to compete in the world pineapple market. Shortly after Murdoch became CEO, the development dramatically accelerated. The tropical paradise now includes two resort hotels: the Lodge at Koele was designed as a mountain retreat with a hunting lodge atmosphere; the Manele Bay Hotel is a more traditional beachfront resort. Both resorts are clearly upscale with room rates beginning at $295 a night. Amenities include horseback trails, tennis, croquet, hunting, and two 18-hole golf courses.

One of the main selling points for Lanai's affluent visitors is its isolation—Microsoft Chairman Bill Gates chose it as the site for his wedding. Unfortunately, the resort has become a little too private—vacancy rates average around 50 percent. By early 1994 Lanai had cost Dole $340 million, 50 percent more than initially planned. Analysts estimate that the resort has lost

$117 million since 1991. The cost overruns are largely attributed to costly construction delays caused by environmental and regulatory issues. To aggravate matters, Dole's Lanai companies are not ordinary resort operations: Dole must run an entire island and maintain the island's infrastructure. When Hurricane Iniki damaged the breakwater at Kaumalapau Harbor, Dole was responsible for repairs. The company also subsidizes workers' housing and, with new hotel workers arriving, has built hundreds of homes for rent. There will also be homes for the more discriminating. Murdoch plans to build 775 homes on the island, with prices ranging up to $900,000. "Projects like that are dead in the water" asserts Darryl Chai, a real estate consultant with PKF Hawaii. Murdoch, however, insists the homes will sell.

So far, Murdoch can't make such claims for some of Dole's other real estate assets, its huge commercial properties. Dole scrapped two separate plans to securitize millions of dollars in commercial and industrial real estate in the form of real estate investment trusts (REITs).

With few big real estate payoffs in sight, Murdoch has lately been trying to wrench more profits from Dole's food business. During 1993, he cut $130 million in annual costs out of Dole's overhead by trimming 5,000 workers, 10 percent of the workforce. Murdoch also planned to boost market share in Europe by spending $125 million, much of it in 1994, to buy small local distributors.

Despite these initiatives, Murdoch has lost credibility with Wall Street. The reason: Poor performance and a seemingly unfocused strategy that ranges from European expansion to REITs. "This guy is all over the lot," claims analyst Timothy S. Ramey of C.J. Lawrence Inc. "This doesn't instill confidence." Meanwhile, back on Lanai, Dole was experimenting with diversified agricultural products, such as oat hay for Oahu's cattle, to bring in more revenue![5]

STRATEGIC TRAP #4: SUBTRACTING VALUE BY ADDING BUSINESSES

Mergers and acquisitions must, in the end, be justified by the creation of value for shareholders. Individual investors can often diversify their portfolios a lot more cheaply than corporations, which, in the case of mergers and acquisitions, usually end up paying expensive takeover premiums. By attempting to diversify into areas of activity that did not add more value *through acquisition* than individual investors could do *on their own*, both Lyonnaise des Eaux and Dole marched directly into Strategic Trap #4: *Subtracting value by adding businesses.*

According to Mergerstat, by the end of 1995, the average premium over market pricing on deals over $500 million was about 37 percent, down from 1994's 41 percent but up quite dramatically from 26 percent in 1993.[6] These huge takeover premiums make it pretty difficult to increase shareholder value even if everything starts to click. A study by Mark Sirower, of the Stern School of Business at New York University, has demonstrated that a buyer, to recover a 50 percent acquisition premium, would have to increase the return on equity of the target by 12 percentage points in the second year and maintain it over the next nine years—just to break even. Sirower notes that "if you pay a premium, the clock is ticking—on the extra money you have paid."[7] Let's look at the track record of diversification over three different time periods:

■ Michael Porter of Harvard University studied the diversification records of 33 large, prestigious U.S. companies over the 1950-1986 period and found that most of them had divested many more acquisitions than they had kept. The corporate strategies of most companies have dissipated rather than enhanced shareholder value—by taking over companies and breaking them up, corporate raiders thrive on failed corporate strategies.[8]

■ Another study evaluated the stock market reaction to 600 acquisitions over a period between 1975 and 1991. The results indicated that acquiring firms suffered an average 4 percent drop in market value (after adjusting for market movements) in the three months following the acquisition announcement.[9]

■ A recent study conducted jointly by *Business Week* and Mercer Management Consulting, Inc., analyzed 150 acquisitions worth more than $500 million that took place from July 1990 to July 1995. Based on total stock returns from three months before the announcement and up to three years after the announcement:[10]

30 percent substantially eroded shareholder returns.

20 percent eroded some returns.

33 percent created only marginal returns.

17 percent created substantial returns.

Clearly, there were some winners and some losers, but overall the record does not look too encouraging. Given the rather dismal performance reported in these studies of corporate diversification, one is tempted to ask: *why diversify at all?* Why take the risk with so little prospect of a reasonable return?

WHY DIVERSIFY? ALL THE WRONG REASONS

There are many good reasons to diversify—we'll address these later—but there are also a number of reasons (excuses?) that just don't hold up under scrutiny. These include: *growth for growth's sake, egocentric machoism,* and a variety of *portfolio management* approaches.

Growth for Growth's Sake

Many have argued that *CEO hubris* at least partly explains the motivation for some of the highest takeover premiums. A recent study conducted by the Columbia University Business School suggested that the bigger the ego of the acquiring company—as indicated by such things as relative compensation and media praise—the higher the premium it is likely to pay. Harvard's Michael Porter notes that "There's a tremendous allure to mergers and acquisitions. It's the big play, the dramatic gesture. With one stroke of the pen you can add billions to size, get a front-page story, and create excitement in markets."[11] Few would argue that CEO interests, backgrounds, and predispositions don't play a role in many diversification moves. What other rationale could there be for David Murdoch's purchase of 9,000 acres in Bakersfield, California, despite his plan to *sell off* Dole's marketable properties? What is the justification for Disney's purchase of the Anaheim Mighty Ducks of the National Hockey League? Are there strong synergies between a professional sports franchise and the Disney Corporation or is it more an example of (avowed hockey fan) CEO Michael Eisner's ego?

Ego-centric Machoism

CEOs are often fiercely competitive, both "on the field" and in the office. There's nothing wrong with a little friendly—or fierce—competition at the golf course or on the tennis court. Sometimes, when pride is at stake, individuals will go to great lengths to win. Sometimes, when the stakes are much higher, a CEO's ego can get in the way of sound strategy. Take the case of Novell CEO Ray Noorda's obsession to take on Microsoft on all fronts:[12]

Noorda's motives appear to have been rooted in his bitterness about failed merger talks between Novell and Microsoft over the period November 1989 to March 1992. When the talks broke off, Noorda decided to challenge Microsoft's dominance in operating systems and applications, rather than to continue to focus on Novell's highly successful networking systems business, where the company had a strong technological franchise and sales organization.

In March 1994, Novell spent $1.4 billion to acquire WordPerfect Corporation, historically a leader in word-processing applications, but under increasing pressure from Microsoft's competitive offering. Novell's goal was to integrate WordPerfect's popular word processing software, Borland's Quattro Pro spreadsheet (purchased in late 1994), and other applications with Novell's networking software. However, severe clashes between the Novell and WordPerfect cultures blocked the smooth integration of the acquisition. Not only were the cultures incompatible, the anticipated synergies in marketing and distribution were not achieved. Novell's sales force was oriented toward the corporate market; WordPerfect's focus was on the retail channel. In the heat of battle, Noorda jettisoned WordPerfect's capable sales force and, when new products were ready, had no channels to the retail market.

Even more damaging, Novell's comparatively limited resources were spread thin, as most of WordPerfect's top management team bailed out shortly after the acquisition. Novell's performance suffered and the stock price fell sharply. Noorda has now departed. New CEO Robert Frankenberg is back to basics. What was left of Wordperfect was thrown overboard. What price did Novell get? About $180 million—mostly in stock and future royalty payments—about a tenth of what it paid less than two years earlier.

Novell is now locked in a titanic battle with Microsoft's Windows NT for control of the corporate networking market Novell virtually owned a few short years ago. Industry analysts project that 15 to 20 percent of Novell's installed base will defect to Microsoft over the next year. A major customer observed: "Novell is at the crossroads. After so many failed initiatives, they've run out of chances, and Windows NT Server is hard on their heels." Paul Gillin, the executive editor of *Computerworld* editorialized that "It's one thing to make a bad business judgement. . . . it's another to throw money down a hole when your investors and advisors are pleading with you not to. Noorda's folly. . . . has hurt Novell deeply and will damage the company's ability to enhance and invest in its product line just when it needs all the resources it can muster. . . . Novell's customers will be the big losers."

Portfolio Management

The results of portfolio analysis, by themselves, provide inadequate justification for diversification. Portfolio analysis includes a number of approaches, each of which seeks to balance a corporation's cash flows, profitability, and growth across a "portfolio" of businesses. Portfolio analysis has been practiced for so many years by so many corporations that it might be viewed as a traditional rationale—albeit, declining in popularity—for diversification. The saying, "old prescriptions have potentially toxic side effects" is clearly applicable to portfolio planning approaches.[13] During the 1970s, many corporations enthusiastically adopted portfolio planning techniques. One study found that by 1979, 45 percent of the Fortune 500 companies employed some type of portfolio planning.[14] Its attractiveness—as well as its dysfunction—lies in its simplicity.[15] Portfolio management approaches provide managers with a common framework for comparing different businesses. The industry attractiveness/business position matrix developed at G.E., the Boston Consulting Group's growth/share matrix, and several other variants have been developed to classify businesses in terms of their present competitive position and future potential. These classifications help managers to set objectives and allocate resources among the various businesses in the firm's portfolio.

The Boston Consulting Group's growth/share matrix is among the best known of these approaches. In the BCG approach, each of the firm's strategic business units (SBUs) are plotted on a two-dimensional grid, in which the axes are relative market share and industry growth rate. Each of the resulting four quadrants of the grid have different implications for the SBUs that fall into the category:

- SBUs competing in high-growth industries with relatively high market shares are labeled "stars." These firms have long-term profit and growth potential and should continue to receive investment funding.

- SBUs competing in high-growth industries, but having relatively weak market shares, are labeled "question marks." They should be invested in to enhance their competitive positions.
- SBUs with high market shares in low-growth industries are labeled "cash cows." These units have limited long-run potential, but represent a source of current cash flows to fund investment in "stars" and "question marks."
- SBUs with weak market shares in low-growth industries are called "dogs." Because they have weak positions and limited potential, most recommend that they be divested.

While colorful and easy to comprehend, the imagery of the BCG matrix can lead to some troublesome and overly simplistic prescriptions. For example,[16]

> The dairying analogy is appropriate for (some cash cows), so long as we resist the urge to oversimplify it. On the farm, even the best producing cows eventually begin to dry up. The farmer's solution to this is euphemistically called "freshening" the cow: he arranges a date with a bull, she has a calf, the milk begins flowing again. Cloistering the cow—isolating her from everything but the feed trough and the milking machines—assures that she will go dry.

There are at least three fundamental problems with an undue reliance on portfolio planning models. *First,* they compare SBUs on only two dimensions, making the implicit, but probably erroneous, assumptions that (1) those are the only factors that really matter; and (2) every unit can be fairly compared on that basis. *Second,* the approach views each SBU as a stand-alone entity, ignoring common core competencies and internal synergies among operating units. *Third,* unless care is exercised, the process becomes largely mechanical, substituting an oversimplified graphical model for the important contributions of the CEO's experience and judgement. The reliance on "strict rules" regarding resource allocation across SBUs can be detrimental to a firm's long-term viability. Take the case of Cabot Corporation, a $1.7 billion industrial corporation:[17]

Today, Cabot Corporation is one of the world's leading producers of chemical products such as carbon black, which is primarily used in rubber products and inks, tantalum powders used in the electronics industry, and plastics concentrates. However, things were not always so rosy. In the 1970s, Cabot enthusiastically embraced the Boston Consulting Group's portfolio planning matrix and decreed that its traditional chemical businesses were cash cows. Subsequently, these divisions were milked and the proceeds were spent in "star" divisions including unrelated acquisitions into metal manufacturing, ceramics, semiconductors, and gas transmission businesses. In effect, "good money" from chemicals was thrown at "bad businesses"—businesses in which Cabot had no expertise and could not add value. Meanwhile, Cabot's chemical operations were starved of the capital necessary to maintain operational efficiencies. Not surprisingly, both morale and return on assets slid during the 1980s.

Fortunately, the Cabot family, which owned 30 percent of the stock, recognized the problem and brought in a new CEO. Many of the BCG-designated stars were divested and the proceeds were used to strengthen the core chemical business. Additionally, research efforts were directed toward Cabot's traditional areas of expertise, organic chemicals, where the emphasis was on enhancing the value of Cabot's commodity products. The result: Cabot's operating costs have fallen dramatically, while a new generation of specialty chemicals, related by common core competencies, has enabled the firm to increase margins. In 1992, Cabot's earnings jumped 55 percent over 1991, despite zero revenue growth due to the effect of divestments. The company's strong earnings growth has continued through 1995.

WHY DIVERSIFY? ALL THE RIGHT REASONS

There are a number of valid—even compelling—reasons for diversification. The overriding guideline, however, should always be that diversification makes sense only when it adds value above and beyond that which could be realized by individual investors through a strategy of diversification in their own equity portfolios.

Central to our discussion is the concept of synergy. In financial terms, the value of synergy is defined as *the incremental value created by business units working together as part of a corporation as compared to the value created by the units operating independently.* Synergy may be created by (1) capitalizing on core competencies (R&D expertise, marketing skills, etc.), (2) sharing infrastructures (production facilities, marketing channels, procurement processes, and the like), and (3) increasing market power (creating a stronger bargaining position vis a vis customers and suppliers).

Capitalizing on Core Competencies

The notion of core competencies is illustrated by the imagery of the diversified corporation as a tree.[18] The trunk and major limbs represent *core products*; the smaller branches are *business units*; and the leaves, flowers and fruit are *end products*. The core competencies are represented by the root system, which provides nourishment, sustenance, and stability. Managers often misread the strength of competitors by looking only at their end products, just as one can fail to appreciate the strength of a tree by looking only at its leaves. Core competencies may also be viewed as the "glue" that binds existing businesses together or, as we see in the case of Mason & Hanger, the engine that fuels new business growth:

Mason & Hanger illustrates the benefits of focusing on core competencies instead of end products.[19] And for good reason. As the prime contractor for the U. S. nuclear weapon system and with 90 percent of their $450 million in revenues derived from military-related business, the company had better know how to do more than build bombs, given the end of the Cold War and the resulting military downsizing. It does. Richard Nathan, the strategic planning chief, broadly defines its business: "We design *high consequence activities*." Essentially, this means that if people botch their jobs, the results are catastrophic in terms of loss of life and property, or as eloquently explained by the *Forbes* writer: "the damned thing will explode."

Defining their core competence in such a manner enables Mason & Hanger to diversify into markets like sophisticated high-security systems. Accordingly, it derives substantial revenues from dismantling weapon systems—conventional, nuclear, and chemical. Presently, it is dismantling missile silos in the Ukraine. It also is supervising security systems at Anheuser-Busch's brewery in Williamsburg, Virginia; it has completed a "threat of vulnerability assessment" of the subway systems for the New York Transit Authority, and its equipment and systems protect Saudi oilfields and refineries. So, despite an expected loss of one-third of the present revenue base due to military cutbacks, its judicious diversification moves should ensure future growth and profitability. Interestingly, this example also proves that "old dogs can learn new tricks"—founded in 1827, Mason & Hanger is the oldest continuously operating construction and engineering firm in the United States.

Core competencies reflect the collective learning in organizations—how to coordinate diverse production skills, integrate multiple streams of technologies, and market and merchandise diverse product and services. The theoretical knowledge necessary to put a radio on a chip does not in itself assure a company the skill needed to produce a miniature radio approximately the size of a business card. To accomplish this, Casio must synthesize know-how in miniaturization, microprocessor design, material science, and ultrathin precision casting—the same skills it applies in its miniature card calculators, pocket TVs, and digital watches.

Core competencies go beyond harmonizing streams of technology, integrating production flows, or coordinating marketing and merchandising efforts. Value activities must be constructively linked to deliver customer value in a timely manner. 3M's adhesives technology, which has played a key role in the company's continuing success, clearly illustrates the many branches nourished by a strong core competence:

Over the years, few organizations have matched 3M's consistent record of innovation.[20] Typically, over 25 percent of the $13.5 billion, Minneapolis-based firm's sales come from products introduced within the most recent four-year period. This impressive level of innovation activity can be traced to 3M's core technologies: adhesives, nonwoven materials, and specialty chemicals—the platforms upon which a majority of 3M's products have been launched. At 3M, the process of research and development stems from a culture in which ideas, methods, and tools transcend business-unit boundaries so that scientists and technicians can draw from the full range of technological resources. They are encouraged to take risks with the recognition that an inventive effort is seldom wasted, even if it produces an outcome different from the one expected.

If there's one technology that has made 3M a household name, it's adhesives. Scotch Tape has been a fixture in homes and businesses for decades, and over the past 13 years, Post-it Notes have earned the same kind of acceptance. From the introduction of masking tape in the 1920s to the development of the first aerosol adhesive in the early 1960s and the first tape closures for disposable diapers in the early 1970s, 3M has been a pioneer in adhesives. Today, adhesives are found in many of the company's 60,000 products, and they are used in virtually every industry, from automotive and aerospace to health care and telecommunications.

3M's adhesives are tailored to solve specific customer problems. The automotive industry uses 3M adhesives to replace more expensive and time-consuming fastening technologies, including rivets and welding. Scotch VHB tapes are used to fasten body side moldings on cars. They're faster and easier to use than metal fasteners, yet withstand harsh weather and slamming doors. In the aerospace industry, Scotch-Weld structural adhesives replace welding in the fabrication of sound-suppression panels in aircraft engines, and adhesive-based sealants are used in airplane fuel tanks. The construction industry uses 3M adhesives on vibration-control materials in skyscraper construction. Fastbond 2000-NF Adhesive is a water-dispersed adhesive for the construction market. It bonds immediately, doesn't require complicated drying equipment, and avoids exposing cabinet makers to unhealthy solvents.

In the telecommunications industry, adhesives bond optical fiber cables used in cable TV and telephone networks. 3M's hot-melt fiber optic connectors, which are faster and require fewer tools than other splicing methods, blend 3M's expertise in advanced adhesives, ceramics, and fiber optics. The first "ouchless" tape for health care led to a broad line of 3M wound management products that today includes tapes, adhesive-backed skin closures, and dressings.

For a core competence to add value and provide a viable basis for synergy among the acquired and existing business units, it must typically meet three criteria:[21]

■ *The core competence must translate into a meaningful competitive advantage.* It must enable the business to develop some strength relative to the competition. Every value chain activity has the potential to provide a viable basis for building on a core competence. At Gillette, scientists developed the Sensor Excel less than four years after the introduction of the tremendously successful Sensor System through a thorough understanding of phenomena that underlie shaving.[22] Among these are the physiology of facial hair and skin, the metallurgy of blade strength and sharpness, the dynamics of a cartridge moving across skin, and the physics of a razor blade severing hair. Consumers have consistently been willing to pay more for such technologically differentiated products.

■ *The new business must be sufficiently similar to existing businesses to benefit from the corporation's core competencies.* It is not essential that the products themselves be similar. Rather, at least one element of the value chain must require similar skills in creating competitive advantage if the corporation is to capitalize on its core competence. While at first glance there would not appear to be very much in common with motorcycles, clothes, toys, and restaurants, at Harley-Davidson, there is.[23] Harley-Davidson has capitalized on its exceptionally strong brand image and merchandising skills to sell accessories, clothing, and toys and has licensed the Harley-Davidson Cafe in New York City—further exposure for its brand name and products.

■ *The bundle of core competencies must be difficult for competitors to imitate.* If the skills associated with a firm's core competence are commonly available or easily replicated, they will be unable to provide a basis for sustainable competitive advantage. Although it is not critical for an individual core competence to be unique, the collection of competencies must be unique, or at least difficult to imitate. Hewlett Packard illustrates this point. According to CEO Lew Platt: "HP is almost unique in its expertise in all three technology axes—measurement, computing, and computation—a potential competitive advantage."[24] These core strengths are found throughout HP's product offerings in mid-range systems, workstations, personal computers, peripherals, and printers.[25]

A core competence is not the same as sharing costs. It has been suggested that the search for shared costs may, at times, be a post hoc effort to rationalize production across existing businesses, rather than a proactive effort to build core competencies to enhance the growth of the business. Nonetheless, sharing infrastructures can significantly enhance a firm's competitive advantage. And it is often a proactive strategic move—many acquisitions are justified on the basis of common infrastructures and shared costs.

Sharing Common Infrastructures

Sharing common infrastructures can create economies of scale when two or more businesses are able to utilize the same resources: distribution channels, production facilities, sales and service organizations, and overhead functions.

Procter & Gamble has profited from its ability to share marketing expenses and delivery systems across multiple product lines. Since its products are destined for the same retail outlets, its various businesses—such as liquid detergents and toothpaste—can share truckloads to reduce costs. The company also benefits from sharing strong brand names. For example, after developing a new detergent with bleach, it introduced the product under the Tide brand.[26] Procter & Gamble's CEO Edwin Artz claims that putting the product under the Tide name strengthened the brand's market share and saved at least $100 million in introductory costs (versus launching a separate new brand).

Another firm that has benefited from sharing infrastructures is $5.1 billion VF Corporation:

Sporting a line of well-known brands such as Lee, Wrangler, Vanity Fair, and Jantzen, VF Corporation is one of the world's largest apparel firms.[27] VF has historically used acquisitions as a means of enhancing its Basset-Walker division's competitive position. Two January 1994 acquisitions—Nutmeg Industries and H.H. Cutler—stand out. What do these companies bring to the party? A great deal. The acquisitions have provided Bassett-Walker with several large customers it didn't have before, increasing its plant utilization and productivity. But more importantly, Nutmeg designs and makes licensed apparel for sports teams and organizations, while Cutler manufactures licensed brand name children's apparel, including Walt Disney kid's wear. States VF President Mackey McDonald: "What we're doing here is looking at value-added knitwear, taking our basic fleece from Bassett-Walker, embellishing it through Cutler and Nutmeg, and selling it as a value added product."

Analysts expect the acquisitions to be quickly and successfully integrated into VF's operations—there is an excellent marketing fit and the newcomers bring strong manufacturing capabilities. Nutmeg's sports logo business is predicted to grow at double-digit rates and Cutler provides VF with new marketing and distribution channels for adult and youthwear. Cutler's advanced high-speed printing technologies will enable VF to be more proactive in the fashion-driven fleece market. Claims McDonald: "Rather than printing first and then trying to guess what the consumer wants, we can see what's happening in the marketplace and then print it up."

Here we have an excellent example of a corporation achieving synergies by sharing production facilities and extending its distribution channels. Not only should VF enjoy greater manufacturing efficiencies, but also the ability to produce higher margin products with branded clothing should also augment both the top and bottom lines of its income statement.

Disney's approach to leveraging the success of the movie *Aladdin* across its many operating units shows how synergy can work in the volatile entertainment industry. Worldwide receipts from the motion picture hit $318 million by the end of 1993, but that was only the beginning!

People wanted to not only see the movie but also read it, wear it, listen to it, and play with it.[28] Disney's many operating units made those things happen—1993 was "the year of Aladdin" for the Walt Disney Company. To meet this demand, Disney Consumer Products licensed a full line of books, apparel, recordings, and toys that, more than a year after the release of the movie, were still selling briskly. To date, more than 4,000 Aladdin products have been created worldwide.

Subscribers to the Disney Channel got an insider's look at the film, thanks to a 30-minute special on the making of Aladdin. The channel also broadcast segments that promoted the film between its regularly scheduled shows. KCAL, Disney's independent Los Angeles TV station, joined the Aladdin parade, producing its own special, "The Magic of Aladdin."

Soon after the movie came out, a new Aladdin parade was unveiled at the Disney-MGM Studios and at Disneyland. Then, in July, Aladdin's Oasis, a popular new restaurant and stage show, opened at Disneyland. Aladdin characters have become instant stars at Disney parks around the world.

On October 1, 1993, Aladdin was released on home video. During its first weekend in release, it sold an astounding 10.6 million units. By November, more than 20 million units had been sold. Original artwork from the film was auctioned by Sotheby's for more than $1.35 million. In October 1993, the Aladdin video game for Sega Genesis was released—the first time that Disney was an active partner in creating a video game. In the fall of 1994, Aladdin returned as the newest entry in the Disney Afternoon, a block of cartoon programming. Every weekday afternoon, Aladdin is featured in a new half-hour television episode, along with Jasmine, Abu, the Magic Carpet, Iago, the Genie, and all the other stars from the film.

Aladdin's success is an excellent example of how the same basic product can be leveraged through the use of different technologies and different distribution channels to maximize revenues and exploit its full potential.

Increasing Market Power

The synergy that results from enhanced market power is a third sound rationale for diversification. Affiliation with a strong parent can strengthen an organization's relative bargaining position versus suppliers and customers and enhance its position versus competitors. Take, for example, the position of an independent confectioner versus the same business as part of Nestle.[29] Membership in the Nestle family of businesses can provide the business with considerable clout: greater bargaining power with suppliers and customers. With access to the parent's deep pockets the business gains strength relative to its rivals and is partially shielded from substitutes and new entrants. Not only would rivals perceive the unit as a more formidable opponent, its association with Nestle also provides greater visibility and improved image.

Market power can also be increased by consolidating an industry. Maytag, a leading United States manufacturer of domestic appliances, sought to improve its power with suppliers and customers by acquiring several businesses that extended and supplemented its core business. Maytag used acquisitions to diversify horizontally into the manufacture of commercial kitchen appliances, supplementing its existing position in appliances for the home. Maytag has also become more vertically integrated through the acquisition of its suppliers—increasing its market by making the suppliers a "captive" part of the same corporation.

Shaw Industries, a dominant manufacturer of carpeting products, shows how a firm can dramatically increase its market power by consolidating its industry. Shaw has flourished in an industry in which overcapacity has forced down wholesale prices 10 percent between 1988 and 1993.[30] While carpet prices have dropped from $6.40 to $5.90 a yard and overall U. S. production has declined 4 percent, Shaw's sales and profits have more than doubled to $2.3 billion and $100 million, respectively, over the same period.[31]

How does Shaw do it? By lowering costs through market domination. According to CEO Robert Shaw: "Control enough of the market and you can ride out the roughest times. Grow big enough so that your costs fall and pricing be damned." Shaw's prescription is no idle boast—the company now commands over 30 percent of its market, a dramatic rise from the firm's 5 percent share in 1984. In the critical builders' residential segment, Shaw's market share is above 40 percent. Today only three large players survive—Shaw, Mohawk, and the private Beaulieu Group—and Shaw is twice the size of its nearest domestic competitor. Shaw has used investment in new technologies and plant modernization to dominate and chase off competitors. Other competing companies were acquired when they couldn't match Shaw's cost structure and pricing strategies. In 1993, all carpet manufacturing operations were consolidated in one location, which was equipped with state-of-the-art looms and design computers. Economies of scale boosted operating margins to 8.5 percent before taxes, about the best in the business!

Not surprisingly, Shaw is not content to focus solely on North American markets. In 1993, Shaw Industries moved into European markets by acquiring Kossett Carpets, Ltd., the largest single-size carpet manufacturer in England, and Abingdon Carpets, another English manufacturer of quality carpets and carpet yarns. A joint venture with Capital Carpet Industries in Melbourne, Australia, ensures participation in a government-supported rationalization of the Australian carpet industry.

To further build its markets and drive down costs, Shaw is becoming more vertically integrated. According to Shaw, "We want to be involved with as much of the process of making and selling carpet as practical. That way, we're in charge of costs." Shaw acquired Amoco's polypropylene fiber manufacturing facilities in Alabama and Georgia. These new plants provided carpet fibers for both internal use and for sale to other manufacturers. With this acquisition, fully one-quarter of Shaw's carpet fiber needs are now met in-house. In early 1996, Shaw began to move down-market, acquiring seven floor-covering retailers in a move that suggests a strategy to consolidate the fragmented industry and increase its influence over retail pricing, as well.

COMBINING THE BENEFITS FROM ALL THREE RATIONALES

For ease of presentation, we have discussed each of the three valid reasons for diversification separately. Our intent, of course, is *not* to imply that the benefits from each rationale are mutually exclusive. Clearly, this is not the case. For example, VF's acquisition of Nutmeg Industries and H.H. Cutler should not only help VF by allowing the production facilities to be shared, but should also produce benefits from building on its core competencies in manufacturing and marketing. The market power that Shaw gains through market domination is complemented by the economies of sale created by consolidating manufacturing operations in a single facility. Furthermore, Shaw's core competence in manufacturing operations will help to increase the productivity and output quality of the acquired units.

Value chain analysis, introduced in Chapter 4, is an essential tool for analyzing and understanding the potential sources of synergy in a diversification strategy. It should be an integral part of the due diligence process, whether considering merger and acquisition candidates, joint venture partners, or investments in diversification through internal development. Managers must look at their existing businesses as parts of the broader value chain system that encompasses the firm, its suppliers, its customers, and the potential acquisition or joint venture candidate, and identiify the sources of synergy. Can synergies be created by (1) capitalizing on core competencies, (2) sharing firm infrastructures, and/or (3) enhancing market power? What important relationships exist or can be created among the primary and support activities of the value chains of the entities (including customers and suppliers) that comprise the firm's "extended" value chain? How can such relationships enhance competitive advantage through cost leadership, differentiation, or quick response. Will the competitive advantage be sustainable? What are the impediments to attaining competitive advantage and how can they be overcome? And, most importantly, can the potential increase in synergies more than offset the takeover premium and the risks associated with the strategy?

General Electric, the firm with the largest market capitalization in the United States (about $120 billion as of early 1996), pursues synergies across its entire organization.[32] GE's business units share technology, design expertise, compensation practices, and customer and country knowledge. The Gas Turbines unit shares manufacturing with Aircraft Engines; Motors and Transportation Systems work together on new locomotive propulsion systems; Lighting and Medical Systems collaborate to improve X-ray tube processes; and GE Capital provides innovative financing packages that help all of GE's worldwide businesses. These coordinated efforts help GE to capitalize on their core competencies, share infrastructures achieve economies of scale, and dominate many of their markets.

IS IT EASY TO GAIN THE BENEFITS OF STRATEGIC DIVERSIFICATION?

Hardly! If it were easy, the track record of companies trying to diversify would not be so dismal. Many things can go wrong. There can be "turf battles" when corporations try to get the benefits from sharing facilities or leveraging core competencies across businesses. Acquired businesses may resent the actual or perceived loss of autonomy that they may experience when they must report to new corporate parents. Inadequate due diligence by the acquirer (or merger partner) may lead to unrealistic expectations regarding potential sources of synergy. Conflicting corporate cultures can also create serious problems, as in the GM-EDS merger in 1984 and the Novell acquisition of WordPerfect in 1994. Even the best of intentions can be led astray by sloppy due diligence and ineffective implementation, as we will see next:

Borden, Inc.—owner of such well-known brands as Cracker Jack, Wise potato chips, Creamette pasta, and Elmer's Glue—is a classic example of a company whose apparently sound strategy was thwarted by poor execution and implementation.[33] Borden's stated objectives echo the successful strategy of Shaw Industries described in an earlier example:

> Growth will be achieved by marketing regional brands beyond their home turf. Consolidating manufacturing and distribution [will] make [Borden] the low-cost producer . . . and provide it with more clout in the marketplace.

In contrast to Shaw's strategic success, Borden's efforts resulted in failure. Borden's stock price peaked at about $39 in 1991. Shortly thereafter it began a free fall than ended only when the company was sold to KKR in late 1994 for about $14.25 a share, a price that reflected a 23 percent premium over the pre-bid market price. Why the precipitous decline in stock value?

Much of the problem lies with CEO Romeo Vantres's acquisition spree. Between 1986 and 1991, Vantres paid nearly $2 billion to acquire 91 regional food and distribution companies. Rather than create value by these acquisitions, Borden was saddled with nearly $2 billion in new debt, and its competitive position was eroded in almost every market.

Although Borden was never considered a "high flyer," it was far more profitable before Vantres's tenure. The acquisition pace accelerated sharply under Vantres. Senior managers were pressured to move quickly—in many cases, the company spent as little as two weeks conducting due diligence before finalizing acquisitions.

Laura Scudder's, acquired in 1987 for nearly $100 million, was one of the strongest regional potato chip brands in the country—it ranked number two in the huge California market. The acquisition was a disaster from the start. In its haste to close the deal, Borden failed to uncover serious union problems. Labor relations soon became so adversarial that Borden closed all of Scudders' California plants within a year after completing the acquisition! Production was shifted to Salt Lake City, but Borden wasn't prepared for the higher logistics costs, and a lot more broken chips, incurred by shipping the product over the Sierra Nevada mountains. Quality problems and intensified competition quickly ate into Scudder's market share. When even deep discounting couldn't halt the slide, Borden sold Laura Scudder's to another regional company for about $15 million. All told, the fiasco cost Borden close to $150 million.

Anthony S. D'Amato took over as CEO in 1991, inheriting a failed diversification strategy, poor integration among the multitude of businesses and brands, and declining positions in its markets. Under his stewardship, performance continued its steady decline. Borden lost both market share and profits as competitors—with more aggressive pricing—invaded Borden's territory. To complicate matters, mounting competition from private label products and an increased consumer focus on price made it increasingly difficult for many national brands to raise prices. Borden's vast collection of tiny brand names in disparate categories made any cohesive marketing program difficult and expensive.

Borden's efforts at promoting a national brand were often ineffective and frequently cannibalized their regional brands. Creamette was a star in Borden's $1.25 billion pasta business. Borden's advertising, however, focused more on increasing overall pasta consumption than on enhancing Creamette's image. While overall pasta demand grew by 5.5 percent, Creamette sales grew by only 1.6 percent. Meanwhile, Borden had neglected its regional brands and their sales declined.

Borden made a similar mistake in its snack business. Here, a national brand of chips and pretzels was launched in 1992; D'Amato hoped this new line could one day replace the company's existing regional brands. Not a good idea. The problem, says Gary M. Stibel of the New England Consulting Group, is that there is not room for another national snack brand beyond Pepsi's Frito-Lay and Anheuser-Busch's Eagle Snacks. Instead, Borden should "hide in the woods and throw sniper fire with regional brands like Jay's and Wise." Borden's management has since agreed with this assessment: They have abandoned their national strategy to refocus on their regional powerhouses. The false start with the national brand, however, consumed important resources and effort.

On the surface, it seemed like a good plan: expand the distribution of regional brands beyond their traditional market areas and consolidate manufacturing and distribution to increase market power. Borden's implementation, however, was a disaster—a textbook case of poorly managed diversification. Predictably, results fell far short of expectations. Among its errors, Borden:

- Failed to conduct due diligence in acquisitions—the striking example being Laura Scudder's Snack Foods.
- Ignored its well-known brands, and missed the move to super-premium brands.
- Spread its marketing resources too thin across many small brands, with little opportunity for increasing market power.
- Created negative synergies (2 + 2 = 3) by allowing national brands to cannibalize the sales of its regionals, as in the case of the pasta division.

MAKING DIVERSIFICATION WORK: GUIDELINES FOR IMPLEMENTATION

There are no panaceas to winning through diversification, no "one size fits all." But there are some guidelines that can improve the chances for success. Our suggestions fall into three broad categories: the corporate parenting role, the effective use of information systems, and the application of horizontal organization concepts.

The Corporate Parenting Role

So far, we have focused largely on how diversification activities can add value for the corporation—we have examined sources of value creation *across* business units. Value can also be created *within* business units as a result of the expertise and support provided by an acquiring parent. The positive contributions of the corporate office have been referred to as the "parenting advantage."[34] Many firms have successfully diversified their holdings without strong evidence of the more traditional sources of synergy. Diversified public corporations like BTR, Emerson Electric, and Hanson, and financial buyers such as leveraged buyout firms Kohlberg, Kravis, Roberts & Company, and Clayton, Dubilier & Rice come to mind.[35] These parent companies justify their roles when their influence creates value through management expertise. How? They improve plans and budgets; promote better linkages among units; provide especially competent central functions such as legal, financial, human resource management, procurement, and the like; and help subsidiaries to make wise choices in their own acquisitions, divestitures, and new ventures. These contributions often help undervalued businesses quickly increase market values through turnarounds.

Texas-based Cooper Industries' acquisition of Champion International, the sparkplug company, provides an example.[36] Cooper applies a distinctive parenting approach designed to help its businesses raise their manufacturing performance. New acquisitions are "Cooperized"—Cooper audits their manufacturing operations; improves their cost accounting systems; makes their planning, budgeting, and human resource systems conform with its systems; and centralizes union negotiations. Excess cash is squeezed out through tighter controls and reinvested in productivity enhancements. As one manager observed: "When you are acquired by Cooper, one of the first things that happens is a truckload of policy manuals arrives at your door." Such hands-on parenting has been effective in transforming the competitive advantages of many kinds of manufacturing businesses.

Using Information Systems

Information processing—the activities necessary to collect, process, and channel the data required to perform a value-creating activity—pervades all value chain activities. The use of sophisticated information systems becomes even more critical when firms expand into multiple industries and markets. The effective design and use of information systems can provide firms with multiple ways to enhance competitive advantage, as the example of Westinghouse illustrates:

To integrate the activities of 18 groups of businesses around the world, Westinghouse developed one of the largest integrated (voice and data) networks in the world, Westinghouse Information Network (WIN).[37] The network provides every employee with the means to contact every other employee in the firm almost immediately. Each day, more than 90,000 people use the system. It provides critical data and technical drawings to different functions and permits integrated operations through video conferencing.

The system is used to make decisions, sell products, and increase customer satisfaction. According to David Edison, executive vice president, the state-of-the-art network is really becoming part of the business, that is, a tool that is part of the product itself. He views Westinghouse as selling more than turbines or refrigeration equipment; it sells the information technologies to order them, to keep them running, and to make sure they are doing what the customer wants them to do.

The network also has led to a reduction in the need for capital spending for new facilities. WIN played a big role in implementing a highly efficient just-in-time inventory system. This has opened up considerable plant floor space—so much that one of the company's groups does not plan any new construction until well into the 1990s.

Applying Horizontal Organization Concepts

The concepts of horizontal organization can be particularly useful in enhancing integration across business units in the diversified firm.[38] We will briefly address three types of horizontal organization: structure, systems and human resources practices. These practices serve to link business units together within the firm's overall organization structure. Properly used, they provide a means to facilitate interrelationships and establish interdependencies among their different subunits.

In applying horizontal structure concepts, the firm is divided into a small number of groups, each of which consists of similar or related businesses. This helps each group to share resources and exploit synergies. Coordination among businesses is attained via mechanisms such as interdivisional task forces and committees. Such mechanisms help integrate activities both with a group and across two or more groups within a firm.

Interrelationships across business units are explicitly recognized and built into planning and control processes through horizontal systems and procedures. Open communication resulting from planning and review sessions (which include managers from multiple business units) facilitates sharing resources as well as concerns.

Cooperation among business units is enhanced further when they develop an understanding of the problems others face. Horizontal human resource practices are designed to improve internal understanding through job rotation of managers among business units, common training programs, and forums in which managers and staff personnel from different business units share ideas or educate each other on developments in their businesses. For example, Sony Corporate Research coordinates the activities of over 20 business groups and hundreds of project teams to eliminate redundant projects and foster technology exchange throughout the corporation. Sony Corporate Research's huge annual exposition—open only to employees—is used as a forum to showcase the technologies Sony's engineers and scientists are working on.[39] This three-day event, a cross between a trade show and high school science fair, serves to cross-pollinate ideas across various business groups.

Recently, Armstrong World Industries sponsored Team Expo '93, a championship competition that brought together 14 quality teams from Armstrong organizations around the world to present their process improvement and customer satisfaction successes.[40] A similar type of competition at Motorola—Total Customer Satisfaction World Wide Team Competition—involved approximately 30,000 employees in 1992, a remarkable 30 percent of Motorola's workforce.[41] Such competitions not only provide a forum to recognize and reward excellence but also encourage the dissemination of innovative initiatives throughout the organization.

Rubbermaid recently acquired Iron Mountain Forge, a manufacturer of commercial playground equipment.[42] After merging it with their Little Tikes division, the two business units were able to build on Iron Mountain Forge's expertise in steel fabricating and Little Tikes' knowledge in plastics technology. A task force consisting of engineers and marketers from both units developed the Little Tikes early childhood play center—a breakthrough in innovative and affordable design—targeted for use in day care centers.

DuPont's Nonwovens unit works in networks and teams to gain insights into potential products.[43] Team members then get together with customers or partners to rapidly deliver the new products. Such flexibility enables the division to seek opportunities in a variety of products and markets. For example, the unit worked with DuPont's Automotive unit to evaluate a Tyvek car cover recently introduced at retail. Nonwovens and Automotive are continuing to work together to design an improved product, and to come up with a cover for new cars enroute to dealers.

A successful diversification strategy must avoid the obvious pitfalls. It is clearly undesirable to erode shareholder value by adding businesses that do not create valid synergies, or by dropping the ball in implementation and causing a valid diversification strategy to self-destruct. Diversification strategies motivated by CEO hubris, the notion of "growth for growth's sake," or rationalized by the use of oversimplified portfolio management approaches often fail to create value through meaningful organizational synergies. Diversification strategies based on leveraging core competencies, reducing overall costs by sharing infrastructures, or increasing market power are more likely to succeed, and when the benefits of two or more of these rationales can be combined, the odds begin to improve dramatically. Implementation remains critical, however. Even the best of diversification strategies, poorly implemented, are doomed to failure. When organizations are combined, extraordinary efforts are often required to ensure that effective communications, coordination and integration are achieved across the inevitable barriers of geography, culture and organizational boundaries.

STRATEGIC INVENTORY

For a diversified firm to create value greater than the sum of its individual parts, managers must address many issues:

- What are the core competencies of the corporation (e.g., technology, manufacturing, marketing)? Are they being successfully leveraged across businesses (present and proposed)?
- What common infrastructures does the corporation have that are or can be effectively shared across businesses (present and proposed)? These include production facilities, shared product platforms (e.g., Chrysler's K-Car), delivery systems, and the like.
- How can diversification enhance a firm's market power vis á vis competitors, suppliers, customers?

- Consider each business (and potential business), along with key suppliers and customers, as parts of an extended value chain system. What activities (both primary and support) and relationships can be strengthened to enhance a firm's sources of competitive advantage and make them sustainable?
- How can the corporate office (i.e., parent) add value to the businesses? Can the parent improve planning and budgeting, promote linkages among businesses, provide excellent central functions, such as legal, human resources, procurement, and so on?
- How can more effective information systems help businesses increase their competitiveness?
- Can further synergies be realized across businesses through the application of horizontal organization concepts? These include horizontal structures, systems, and human resource practices.

ENDNOTES

1. Pare, T.P. November 28, 1994. The new merger boom. *Fortune:* 96.
2. Anonymous. June 18, 1994. Tally eaux. *The Economist:* 75–76; Norman, R. and Ramirez, R. July-August, 1993. From value chain to value constellation: Designing interactive strategy. *Harvard Business Review:* 73–77; Mao, P. September 12, 1992. Water with a French touch. *Business Week:* 212–214; Reier, Sharon, October 24, 1995. French rules. *Financial World* 164(22): 40–42;
3. Figures converted to dollars on the basis of $1 U.S. = 5.92FF — the exchange rate as of December 31, 1993.
4. Barrett, A. February 7, 1994. Dole's stunted harvest. *Business Week:* 116–117; Bartlett, T. February 18, 1993. Lanai markets itself as a 'dramatically different' destination. *Travel Weekly:* 18–19; Bartlett T. February 18, 1993. Lanai, once the pineapple island, makes transition to tourism. *Travel Weekly:* 17–19; Lyons, John T. Dole Food Company, Inc. February 18, 1996. *Value Line:* 1471.
5. In December 1995, Dole completed a spinoff of its real estate and resorts operations. Subsequently, its stock price has recovered to approximately 85 percent of its 1991 peak levels.
6. Zweig, P. L. October 30, 1995. The case against mergers. *Business Week:* 122–130.
7. Ibid.

8. Porter, M.E. May-June 1987. From competitive advantage to corporate strategy. *Harvard Business Review*, 65: 43.

9. A study by Dr. G. William Schwert, University of Rochester, cited in Pare, T.P. November 28, 1994. The new merger boom. *Fortune:* 96.

10. Pare, T. P. op.cit.: 125.

11. Porter, M.E. May-June 1987. op cit.

12. Lewyn, M., and Brandt, R. September 27, 1993 Novell vs. Microsoft: What's behind the hate. *Business Week:* 124, 126, 128; Henry, A.M. January 8, 1996. Novell's road ahead. *LAN Times:* 1–8; Clark, D. January 12, 1996. Novell Noveau. *Wall Street Journal:* A2, A6.; Picarille, Lisa, February 5, 1996. WordPerfect users say "show me" to Corel. *Computerworld:* 4; DiDio, L., and Ouellette, T. March 11, 1996, All Eyes are on Novell. *Computerworld:* 14; Gillan, Paul, February 5, 1996, Noorda's Folly. *Computerworld:* 36.

13. Prahalad, C.K., and Hamel, G. 1990. The core competence of the corporation. *Harvard Business Review*, 68: 79–91.

14. Haspelagh, P. 1982. Portfolio planning: Uses and limits. *Harvard Business Review*, 60: 58–73.

15. There are many other limitations of portfolio models. Among those are that they tend to trivialize strategic thinking, it is difficult to properly identify individual businesses, the models are often not accurate, they ignore linkages and sources of synergy, and so on. For an excellent review, refer to Haspelagh, P. Ibid.

16. Seeger, J.A. 1984. Reversing the images of BCG's growth-share matrix. *Strategic Management Journal*, 5: 93–97.

17. Hill, C.W.L. and Jones, G.R. 1995. *Strategic Management: An Integrated Approach* (3rd edition). Boston: Houghton Mifflin; Plishner, Emily S. August 1, 1995. Cabot: Carbon updating. *Financial World*, 164(17): 26.

18. This section draws on the seminal work of Prahalad, C.K., and Hamel, G. 1990. The core competence of the corporation. *Harvard Business Review*, 70: 79–91.

19. Berman, P. January 22, 1996. A proud record. *Forbes:* 56, 58.

20. *1993 3M Corporation Annual Report;* Giglio, John. March 1, 1996. 3M Corporation. *Value Line:* 1893.

21. Dess, G. G. and Miller, A. 1993. *Strategic Management*. McGraw Hill: New York, Chapter 6.

22. *1993 Gillette Company Annual Report:* 18.

23. *1993 Harley-Davidson Annual Report.*

24. Speech by Lew Platt, CEO of Hewlett-Packard, to CSO Consultants, May 12, 1994.

25. *1993 Hewlett-Packard Annual Report.*
26. Artz, E.L. May 21, 1990. Strategies for global growth. A speech delivered as a meeting for leading financial analysts in Cincinnati, Ohio.
27. Henricks, M. August, 1994. VF seeks global brand dominance. *Apparel Industry Magazine:* 21–40; VF Corporation, 1st Quarter, Corporate Summary Report. *1993 VF Annual Report.*
28. *1993 Walt Disney Company Annual Report.*
29. The examples of Nestle and Maytag draw on Miller, A. and Dess, G.G. 1996. *Strategic Management,* 2nd ed. New York: McGraw-Hill: 268–9.
30. Server, A. June 13, 1994. How to escape a price war. *Fortune:* 88, and *Shaw Industries 1993 Annual Report.*
31. *1994 United States Industrial Outlook.* Washington, D.C.: 9–7 ; Joseph, C. M. January 19, 1996. Shaw Industries, Inc. *Value Line:* 908.
32. *1993 General Electric Annual Report:* 3.
33. Dereny, K., and Hwang, S. L. January 18, 1994. A defective strategy of heated acquisition spoils Borden's name. *The Wall Street Journal:* A1. Lesly, E. November 22, 1993. Why things are so sour at Borden. *Business Week:* 78–81; Royce, M.M. November 18, 1994. Borden Inc. *Value Line:* 1455; Zinn, L., Burns, G., and Alexander, K.L. September 25, 1994. Elsie may be ailing, but KKR is thinking whipped cream. *Business Week:* 55.
34. This section draws on Campbell, A., Goold, M. & Alexander, M. March-April 1995. Corporate strategy: The quest for parenting advantage. *Harvard Business Review:* 120–132.
35. Anslinger, P.A. & Copeland, T.E. January-February, 1996. Growth through acquisition: A fresh look. *Harvard Business Review:* 126–135.
36. Campbell, A., Goold, M. & Alexander, M. March-April 1995., op. cit.
37. Ruffin, W.R. January 1990. Wired for speed. *Business Month:* 56–58.
38. Porter, M.E. 1985. *Competitive advantage.* Free Press: New York.
39. Schlender, B.R. February 24, 1992. How Sony keeps the magic going. *Fortune:* 76–84.
40. *1992 Armstrong World Industries Annual Report.*
41. Brewer, G. May 1992. On with the show. Incentive.
42. *1993 Rubbermaid Annual Report:* 16–17 and author's discussion with Ms. Linda Ragsdale, Sales Supervisor, Iron Mountain Forge, November 15, 1994.
43. *1993 DuPont Annual Report:* 13.

6

CHAPTER

Tripping Over the Barriers

Boundaries are an essential element in the description and definition of organizations. Organizational boundaries are defined in a variety of ways: by product, by function, by geography and, ultimately by ownership, control and an organization's existence as a legal entity. For the most part, organizational boundaries serve useful and essential functions, but when the boundaries become barriers to effective coordination and integration, they often emerge as major impediments to the successful implementation of strategy. Organizations that fail to ensure effective coordination and integration of core processes across organizational boundaries frequently end up tripping over these barriers enroute to a failed implementation of their strategies.

THE DENVER INTERNATIONAL AIRPORT

The futuristic Denver International Airport (DIA)—initially heralded as a paragon of civic pride—has instead become the butt of jokes in newspapers, magazines, and talk shows across the United States.[1] More frequently cited by Letterman and Leno than by *Forbes* and *Fortune*, the story of DIA is a classic tale of strategic errors, with one blunder after another—a colossal tale of

131

mismanagement! As the story has evolved, punsters have suggested over 150 variations on the initials of DIA, including *Doing It Again, Dinosaur in Action, Debacle in Aviation,* and *Denver is Awaitin'.*

Originally scheduled for completion in October 1993 at a cost of $1.3 billion, Denver International finally opened for business in February 1995—not yet completed, 16 months behind schedule, and $2.9 billion over budget! The delays were estimated to have cost the city over $1 million per day. Flaws in the baggage system designed and built by BAE were the most visible and frequently cited problem. However, when the finger-pointing was over and the dust finally settled, it was clear that a series of strategic errors, made early in the process by Denver city officials and the management of DIA, also deserved a fair share of the blame. Let's take a brief look at the history:

After three years of planning, construction began on DIA in 1989, with completion targeted for October 1993. Two years later, in the fall of 1991, Boeing Aircraft Equipment (BAE) signed a contract with United Airlines to build a baggage system for United at the new airport. Only after BAE began work on United's system did the City conclude that an airportwide baggage system would be more efficient. Ginger Evans, DIA's director of engineering at the time, acknowledged that the baggage system plans came late, but explained that *the airport had originally expected the individual airlines to build their own systems.*

Specifications were developed and requests for bids were solicited from 16 companies around the world. The project was huge: over 22 miles of track, 10,000 motors, and six miles of conveyors would be controlled by over 100 computers as baggage moved through underground tunnels between the main terminal and three giant concourses. By the end of 1991, the scheduled opening date was less than two years away, but DIA had not yet awarded a contract. Why? Not a single company was willing to make a bid. Each had the same concern: there was not enough time to build the complex system.

Meanwhile, Denver was getting disturbing feedback from the new Franz Josef Strauss Airport in Munich. This airport, opened in May 1992, had a baggage system similar to that planned for Denver. Over two years of testing had been required to eliminate the bugs in Munich's system, including continuous 24-hour a day trials for six months prior to the airport's opening. Denver didn't have the time—the contractor would have to get it right the first time.

According to BAE's CEO, Gene DiFonso, "The city got caught in a trap. They were lulled into believing they'd find companies to build the system. They were shocked when they were told it couldn't be done." Breier, Neidle, and Patrone, a New York-based consulting firm hired by DIA, suggested that BAE—already at work on United's system—build the system for the entire airport. A contract was hammered out with BAE in early 1992. For $193 million, BAE would build an expanded version of the United system for the entire airport.

"We placed a number of conditions on accepting the job," stated DiFonso. "The design doesn't change beyond this date, and there would be a number of freeze dates for mechanical design, software design, permanent power requirements and the like." The success-oriented schedule was tight, with little room for error. Shortly after work began in April 1992, nearly all of the promises evaporated. The airlines requested numerous changes, including the removal of an entire loop by United (cutting the cost by $20 million), relocation of outside stations, and a request by Continental Airlines for a larger baggage link. By opening day the costs had ballooned to $232 million, with a third of the system still to be built.

When the magnitude of the problems and delays began to surface, the finger-pointing began in earnest. After a failed test in July 1994, Denver's Mayor commented, "I won't hazard a guess" about when DIA would open. With the costs of the delay pegged at $33 million per month, the city hired Logplan, from Germany, to monitor and review BAE's work, and awarded a $53 million contract for a backup "tug and cart" baggage handling system. On opening day, the baggage system was complete on only one of three concourses, and that system was only partially operational. The backup system was put to the test. It also failed.

Denver Mayor Wellington Webb was on hand to greet the first arriving passenger, 88-year-old Capt. Elrey P. Jeppesen, for whom the terminal was named. The ceremonies were delayed briefly when the boarding bridge malfunctioned and the aircraft had to be towed to an adjacent gate. Jeppesen remarked, as he greeted the Mayor, that he was "awfully glad he had lived long enough [to attend the opening ceremonies]."

The Denver International Airport was a project of major strategic importance to the city of Denver. The baggage-handling system, as a critical link in the complex chain of services provided to the public, clearly had to be a priority—but apparently it wasn't. It almost fell through the cracks in the planning and construction of the airport and turned out to be a major embarrassment for all concerned. In early 1996, a year after the airport opened, the system was still incomplete, plagued with problems, and the subject of an ongoing series of legal disputes, suits, and countersuits.

> So what went wrong? Whose fault was it, anyway? Did the planners fail to plan? Was the system just too complex—too grand in scope—to succeed on the first try? Was there no prior experience to draw upon? Were the specs inadequate? Did BAE promise more than they could deliver?

WHAT WENT WRONG IN DENVER?

DIA's experience with the baggage-handling system is a textbook case of "how not to do it," with shortfalls in coordination, integration, and strategic control. *Coordination* refers to the management activities by which consistency in goals and objectives is achieved among individuals and functions, both within organizations and across organizational boundaries. *Integration* is concerned with issues of process: systems, procedures, and working relationships that determine how effectively participants and diverse organizational components work together to achieve the common goal. *Strategic control* refers to the management tools and techniques used to steer the organization consistently in the direction of its defined objectives. Successful strategic management requires an appropriate mix of coordination, integration, and strategic control; all are essential, and a judicious balance must be maintained among them.

Much of the problem with the baggage system can be traced to the way DIA's designers and engineers understood and interpreted their mission and role in the project. It appears that DIA saw the construction of the airport as an undertaking quite separate and apart from its ultimate operation. Construction came first. DIA saw its role primarily as the architect of a facility—its role was to design the airport, contract for its construction, and monitor the performance of the contractors while it was being built.

When the airport was completed, DIA would assume the role of landlord. Its relationships with the airlines would be contractual, not operational. The airlines, as tenants, would be responsible for furnishing (equipping) the facility and conducting their operations within it. From this perspective, there were no significant interdependencies to be considered between the airport authority, the contractors, and the airlines that would eventually occupy the facility. Neither was it unreasonable for DIA to expect the airlines, individually, to contract for and install their own baggage-handling systems.

DIA's management approach was consistent with this perspective. Management followed the traditional government procurement cycle: defining requirements, preparing detailed specifications, soliciting bids, awarding contracts, and monitoring performance. Things began to go wrong fairly early in the process, however, and only got worse as the time pressures increased. Coordination between DIA and the airlines was an obvious weak link. Early on, it was not clear who would be responsible for the baggage-handling system—DIA or the airlines—so many of the key players were not involved in the planning. DIA initially expected that each airline would build its own system; it belatedly decided that an airportwide system would be more efficient and took over the project's management.

Once the project was underway, the lack of effective integration became a problem. BAE had accepted a contract to build the system with the stipulation that no changes would be made in the requirements. Once the airlines got involved, however, each wanted its section of the system to function in a different way. BAE also complained that its efforts were hampered by DIA's mechanical problems: unreliable power generation, inadequate communications systems, and incomplete security and fire protection systems. Although the success-oriented schedule required close coordination and tight integration of activities, by relying on the traditional contract management model DIA's approach encouraged adversarial, rather than cooperative relationships.

DIA's mechanisms of strategic control were based on specifications and schedules, but as the time pressures increased and multiple cooks began stirring the pot, DIA's control systems began to break down. It became increasingly difficult to track progress or estimate costs and schedules. When BAE began to stumble in implementation, the finger-pointing began in earnest, and the engineers turned the dialogue over to the contract administrators and the lawyers. DIA's response was to add another contractor, effectively an additional layer of management, to oversee and coordinate BAE's efforts.

Had DIA taken a broader view and initially defined the construction and ongoing operation of the airport in terms of a long-term strategic partnership among the city, the airport authority, and the airlines, a much different understanding of the roles and relationships among the parties might have been developed. Both the airport and the airlines are involved in delivering a service—air transportation for the traveling public—and significant operational interdependencies are present. The broader value chain for air transportation services, as illustrated in Figure 6–1, clearly shows the degree of interdependence that exists.

The delivery of air transportation services involves multiple organizations and activities, including the departure airport, the destination airport, and the airline providing the service. Typically the airport authority has primary responsibility for control of exter-

FIGURE 6–1

Value Chain Analysis of Air Transportation Services

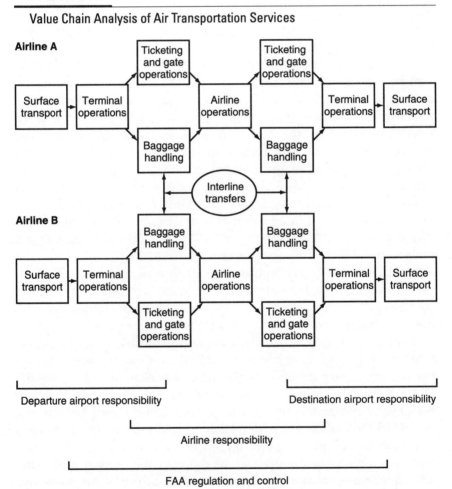

nal access, interface with surface transportation, parking, and terminal operations (physical plant, concessions, and the like). The airport authority and its airline tenants usually share responsibilities for gate operations and passenger and baggage handling, with the airport authority responsible for providing facilities, utilities, and security, and the airline responsible for staffing, ticketing, and other operational matters. Airline operations are conducted within a framework of FAA and local procedures and regulations, many of which are established by the airport authority. If more than one airline is involved, passenger and baggage transfers must take place. Interline agreements negotiated between the airlines cover these matters, but operations are governed partially by the facilities and local regulations established by the airport authority.

Had DIA initially recognized the high degree of operational interdependence involved in the baggage-handling process, it would have made sense to have ensured effective coordination by getting the airlines involved in the initial planning. Given the obvious requirement for efficient interline baggage transfers, the need for an airportwide baggage-handling system might have been apparent at the beginning. Early involvement of all participants in the planning stages would, no doubt, have helped to ensure more effective integration during design and implementation.

STRATEGIC TRAP #5: TRIPPING OVER THE BARRIERS

In our view, DIA's problems with the baggage-handling system began with an inadequate conceptualization of the problem. DIA viewed its role too narrowly and failed to recognize the significant interdependencies that existed between the airport authority and the airlines. With an overly narrow view of its role and mission, DIA's approach to coordination, integration, and strategic control was woefully inadequate. Because DIA failed to recognize that the full participation of several separate organizations was critical to the success of the project, it blundered right into Strategic Trap #5, as it *failed to structure and implement appropriate mechanisms to ensure the coordination and integration of core processes and key functions across organizational boundaries.*

DIA's problems are not unique, nor are they limited to the public sector—many organizations, public and private, have experienced similar problems though few have achieved incompetence on so grand a scale! Most complex activities are characterized by a considerable degree of interdependence among the organizational elements involved. As organizations become more complex (in terms of functional diversity, competing objectives, project complexity, or product-market scope and geographic domain), there is a corresponding need to develop structures, systems, and mechanisms to coordinate and achieve integration of both ongoing activities and strategic projects across the internal and external boundaries of the organization. Major strategic programs, such as the development and introduction of a complex system or a new product, are particularly dependent upon effective cross-functional integration of activities.

Many fall into the trap of an overly narrow conceptualization of their organization's role in the larger scheme of things. A fundamental problem arises when an organization defines and understands its business only in the context of those activities under its direct operational or strategic control and fails to take proper account of the contributions of other organizations to the product or service delivered to the end-user. We will label this perspective, in which the scope of organization's value chain is conceptualized primarily within the boundaries of its span of direct control, as the *traditional model*. The traditional model is predominant in the thinking of many managers today, and is a frequent contributor to the kinds of strategic errors illustrated in the example of the DIA. In the section that follows, we will discuss the essential features and highlight the limitations of the traditional model.

LIMITATIONS OF THE TRADITIONAL MODEL

The organizing principle of the traditional model is *control*: tasks and responsibilities are divided among relatively specialized managers, functional departments, and business units arranged in a hierarchical structure that defines reporting relationships and patterns of internal communication. Clear definitions of authority and responsibility delineate organizational boundaries and avoid redundancies. Coordination is achieved by institutionalizing organizational goals and expectations through formalized planning. Integration of activities is achieved by formalizing processes in terms of rules and procedures. Performance is typically monitored by "plan versus actual" controls.

Arms-length relationships with suppliers and customers are clearly defined and highly structured. The external boundaries of the firm are important in framing strategy—it's the organization vs. the external environment, the firm vs. the competition, and so on. Strategic control is focused primarily on internal operations. The performance of self-contained business units operating as profit centers is easy to measure, and such measurements help to focus managers on local performance goals. Each functional area, business unit, and organizational entity in the value chain is expected, with single-minded focus, to pursue the optimization of its own well-defined sphere of responsibility.

Many of these traditional perspectives were evident in DIA's reliance on comprehensive planning and highly structured procurement and contracting systems and its use of formal schedules and milestones for project control. These traditional management approaches have their downside, however, and are often inadequate in complex and dynamic environments. High degrees of organizational specialization and the optimization of processes and procedures to maximize local efficiencies may create strong organizational barriers that limit flexibility, impede communications, and create intolerable delays in accomplishing even routine tasks.

Even when routine tasks are handled with relative efficiency, systems and procedures often break down when confronted with an out-of-the-ordinary requirement. Complex tasks such as the design and development of new products require the close coordination and integration of R&D, engineering, manufacturing, marketing, and sales activities and are virtually impossible to accomplish with efficiency under a traditional structure. Memos and meetings consume more managerial time than productive activity, and political "turf battles" often become more important, on a daily basis, than the goals of the organization. In fast-moving competitive environments, or in situations where organizational interdependencies are high, these traditional structures and perspectives may become a millstone around the organization's neck, sapping its productivity and constraining its ability to compete.

In complex and rapidly changing environments, successful managers must frequently coordinate efforts and achieve effective integration not only across functional departments but also within collaborative groups (teams) and across multiple business units. Firms that fail to coordinate and integrate the activities essential to their success may fall prey to what has been referred to by ecologist Garret Hardin as "the tragedy of the commons."[2] This idea asserts that, given unrestricted access to shared town commons, farmers would graze too many sheep there, ultimately depleting the grass and ruining the grazing for all. Why? Since no single farmer felt any incentive to reduce the number of sheep, everyone would have to suffer. Similarly, if managers "graze" independently within the confines of their own "fiefdoms," their organization's resources will be depleted and competitive positions eroded.

It is often argued that smaller organizations, by virtue of their size alone, should have more efficient patterns of internal communication and less need to develop formal mechanisms of coordination and integration. Small size does not, however, guarantee effective integration across functional boundaries, as illustrated in the failure of Frox, a well-funded high-tech start-up based on an innovative new product concept:

Frox was founded in 1988 by Hartmut Esslinger, an industrial designer whose resume included the casing designs of Sun workstations, Apple's first Macintosh, and the aesthetic, but ill-fated Next PC.[3] The target for Frox's "smart TV" was the U.S. home-theater market, worth about $1 billion in the early 1990s, and growing at an annual 20 to 30 percent clip. With near-HDTV (high-definition television) screen resolution, compact disc quality sound, and the promise of access to innumerable databases, Frox's "living room supercomputer" was conceived as the ultimate marriage of television and computers—equally suited for programming a VCR or searching the databases of a remote network. Key staff were recruited from leading high-tech firms like Sun Microsystems, Apple Computer, LucasFilm and Xerox, as well as Stanford University and MIT's Media Lab. In 1991, Frox was heralded as the kind of firm that could regain the consumer electronics market from the Japanese. With all the hype over the Information Superhighway, where is Frox today? Unfortunately for Frox's investors, $43 million in venture capital yielded sales of a mere 100 units before the firm closed its doors in early 1994.

So, what went wrong? Frox's failure cannot be explained by a lack of resources, expertise, or market opportunity. Instead, Frox fell victim to a one-dimensional focus on engineering excellence and weak internal integration between product design and the downstream activities of marketing, production, and sales. Managed by engineers, Frox failed to recognize that excellence in engineering did not, by itself, guarantee success. Unwilling to compromise on any aspect of the product, the engineers custom designed everything from the screen to the speakers—even the remote control. The result? The product's projected retail price quickly rose from $5,000 to $7,000, and then to $10,000. By the time the product was released at Christmas 1991, the retail price had risen to $30,000, well beyond what the market would bear.

In the meantime, scant attention was paid to market research, production, quality assurance, or sales and marketing. Joanna Hoffman, Frox's product marketing manager, observed that: "There were some very good people and some very flaky people. The academic people had no concept of how to do a product, and there was no one who understood how to run a business." Weak integration between engineering and production resulted in a product, rushed to market with inadequate testing, that was plagued by software bugs and mechanical defects. Many of the machines were in use for only a few weeks before being returned for repair.

In the end, Frox failed, in part because its engineering-oriented management failed to recognize the importance of other activities in the value chain. An "if we build it, they will come" strategy will fail without close integration of engineering and marketing to determine whether the target market actually exists. Equally important is close coordination and integration of engineering and production operations, to ensure that the product is sufficiently reliable for release.

While the issues of coordination at Frox were inherently less complex than those at DIA, and all of the functions were directly under management's control, the failure to integrate activities across functional boundaries contributed significantly to the unsuccessful product launch and the ultimate demise of the company. Even in a small entrepreneurial organization, a one-dimensional management emphasis carried to extremes will result in failure. The problems are inherent in the traditional model—the organizational architecture and the control-oriented managerial mindset create barriers that frequently stand in the way of effective coordination and integration.

I'm beginning to understand the problem—but how do I address it? How does an organization ensure coordination and integration? How does it maintain strategic control?

A NEW MANAGEMENT MODEL: THE "BOUNDARYLESS" ORGANIZATION

Many leading organizations are beginning to address the limitations of the traditional management model with new management techniques and organizational architectures. GE's concept of the boundaryless organization is particularly noteworthy. This innovative organizational perspective was first described in GE's 1990 Annual Report: "Our dream for the 1990s is a boundaryless company . . . where we knock down the walls that separate us from each other on the inside and from our key constituencies on the outside." CEO Jack Welch's emphasis on multiple stakeholders enhances GE's reputation as well as its growth and profits. The following excerpt from GE's 1993 Annual Report describes the concept and highlights the progress the company has achieved in its implementation:[4]

Boundaryless behavior is the soul of today's GE. We've described it to you in past years. Simply put, people seem compelled to build layers and walls between themselves and others, and that human tendency tends to be magnified in large, old institutions like ours. These walls cramp people, inhibit creativity, waste time, restrict vision, smother dreams and, above all, slow things down.

The challenge is to chip away at and eventually break down these walls and barriers, both among ourselves and between ourselves and the outside world. The progress we've made so far has released a flood of ideas that is improving every operation in our Company. We've adapted new product introduction techniques from Chrysler and Canon, effective sourcing techniques from GM and Toyota, and approaches to quality from Motorola and Ford. We've moved more effectively into the immense potential markets of China with advice and best practices from pioneers like IBM, Johnson & Johnson, Xerox and others.

The removal of those walls means we involve suppliers as participants in our design and manufacturing processes rather than treat them as vendors, left to cool their heels in waiting rooms. It means having major launch customers like British Airways, Tokyo Electric Power or CSX in the room and involved in the design of a new jet engine, a revolutionary gas turbine or new AC locomotive, or a panel of doctors helping us develop a new ultrasound system.

Internally, boundaryless behavior means piercing the walls of 100-year old fiefdoms and empires called finance, engineering, manufacturing, marketing, and gathering teams from all those functions in one room, with one shared coffee pot, one shared vision and one consuming passion—to design the world's best jet engine, or ultrasound machine, or refrigerator.

Boundaryless behavior shows up in the actions of women from our Appliances business in Hong Kong helping NBC with contacts needed to develop a satellite television service in Asia. On a larger scale, it means labor and management joining hands in the unprofitable Appliance Park complex in Louisville in a joint effort to "Save the Park," with a combination of labor practice changes and GE investment—not two people making a "deal," but 10,721 making a commitment.

And finally, boundaryless behavior means exploiting one of the unmatchable advantages a multibusiness GE has over almost every other company in the world. Boundaryless behavior combines 12 huge global businesses—each number one or number two in its markets—into a vast laboratory whose principal product is new ideas, coupled with a common commitment to spread them throughout the Company.

To succeed in implementation, the boundaryless organization must not only create flexible, porous organizational boundaries, but also establish communication flows and mutually beneficial relationships with suppliers, customers, and other external constituencies.[5] That's an issue of perspective—recognizing that your own organization doesn't stand alone, but is rather one of several links in a larger value chain involved in the creation and delivery of value to the ultimate consumer. Stepping back—taking a broader view—and understanding the relationships and interdependencies between your organization and your suppliers, customers, and competitors is a critical first step in breaking down the barriers.

In today's rapidly changing environment, a key management challenge is to design more flexible organizations.[6] If traditional structures (e.g., functional, divisional, matrix) are failing, managers must evaluate innovative types of organizational designs to see if they can deliver on promises of enabling strategic implementation. The need for more rapid response to a changing environment calls for more effective communications and greater interdependence, both within and outside the firm. Later in this chapter, we will address three innovative new architectures that promise greater flexibility than the traditional model.

A wide variety of management tools and techniques is available. Some are focused on achieving more effective coordination, others address the barriers to more effective integration, and some provide new approaches to strategic control. GE's description of the boundaryless organization suggests that a number of different approaches have been successful within that organization: experimenting with new ideas, adopting "best practices" from other organizations, involving customers and suppliers in design and production decisions, using multifunctional teams, developing cooperative labor-management practices, and sharing expertise among business units throughout the organization. Total quality management (TQM), process reengineering, and cycle time reduction all seek to improve internal coordination and integration by identifying and eliminating internal barriers to organizational improvement and external impediments to cooperative endeavor.

Others advocate leveraging core competencies, using information technology to facilitate cross-functional integration, outsourcing nonstrategic functions, and developing strategic partnerships and alliances. No one tool or technique, by itself, is likely to be the total solution; rather, a combination of several techniques must be used, as building blocks, to achieve the desired result. The recipe is likely to be unique for each organization and strategic environment—the art of strategic management is to select and apply an appropriate and balanced mix of tools and techniques to the situation at hand.

ENSURING EFFECTIVE COORDINATION AND INTEGRATION

Achieving effective coordination and integration in a complex and interdependent strategic environment involves three separate and distinct management activities:

- Defining the strategic context—identifying the key players and understanding the interrelationships among them.

- Designing an organizational architecture—defining, structuring, and implementing critical relationships among the key players.

- Selecting and implementing an appropriate set of tools and techniques—enabling the coordination of objectives and integration of activities, both within and among organizations.

First, the strategic situation must be evaluated and important relationships and interdependencies identified and understood in the context of the broader strategic environment. The process is not unlike taking attendance in a lifeboat: "OK, guys—we're all in this together—let's see what we have to work with."

A useful approach to the development of an appropriate understanding is to work backward through a value chain, conceptualized at the highest level, from the end product or service delivered to the customer. For this purpose, the value chain must be conceptualized in its broadest context, without regard to organizational boundaries. Recall, from Chapter 4, our definition of the value chain as *a sequential arrangement of processes or activities that operate on inputs, add value, and collectively produce outputs—a product or service—created for and delivered to an end-user.*

In most cases, this value chain will involve multiple organizations, each of which makes an incremental contribution to the final product or service. These are the organizations—suppliers, customers and competitors—that must be considered in the definition of the organization's strategic context. Each of these organizations will, in turn, have its own internal value chain consisting of the sequence of activities that produces the set of outputs that become the inputs for the next link in the overall chain. In identifying interdependencies, it is important to distinguish between the set of all possible relationships and those that are strategically relevant. A careful analysis of your own organization's strengths and weaknesses and an identification of its core competencies will be helpful in identifying those relationships that will be most important to the successful implementation of your strategic objectives.

Recognizing interdependencies and achieving effective coordination and integration is vital to sustaining competitive advantage.

Multiple relationships and interdependencies must be considered, often at three different levels of analysis. Within each business unit, activities must be coordinated and integrated *across functional departments*. In organizations composed of multiple business units, common activities must be coordinated *among business units* and *across geographic boundaries*. Finally, close ties of coordination and integration must often *cross external organizational boundaries* to effectively link the organization to its suppliers and customers.

Second, an organizational architecture must be selected and implemented. A variety of organizational architectures are available. In addition to the traditional model described above, we will consider a number of alternatives, including the *modular, virtual* and *barrier-free* organizational types. The choice of an organizational architecture is important, for each structure creates different opportunities and places different constraints on management's subsequent choices. The dimensions to be considered are the organization's strategic objectives, its core competencies and limitations, and its need to retain, or willingness to relinquish, strategic control over the key activities in its value chain.

Third, management must select and implement an appropriate mix of tools and techniques to achieve the desired mix and balance of coordination, integration, and strategic control.

Chapters 2 through 5 addressed the use of value chain concepts and other approaches to develop an understanding of the strategic context and devise strategies that would result in sustainable competitive advantage. In the sections that follow, we will describe the building blocks—the organizational architectures, tools, and techniques—available to strategic managers as they design and implement an appropriate framework for coordination, integration, and strategic control within their organizations.

NEW ORGANIZATIONAL ARCHITECTURES

The purpose of organizational architecture is to provide a structure within which the roles and interrelationships of the key players (individual or organizational) are defined, structured, and implemented. The traditional model represents one of the several possible architectures available to the strategist. The advantages of this model lie in its clear definition of responsibility and authority, the use of efficient functional organization structures, task specialization and well-defined processes, policies, and procedures, and the relatively direct approach to both operational and strategic control. Its limitations lie in the tendency to develop organizational barriers that limit flexibility, impede communications, create local "fiefdoms," and slow organizational response patterns.

As managers have sought to overcome the limitations of the traditional structure, new organizational forms—boundaryless organizations—have emerged. The term *boundaryless organization* may bring to mind a chaotic reality in which "anything goes." Such is not the case. The term *boundaryless* does not imply that all internal and external boundaries vanish altogether. Although boundaries may continue to exist, they must become more open and permeable. In the following sections, we describe three distinct structural forms that can contribute to reducing boundaries.

The *modular* and *virtual* organization structures represent different approaches to modifying or breaking down *external* organizational boundaries. The modular type outsources nonvital functions, but the organization retains full strategic control. The virtual type emphasizes the development of strategic alliances among firms with complementary core competencies; but some strategic autonomy is sacrificed. The *barrier-free* approach addresses the limitations of the traditional model through techniques designed to break down the *internal* boundaries of organizations.

These three organizational forms are all, to varying degrees, "boundaryless." They differ from each other, and from the vertical hierarchy of the traditional model, in terms of the relative emphasis placed upon, and the mechanisms used to achieve, coordination, integration, and strategic control. Each relies, not only on new forms of structure, but also on various tools and techniques to improve communications, reduce costs and investments, lever core competencies, and achieve increased speed and flexibility in the implementation of corporate strategies. The modular, virtual, and barrier-free organization types are not mutually exclusive. Rather, as we shall see, they are but a few of the available building blocks for the ideal of the boundaryless organization.

The Modular Organization

In modular organizations, selected noncore functions are outsourced to specialist firms that can perform these functions more effectively and more efficiently than the organization could do them on its own. Examples abound—organizations have outsourced, in whole or in part, their manufacturing operations, distribution and outbound logistics, data processing, and so on. These organizational designs minimize investment in fixed assets and maximize flexibility and responsiveness to a volatile market. They achieve coordination and integration through cooperative relationships while maintaining full strategic control over the core competencies that comprise the key links in their value chains. The central concept in the modular organization is focusing effort and investment primarily on those activities that create the most value and are critical to the success of the firm, while minimizing investment and management effort on noncore activities that contribute only marginally to the final product or service.

Many companies are moving away from vertical hierarchies and shifting toward lean and responsive structures centered on what they do best. Such companies develop a few core activities and depend on outsiders to do everything else. The organization becomes a central hub surrounded by a network of specialist organizations. Outsourcing the noncore functions offers three basic advantages. *First,* it enables a company to achieve cost savings in noncore activities and focus its scarce resources on the core activities where competitive advantage is created. These benefits can translate into more money for research and development, hiring the best engineers, and providing continuous training for sales and service staff. *Second,* the modular type enables a company to leverage relatively small amounts of capital and a small management team to achieve ambitious strategic objectives. Freed from the need to make big investments in fixed assets, modular companies can achieve rapid growth, and, at the same time, minimize the risks of technological obsolescence. *Third,* a modular structure provides increased flexibility. In uncertain environments, outsourcing may help a firm reduce inventories and avoid idle capacity due to cyclical demand patterns, and may provide the flexibility to rapidly redeploy assets as market and competitive conditions change.

Certain preconditions must exist, or be created, before a modular organization can be successful. First, the organization must work closely with its chosen suppliers in order to ensure that the interests of each party are being fulfilled. Companies need to find loyal, reliable vendors who can be trusted with trade secrets and who will dedicate their financial, physical, and human resources to satisfy the mutually agreed-upon strategic objectives. Second, the modular organization must make sure that it chooses the right competence to keep in-house. A company must be wary of outsourcing key value activities that may compromise long-term competitive advantage.

Apparel and computers are two industries where modular organizations have been successful. Nike and Reebok have succeeded by concentrating on their strengths: designing and marketing high-tech, fashionable footwear. These companies contract virtually all their production to independent suppliers in Taiwan, South Korea, and other low-cost labor countries. Thus, they gain flexibility to keep pace with changing tastes in the marketplace by expanding or contracting production rapidly without significant investments in new facilities or the need to manage a large workforce.[7] Apple Computer relied heavily on outsourcing to fuel the rapid growth of its early years. In 1990, Apple achieved sales of $370,000 per employee, and its net plant, property, and equipment totaled only 18.4 percent of sales. By contrast, the highly integrated IBM Corporation's net property, plant and equipment equaled 63 percent of its revenues and its sales per employee were only $139,000.

Other industries are also becoming increasingly modular. The automobile industry has traditionally been highly integrated, but Chrysler now purchases 70 percent of its parts from outside suppliers. It avoids buying thousands of separate items, however, as its suppliers provide preassembled sections such as brake systems and door panels. In an effort to regain its competitive advantage, even IBM has shaken up its business in response to more nimble competitors such as Dell and Compaq. It spun off its huge human resource operation into a separate company called Workforce Solutions, forcing its former employee benefits staff to become more entrepreneurial and saving IBM about $45 million annually in the process.[8]

Adopting the modular type does not mean outsourcing every activity. Mindless outsourcing in the pursuit of temporary cost advantages can lead to firms becoming "hollow" and losing their competitive advantage. Semiconductor firms like Chips & Technologies and Weitek flourished in the late 1980s by focusing solely on chip design and outsourcing production.[9] Their competitive advantage eroded substantially in the early 1990s, however, as other firms imitated their design-focused strategy and fabricators gained greater bargaining power.

Another outsourcing strategy that backfired is that of the Schwinn Bicycle company.[10] The world leader in the bicycle business for almost a century, Schwinn filed for bankruptcy in October 1992. Schwinn outsourced most of its production in 1991, in response to a labor strike, and turned over much of its technology to the Giant Manufacturing Company of Taiwan and the China Bicycle Company. These firms now dominate the world bicycle business. Schwinn's demise can be traced to its inability to protect its technology, its failure to establish global brand equity, its lack of innovation, and severe labor-management problems. Instead of addressing these basic problems, Schwinn responded with a poorly designed outsourcing strategy that failed to keep high value activities in-house and build on its core competencies.

The Virtual Organization

The virtual organization relies primarily on strategic alliances: a continually evolving network of independent companies that includes suppliers, customers, and even competitors linked together to share skills, costs, and access to one another's markets in pursuit of a common strategic objective. By assembling resources from a variety of entities, a virtual organization may appear to have more capabilities than it really possesses. Participating firms may be involved in multiple alliances at any one time. Virtual organizations may involve different firms performing complementary value activities or different firms involved jointly in the same value activities such as production, R&D, advertising, and distribution. The mix of activities that are jointly performed may vary significantly from alliance to alliance.

Virtual organizations demand a unique set of managerial skills. Managers must build relationships with other companies, negotiate win-win deals for all parties involved, find the right partners with compatible goals and values, and provide the temporary organization with the right balance of freedom and control.

An ever-changing pattern of alliances that are constantly being formed and dissolved does not necessarily imply mutually exploitative arrangements or lack of long-term relationships. The key is to be clear about the strategic objectives when the alliances are being formed. Alliances focused on narrow short-term goals should be dissolved once the objective has been accomplished. Other alliances may have relatively long-term objectives and must be nurtured and protected to maintain mutual commitment over time. The highly dynamic PC industry, for example, is characterized by multiple temporary alliances among hardware, operating systems, and software producers. But alliances in the more stable automobile industry, such as those involving Nissan and Volkswagen as well as Mazda and Ford, have long-term objectives and tend to be relatively stable.

The virtual type of organization can be distinguished from the modular type in two respects: the *nature of the relationships* and the *locus of strategic control*. In the modular type, supplier-customer relationships predominate and the focal firm retains full strategic control. The virtual organization, however, is characterized by alliances in which participants share responsibilities, give up part of their strategic control and accept interdependent destinies. Such collective strategies enable firms to cope with uncertainty in their environments through cooperative efforts that enhance the capabilities of the participating firms and create competitive advantage through synergies across organizational boundaries. Each company that links up with others to create a virtual organization contributes only its core competencies to mix and match what it does best with the strengths of other firms and bolster its areas of relative weakness.

Paramount Communications, Inc., is positioning itself to use strategic alliances to exploit as many stages of the entertainment industry value chain as possible.[11] The entertainment industry is rapidly converging with the computing, communications, consumer electronics, and publishing industries. In anticipation, Paramount is busy converting its movies, textbooks, and other "software" into digital format, and has already entered into an alliance with Hughes Aircraft to put its movies on compact discs and distribute them over a satellite system. It is also discussing possible alliances with communication companies. Other examples of virtual organizations include:[12]

- MCI Communications Corporation, which uses partnerships with as many as 100 companies to win major contracts.
- The R&D alliance among IBM, Apple Computer, and Motorola to develop the Power PC microprocessor.
- The Apple Computer-Sony alliance to produce the low end PowerBook notebook computer line. By linking Apple's software and design technologies with Sony's skills in manufacturing and miniaturization, Apple was able to get the PowerBook to market more rapidly.
- The many strategic alliances of Time Warner, which has teamed up with Toshiba, Silicon Graphics, Sega, AT&T, and others to establish multiple beachheads in the emerging multimedia market.

Despite their many advantages, alliances often fail to meet expectations. An IBM-Microsoft alliance to develop the OS/2 operating system soured in 1991 when Microsoft began shipping Windows in direct competition to the jointly developed product.[13] In retaliation, IBM entered into an alliance with Microsoft's archrival, Novell, to develop network software to compete with Microsoft's LAN Manager.

The Barrier-Free Organization

The barrier-free organization, without changing the basic relationships among organizations, seeks to eliminate the boundaries, within and between them, that impede communications, stifle productivity, and choke off innovation. In the traditional organization model, boundaries are clearly drawn into the design of an organization's structure. These boundaries are rigid. Their basic advantage is that the roles of managers and employees are simple, clear, well-defined, and long-lived. In today's fast-changing world, however, such organizational designs are becoming increasingly impractical. New technologies, rapidly changing markets, and global competition are revolutionizing the way business is conducted. Mirroring these environmental changes, effective barrier-free organizations achieve close integration and coordination both within the organization and with its suppliers, customers, and other external constituencies, encouraging inter-divisional coordination and resource sharing. As noted in Chapter 5, multibusiness firms have the potential to benefit greatly from sharing resources and integrating activities across businesses.

The internal structures of barrier-free organizations are often characterized by fluid, ambiguous, and deliberately ill-designed tasks and roles. Just because work roles are no longer defined by traditional structures, however, does not mean that differences in skills, authority, and talent disappear. Cross-functional teams; inter-divisional task forces and committees; increased involvement of production workers in setting objectives, designing processes and procedures, and structuring work environments; and reward and incentive systems that encourage cooperative behavior are commonly used techniques to improve internal coordination. Equally important are mechanisms for lateral communications, employee training and skill development, and top-management leadership that creates an environment of trust and openness and a sense of shared values and common purpose. A barrier-free organization enables a firm to bridge real differences in culture, function, and goals to find common ground that facilitates cooperative behavior. Technology can play an important role, as e-mail and video-conferencing can enhance communications and electronic data interchange (EDI) can eliminate paperwork and speed transaction flows with suppliers and customers.

Effective barrier-free organizations achieve close integration and coordination both with internal constituencies and external stakeholders. To be successful, the organization must go well beyond traditional forms of coordination across internal functions and focus on promoting shared interests and mutual trust throughout the organization. Chrysler's Neon project is an excellent example of the results that can be achieved by breaking down internal barriers:

Throughout the 1970s and 80s, the U.S. automobile industry steadily lost market share to the Japanese, particularly in smaller models. On the afternoon of July 31, 1990, however, in a test-track garage in Highland Park, Michigan, Robert P. Marcell, head of Chrysler's small car engineering team, convinced Lee Iacocca, then the company's CEO, that a subcompact *could* be built and sold at a profit, without a partner. Marcell passionately argued that American manufacturers, in toe-to-toe combat, could beat the Japanese. Pointing out that continued failure in the small car segment could hasten the demise of the U.S. auto industry, he asserted, "If we dare to be different, we could be the reason the U.S. auto industry survives. We could be the reason our kids and grandkids don't end up in fast-food service." As he ended the pitch, he thought he saw a tear in Iacocca's eye. Thus began one of the most remarkable development efforts in Detroit's history.

Marcell's core group of 150 colleagues mobilized internal and external stakeholders—600 engineers, 289 suppliers, and hundreds of blue-collar workers. The mission was clear: to deliver a competitive new subcompact in only 42 months and at a fraction of the development cost for any recent small car. From the beginning, Marcell applied the concept of concurrent engineering, which required personnel from diverse functional areas to work together and with suppliers to avoid later delays, disagreements, or misunderstandings. Specific goals and cost targets were established at the beginning. Higher component costs would not be accepted unless they resulted in a lower overall cost. Chrysler's approach dissolved traditional barriers and involved engineers, marketers, purchasing, finance, and labor as well as suppliers and customers (including subcompact owners in San Diego, California) in Neon's design. Union workers proposed more than 4,000 changes in the car and production process, many of which were implemented.

In the end, Chrysler spent $1.3 billion to develop the widely acclaimed Neon in only 42 months, comparing very favorably with Ford's $2 billion investment over five years to develop the Escort and GM's $5 billion, seven year effort to develop the Saturn.

Chrysler's Neon project illustrates the benefits of horizontal coordination across activities (e.g., design, manufacturing, marketing) that have often been viewed as sequential in many organizations. While this example primarily involves coordination among professional employees, many organizations have benefited by effectively using teams of production and clerical workers.[14] For example, General Mills has increased the productivity of its plants by

40 percent using self-managed teams. The cost savings mostly reflect a decrease in the number of middle-level managers. At its cereal plant in Lodi, California, the workers are in charge of all activities including scheduling and maintenance. Further, the firm has found that teams generally set higher goals than management. Federal Express used the team concept to organize its 1,000 clerical workers into teams of 5 to 10 people each. This new structure played a key role in achieving a 13 percent reduction in service problems such as incorrect bills and lost packages.

In spite of its potential benefits, many firms are discovering that creating and managing a barrier-free organization is a frustrating experience.[15] Puritan-Bennett Corporation, a manufacturer of respiratory equipment located in Lenexa, Kansas, found that its product development time more than doubled after they adopted team management. Roger J. Dolida, Director of R&D, attributes this failure to lack of top management commitment, high turnover among team members, and infrequent meetings. Similarly, efforts to switch to entrepreneurial teams at Jerome Foods, a turkey producer in Barron, Wisconsin, have largely stalled due to a failure to link executive compensation to team performance. The apparent difficulties inherent in creating a barrier-free environment suggest that we need to take a closer look at the tools and techniques available for achieving effective coordination and integration.

MANAGEMENT TOOLS AND TECHNIQUES FOR COORDINATION AND INTEGRATION

Achieving coordination and integration involves more than just creating a new organization structure. Often managers trained in rigid hierarchies find it difficult to make the transition to the more democratic, participative style that teamwork requires. As Douglas K. Smith, co-author of *The Wisdom of Teams* points out, "A completely diverse group must agree on a goal, put the notion of individual accountability aside and figure how to work with each other. Most of all, they must learn that if the team fails, it's everyone's fault." Within the framework of an appropriate organizational architecture, managers must select a mix and balance of tools and techniques to facilitate the effective coordination and integration of key activities. Many of the techniques listed below

are described in detail in Chapters 7 and 8, and will be addressed
only briefly here:

- Understanding the strategic context.
- Clear communication of goals and objectives.
- Common culture and shared values.
- Horizontal organization structures.
- Horizontal systems and processes.
- Communications and information technologies.
- Human resource practices.

Understanding the Strategic Context. An appropriate understanding
of the strategic context, and of the relationships and interdependencies among organizations is critical to effective coordination
and integration of activities, both within and across organizational
boundaries. This understanding must be communicated, understood, and accepted throughout, to facilitate and ensure consistent
behavior and interaction among the parties involved, at multiple
levels throughout each organization.

Clear Communication of Goals and Objectives. Effective coordination
and integration begins at the top. Senior managers must clearly ar-
ticulate organizational goals, objectives, and values, and employees
must identify with and buy into these goals and objectives. In the
traditional approach, objectives and goals are defined in terms of a
single organization and broken down into divisional and functional objectives that support the higher level goals. A broader view
is required in implementing the modular, virtual, or barrier-free organizational architectures, as a sense of common purpose must
transcend traditional organizational boundaries to include customers, suppliers, alliance partners, and team members, regardless
of the structure. Clear and effective communications and the careful avoidance of goal conflicts are essential.

Common Culture and Shared Values. Shared goals, mutual objectives,
and a high degree of trust are essential to the success of boundaryless organizations. It is neither feasible nor desirable to attempt to
"control" suppliers, customers, or alliance partners in the traditional sense. In the fluid and flexible environments of the new or-

ganizational architectures, common cultures, shared values, and carefully aligned incentives are usually easier to implement and often a more effective means of strategic control than rules, boundaries, and formal procedures.

Horizontal Organization Structures. Horizontal organization structures, which group similar or related business units under common management control, facilitate sharing resources and infrastructures, exploit synergies among operating units, and help to create a sense of common purpose. Consistency in training and the development of similar structures across business units facilitates job rotation and cross-training and enhances understanding of common problems and opportunities. Cross-functional teams and interdivisional committees and task groups represent important opportunities to improve understanding and foster cooperation among operating units. Service strategies based on the "smallest replicable unit" are perhaps the ultimate expression of horizontal structure. These strategies often achieve extraordinary levels of quality, flexibility, and customer service, while maximizing efficiency through shared infrastructures and the leveraging of organizational experience and learning.[16]

Horizontal Systems and Processes. Organizational systems, policies, and procedures are the traditional mechanisms for achieving integration among functional units. Too often, however, existing policies and procedures do little more than institutionalize the barriers that exist from years of managing within the framework of the traditional model. The popular concept of business reengineering focuses primarily on these internal processes and procedures. Beginning with an understanding of basic business processes in the context of "a collection of activities that takes one or more kinds of input and creates an output that is of value to the customer," Michael Hammer and James Champy's 1993 best-seller, *Reengineering the Corporation*, outlined a methodology for redesigning internal systems and procedures that has been embraced, in its various forms, by many organizations. Proponents claim that successful reengineering lowers costs, reduces inventories, improves quality, speeds response times, and enhances organizational flexibility.[17] Others advocate similar benefits through the reduction of cycle times, total quality management, and the like. GE and others have used benchmarking and adopted "best practices" from leading companies around the world in their efforts to streamline their internal systems and procedures.

Communications and Information Technologies. Improved communications through the effective use of information technologies can play an important role in bridging gaps and breaking down barriers between organizations. Electronic mail and video-conferencing can improve lateral communications across long distances and multiple time zones and, by short-circuiting vertical structures, tend to circumvent many of the barriers of the traditional model. Information technology can be a powerful ally in the redesign and streamlining of internal business processes and in improving coordination and integration between suppliers and customers. Electronic data interchange (EDI) has eliminated the paperwork of purchase order and invoice documentation in many buyer-supplier relationships, enabling cooperating organizations to reduce inventories, shorten delivery cycles and reduce operating costs. On the other hand, ineffective implementation that uses technology to automate existing processes, without thoughtful redesign, often has the opposite result, increasing cost and reducing flexibility. Regardless of the methodology, the basic principles are the same. The key is in the perspective—looking at business processes as a sequence of activities that add value to the ultimate product or service, and then optimizing those processes without regard to organizational boundaries.

Human Resource Practices. Change, whether it be in structure, process or procedure, always involves and impacts the human dimension of organizations. Training and education of the workforce must be an important part of any effort to improve organizational coordination and integration. As new architectures are implemented, processes are reengineered and organizations become increasingly dependent on sophisticated information technologies, the skills of workers and managers alike must be upgraded to realize the full benefits. Both the GE and Chrysler examples testify to the value of close labor-management cooperation in realizing operational efficiencies.

MOVING TOWARD THE BOUNDARYLESS ORGANIZATION

Today's competitive business environment requires managers to embrace new organizational architectures, reengineer internal processes, and upgrade the skills of the workforce to gain competitive advantage by improving coordination and integration and enhancing strategic control. The issue is not one of choosing a specific architectural form, of redesigning a single process, or addressing skills in one department. Rather, all must be addressed in concert, in the light of a clear understanding of the strategic context and the strengths and core competencies of the organization. The pursuit of the boundaryless organization may, in some cases, involve the simultaneous considerations of the *modular, virtual,* and *barrier-free* approaches to organizational design, closely coordinated with the implementation of a number of different tools and techniques to strengthen organizational coordination and integration. Careful consideration must be given to maintaining strategic control over core competencies and the critical links of the organization's value chain.

When organizations face harsh competitive pressures, resource scarcity, and declining performance, managers often "pull in the reins"—increasing control and reducing experimentation with new strategies. There is a tendency to focus internally, rather than to manage and further external relationships with existing and potential partners and stakeholders. To the contrary, we suggest that difficult times may become the most opportune time for managers to carefully analyze their value chain activities and evaluate the potential for the development of strategic alliances. Such endeavors may help an organization to enhance or establish multiple forms of competitive advantage—differentiation, overall low cost, quick response—at a time when they are needed most.

STRATEGIC INVENTORY

Understanding the strategic context (taking attendance in the lifeboat)

- Who is the ultimate customer? What goods and services does he need?

- What are the key elements in the overall value chain (disregarding organizational boundaries)?
- Who are the key players? What are the interdependencies?
- Is there a common vision? Do all the players have the same objectives?
- Who is in charge? Will everyone else accept their leadership?

With regard to the modular type:

- Are the firm's assets and human resources directed toward the firm's most critical value chain activities?
- Is the firm striving to attain "best in class" performance in each value chain activity (through internal development or outsourcing)?
- Are the firm's core competencies leveraged through outsourcing while capital requirements are reduced?
- Do the firm's outsourcing efforts enable it to focus more effectively on its customers and markets?
- Is the firm *not* outsourcing technologies that are critical for present (or future) sustainable competitive advantage?

With regard to the virtual type, can participation (or has participation) in networks of organizations enabled the firm:

- To share costs and skills?
- To improve access to global markets?
- To increase market responsiveness?
- To avoid a loss of operational control?
- To avoid a loss of strategic control over emerging technology?

With regard to the barrier-free type:

- Does the firm effectively leverage the talents of all of its employees?

- Has the firm improved cooperation and coordination across functions, divisions, strategic business units (SBUs), and external constituencies?
- Are the inherent democratic processes *not* becoming too time consuming or difficult to manage?
- Do shared goals and objectives enable faster response to market demands?
- Have appropriate mechanisms been established to resolve disputes in the absence of more traditional authority structures?
- Have appropriate information systems been designed and implemented to improve collaboration across functions and business units?

Are we using the right tools and techniques:

- Does everyone understand the goals and objectives? Do they buy in to them?
- Have we made the best use of horizontal structures?
- Do our systems, policies, and procedures support our objectives, or do they get in the way and slow our progress?
- Does our information infrastructure facilitate cross-functional communications?
- Do we have the right skills in place? Have we provided the training required to ensure that our people have the skills they need to do the job?
- Are all our tools and techniques working together—or are they competing with each other?

ENDNOTES

1. Anonymous, June 6, 1994. Doesn't it amaze? The delay that launched a thousand gags, *Travel Weekly*: 16; Knill, B. August 1994. Reality checks into baggage handling system. *Material Handling Engineering*: 51; Rifkin, G. August 29, 1994. It's in the bag(s), *Air Transport World*: 54–58; Henderson, D.K. September 1994. What really happened at Denver's airport? *Forbes ASAP*: 110–114; and Henderson, D.K. May 1995. Better late . . . *Air Transport World*: 76–77.

2. Dumaine, B. October 17, 1994. Mr. Learning Organization. *Fortune*: 156.

3. References for this section include: Gilder, G. October 14, 1991. Now or never, *Forbes*: 188–189; Pitta, J. May 9, 1994. Choking on a silver spoon, *Forbes*: 173–174; Anonymous, October 26, 1991. Out Froxed, *The Economist*: 86; Anonymous, March 15, 1993. Smart TV, *Forbes*: 14–15; and Johnstone, B. December 19, 1991. Rescue programme, *Far Eastern Economic Review*: 42.

4. *1993 General Electric Company Annual Report*: 2.

5. References for this section include: Woodruff, D. May 3, 1993. Chrysler's neon: Is this the small car Detroit couldn't build? *Business Week*: 119; and *1993 Chrysler Corporation Annual Report*.

6. This chapter draws on: Dess, G.G., Rasheed, A.M.A., McLaughlin, K.J., and Priem, R.L. August 1995. The new organizational architecture, *The Executive* 9: 7–18.

7. Tulley, S. February 8, 1993. The modular corporation, *Fortune*: 106.

8. Smart, T. May 10, 1993. IBM has a new product: Employee benefits, *Business Week*: 58.

9. Pitta, J. January 18, 1993. Score one for vertical integration, *Forbes*: 88–89.

10. Tanzer, A. December 21, 1992. Bury thy teacher, *Forbes*: 90–95.

11. Yoder, S. K., and Zachary, G. P. July 14, 1993. Digital media business takes form as a battle of complex alliance, *Wall Street Journal*: A1, A6.

12. Peters, T. 1994. *Liberation Management*, New York: Knopf; Byrne, J.A. February 8, 1993. The virtual corporation, *Business Week*: 58; and Lander, M. May 10, 1993. Time Warner's Techie at the top, *Business Week*: F8.

13. Anonymous, February 23, 1991. Young love, great riches, first tiff, *Economist*: 63–64.

14. Dumaine, B. July 12, 1993. Who needs a boss? *New York Times*: 16.

15. Stern, A. L. July 12, 1993. Team spirit is no easy goal in business, *New York Times*: 16.

16. Service strategies based on the "smallest replicable unit" are described by James Brian Quinn in *Intelligent Enterprise*, 1992, The Free Press, New York, 103–113.

17. Hammer, M. and Champy, J. 1993. *Reengineering the Corporation: A manifesto for business revolution*, HarperCollins, New York.

7

CHAPTER

Out of [Strategic] Control

Charles Handy, one of today's foremost business visionaries and author of *The Age of Unreason* and *The Age of Paradox*, recently shared an interesting story:[1]

> The other day, a courier could not find my family's remote cottage. He called his base on his radio, and the base called us to ask directions. He was just around the corner, but his base managed to omit a vital part of the directions. So he called them again, and they called us again. Then the courier repeated the cycle a third time to ask whether we had a dangerous dog. When he eventually arrived, we asked whether it would not have been simpler and less aggravating to everyone if he had called us directly from the roadside telephone booth where he had been parked. "I can't do that," he said, "because they won't refund any money I spend." "But it's only pennies!" I exclaimed. "I know," he said, "but that only shows how little they trust us!"

Handy's story emphasizes the extent to which some organizations waste resources and stifle creativity by overmanaging and overcontrolling their employees. Henry Ford once lamented: "Why is it that I always get the whole person when what I really want is a pair of hands?"[2] Unfortunately, this implicit "park your brain at the door" message is still the gospel in many organizations. Such "solutions" to the control problem harken back to the 1950s and 1960s, when machinelike bureaucracies were in vogue.[3] Then, managers exercised control by telling people how to do their jobs and monitored them with constant surveillance to guard against any surprises. Idiosyncratic behavior and unintended consequences were anathema to the efficient functioning of organizations. An overemphasis on task specialization, standardization, and rigid control tends, however, to stifle creativity, inhibit organizational flexibility, and breed employee resentment. Further, it takes a lot of middle managers and supervisors to effectively implement a system based solely on monitoring and control—and most organizations can no longer afford the overhead.

Today's global competitive environment is far more complex, interconnected, and unpredictable—times have changed since the 1950s—and different approaches to control are indicated. Managers have a number of tools at their disposal, as illustrated in Figure 7-1, below. Effective strategic control involves the use—and balancing—of three separate, but closely interrelated elements: boundaries, culture, and rewards.

Each of these elements plays a different role in the development and implementation of an effective system of strategic controls—alignment and balance among them is essential. If culture, rewards, and boundaries are not consistent, they will work

FIGURE 7-1

Essential Elements of Strategic Control

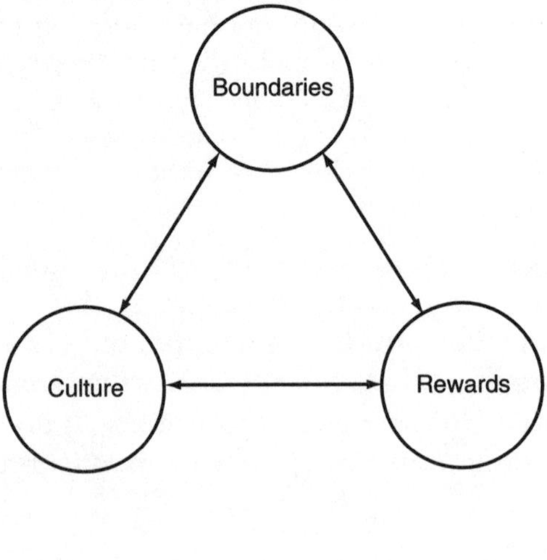

at cross purposes. If one or more dimensions are neglected or overemphasized, the system of controls may become dysfunctional. Organizational flexibility is highly desirable in many environments, but an overemphasis on controls often gets in the way. By contrast, the advocates of empowerment argue that managers should, in essence, trust their employees to "do the right thing" and just "get out of the way." Sounds pretty simple—just install capable managers, hire the right employees, set goals, align incentives, and empower them to produce the results. Avoid micromanagement and let those who do the work choose the means to achieve the ends. The beauty of empowerment is in its parsimony. But if it sounds too good to be true, it probably is! Consider the case of Bausch & Lomb:

Bausch & Lomb and its CEO, Dan Gill enjoyed a great run between 1981 and 1991.[4] Rapid growth in high-margin contact lenses and the Ray-Ban Wayfarer sunglass line, popularized in movies such as *The Blues Brothers*, tripled sales and earnings to $1.5 billion and $150 million, respectively. Shareholders were rewarded with a fivefold increase in value, and Gill's compensation soared from $362,000 in 1981 to $6.5 million by 1991.

Achieving double-digit annual growth was Gill's overriding goal. Typically, all divisions were expected to post impressive annual gains. How was such growth attained? The culture at B&L became a mirror image of Gill: tenacious, demanding—and very numbers-oriented. Harold Johnson, the former head of the contact-lens unit, recalls: "Each year, the top executives would agree on what number they wanted to make. The numbers would be divided out by operating units and then assigned." Once goals were set, there was little tolerance for shortfalls. "Once you signed up for your number, you were expected to reach it," according to former President Tom McDermott.

So far so good. But, things started to unravel in the early 1990s as growth slowed in the United States and Europe, competition intensified, and Gill's strategy of diversification failed (several key acquisitions were either marginally profitable or losing money). But the unyielding growth targets remained. How did the operating managers cope? What actions did they take? Let's look at three examples.

First, at the Ray-Ban division, deal making became frantic and one end-of-quarter promotion was tried after another. One large distributor claimed, "we had nine months' inventory. I bought extra insurance and sweated a lot at night." In a late 1993 deal, six months' worth of Ray-Bans were shipped to a Chilean distributor. Although Gill denied that such distributor loading took place, others viewed it as all too typical.

Second, in December 1993, according to more than a dozen sources, Harold Johnson called 30 of B&L's U.S. distributors to the company's Rochester headquarters. They were, in effect, ordered to take immense stocks of the older Optima lenses—up to two years' worth—or face the cancellation of their distributor agreements. Many were given verbal assurances they wouldn't have to pay for the lenses until they sold them. All but two agreed—they were terminated—and Johnson booked an extra $23 million in sales in the final days of 1993. By mid-1994, most of the unwanted inventory had made its way back to B&L, as the distributors refused to pay. These actions became the core of both an SEC investigation and a shareholder class action suit that accused the company of misleading investors by falsely inflating sales and earnings.

Third, B&L's Hong Kong operations—the long-time star of the international division—racked up annual growth rates of 25 percent. A good chunk of its 1993 sales were, however, bogus. The unit would pretend to book huge sales to Southeast Asian distributors, but product would never be shipped. Instead, the goods were moved to an outside warehouse from which B&L sales managers attempted to persuade distributors to buy the excess. Some of the glasses may have also been funneled into the gray market—buyers could profit because wholesale prices were higher in Europe or the Mideast. By mid-1994, B&L headquarters was tipped off by declining revenues and soaring receivables. Since no one was paying for many of the glasses booked as sales, receivables ballooned to 90 days' sales. There was no let-up on the pressure for sales results—1994 sales were targeted to rise to $176 million from $151 million. But with bulging distribution channels, the sales came in at only $85.8 million coupled with a $61.7 million loss. Internal auditors belatedly discovered significant irregularities including half a million pairs of sunglasses stashed in a Hong Kong warehouse!

Isolated problems? Some think so. According to Kenneth Wolfe, head of B&L's audit committee: "Unfortunately, when you have operations scattered throughout the world, people do things they shouldn't. But I don't think there's a larger problem." Gill denied accountability: "It's generally accepted that day-to-day operations of a company are overseen by the chief operating officer. I don't mean to pass the buck, but . . . as chairman, I'd have only a general understanding of what happened."

A brief postscript. Near the end of a highly acrimonious seven-hour meeting with investors, Gill was asked, after several charges had been made: "What else has to happen for you to resign?" After a stunned silence, he stammered that he would remain until he lost his board's confidence. A week later, B&L announced Gill's retirement. The stock market reacted: B&L's shares jumped 7.2 percent on the announcement!

WHAT WENT WRONG AT BAUSCH & LOMB?

At Bausch & Lomb, an aggressive culture and an emphasis on performance and rewards drove the organization—drove it too far, too fast, and nearly off a cliff. The key to financial rewards was straightforward: making the numbers. The focus on the ends—growth at all costs—caused any concern about the appropriateness of the means to take a back seat. There's nothing wrong with stretch targets, management incentives, or an aggressive culture, but organizations must also maintain standards of ethical behavior and a sense of "fair play."[5] Bausch and Lomb's organizations in Europe and the Mideast were probably not very happy about the gray market sunglasses that showed up in their markets—diverted from the secret Hong Kong warehouse.

Rewards and incentives are fine, but organizations also need to set boundaries. The imagery of a race car has been suggested: The more culture and rewards drive ambition and goal-seeking behavior, the better tuned and stronger the brakes, i.e., a system of boundaries and constraints, must be.[6] At Bausch & Lomb, the boundaries were set rather late in the game, after the SEC investigation began. Only then did Gill and his top executives order the company to follow more conservative practices, eliminate quarter-end wheeling and dealing, reduce distributor inventories, and change bonus guidelines to incorporate broader, longer-term goals.

The lack of alignment and balance among culture, rewards, and boundary systems was only part of Bausch & Lomb's problem. Rigid and arbitrary goal-setting also contributed. Once the goals and objectives were set, little time or effort was devoted to evaluating their reasonableness, and a change in circumstances brought no relief. In fact, Gill rarely discussed specific actions that a division might take to rectify a shortfall. A famous Gill line was: "Make the numbers, but don't do anything stupid." Unfortunately, many executives read the message differently, including one ex-marketing executive who commented, "I'd walk away saying, 'I'd be stupid not to make the numbers.'"

The notion that well-managed companies should move forward in accordance with detailed and precise plans has come under attack.[7] Brian Quinn of Dartmouth has argued that grand designs with precise and carefully integrated plans seldom work. Rather, most strategic change proceeds incrementally—one step at a time. Leaders can best serve their organizations by introducing some sense of direction, some logic to the incremental steps. His research described the messy, political nature of decisions, the need for flexibility and opportunism, and the difficulty of controlling strategic change.[8]

McGill's Henry Mintzberg has written about leaders "crafting" a strategy.[9] Drawing on the parallel between the potter at his wheel and the strategist, he contends that as the potter commences work, he has some general idea of the artifact he wishes to create. However, the detailed design evolves as the potter works with his clay. New possibilities emerge as his work progresses. Uncertainty about how a given design will work out in practice, and the need to allow for the creative element suggests that the view of a rational planner should be replaced by the craftsman analogy.

Quinnis and Mintzberg's arguments cast doubt on the value of a rigid planning process and goal setting. Fixed strategic goals also become dysfunctional for firms competing in highly unpredictable competitive environments—strategies need to change frequently and opportunistically. An inflexible commitment to predetermined goals and milestones can prevent the very adaptability that is often the essence of a good strategy.

STRATEGIC TRAP #6: ARBITRARY GOALS; UNBALANCED CONTROLS

Looking back, it is apparent that weaknesses in the goal-setting process and inadequate strategic controls both contributed to Bausch & Lomb's difficulties. The fundamental strategic error resulted from the combination of two defects: *(1) the blind pursuit of an arbitrary and inflexible set of objectives; and (2) an unbalanced system of strategic controls that drove the organization with culture and rewards, but failed to define the boundaries of acceptable behavior.* By placing too much emphasis on "making the numbers" and failing to implement a balanced system of strategic and operational controls, Bausch & Lomb fell right into Strategic Trap #6.

FIGURE 7–2

Traditional Approach to Strategic Control

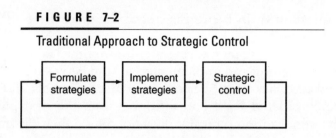

How did this happen? Our discussion will focus on two issues. *First,* we'll address the inherent limitations of the traditional approach to strategic control: the measurement and assessment of performance against predetermined and inflexible goals. We contrast this approach with a perspective that stresses the need to constantly monitor changes both within the firm and in the competitive environment and to adapt both goals and strategies to the changing realities. *Second,* we will address the need for an appropriate balance between the three elements of strategic control: culture, rewards, and boundaries.

Figure 7–2 illustrates the traditional approach to strategic control. The process is sequential: (1) strategies are formulated and goals are set; (2) strategies are implemented; and, (3) performance is monitored against the predetermined goal set. The feedback loop from strategic control to strategy formulation typically involves lengthy time-lags, often tied to the annual planning cycle. The analogy in everyday life is a thermostat. You set it at a predetermined position and if there is a deviation between the actual and prescribed temperatures, the preprogrammed activities of heating or cooling are activated. The thermostat doesn't question the appropriateness of the preset temperature.

In the same way, traditional control systems, termed single-loop learning by Chris Argyris, simply compare actual performance to a predetermined goal.[10] They are most appropriate when the environment is stable and noncomplex, goals and objectives can be measured with certainty (units of output, dollars of sales or profits), and there is little need for multiple measures of performance. Sales quotas, operating budgets, production schedules, and similar control mechanisms are representative of this type. The appropriateness of the strategy and the standards of performance are seldom questioned. In B&L's case, once the goals were set, there was "no looking back."

Without ongoing monitoring, significant time lags often occur between goal setting and implementation, and between implementation and feedback about performance. Because goals and objectives are considered fixed and inflexible until the next planning cycle, the organization typically does not alter either its strategies or its objectives to deal with the realities of a changing environmental context. Rigid and inflexible objectives are often out of touch with the realities of the competitive situation, as this story from a speech by Norman R. Augustine, CEO of Martin Marietta Corporation suggests:

> I am reminded of an article I once read in a British newspaper . . . which described a problem with the local bus service between the towns of Bagnall and Greenfields. It seemed that, to the great annoyance of customers, drivers had been passing long queues of would-be passengers with a smile and a wave of the hand. This practice was, however, clarified by a bus company official who explained, "It is impossible for the drivers to keep their timetables if they must stop for passengers."[11]

When rigid controls no longer fit the situation, organizations often find ways to compensate. One of the authors recalls his early experience as an engineer at Western Electric where the first line supervisors seldom questioned the time standards established by industrial engineering for warehouse operations. With little incentive to exceed standards, but hell to pay if you fell short, the supervisors worked together to transfer input hours from one section of the distribution center to another each week so that each supervisor could meet his efficiency goals.

In the late 1970s, one of the authors was hired as CFO of a recently acquired subsidiary of Houston-based Cooper Industries, Inc., a manufacturer of heavy mining, oilfield, and construction equipment. Multimillion dollar pieces of equipment were designed and built in the United States, and shipped in pieces to one of 14 sales companies around the world. The sales companies were responsible for assembly and delivery of the equipment and for ongoing support and warranty service. Each unit's performance had been measured against predetermined profit objectives, and little attention was paid to the balance sheet. All costs incurred in the field for warranty support were charged back to the factory through intercompany accounts and immediately credited against the sales company's operating expenses. Because warranty costs were charged against the factory's cost of sales, each plant scrutinized the chargebacks in detail. One way to solve a short-term profit problem at the factory was to slow down the processing of warranty claims by leaving them unresolved in the intercompany accounts. Because of the time lags involved, if a sales company's profits were down, it could "get well" quickly by overcharging the factory for warranty work, confident that the overcharge would not be detected for months. Frequently the factory "disallowed" warranty claims for minor discrepancies and charged them back to the subsidiary, which would correct the problem and rebill it to the factory. When uncovered, this warranty-claim "ping-pong" had been going on for years. Over $50 million of expenses were hung up in an unreconciled "warranty claims in process" account on the balance sheet—an amount that exceeded the subsidiary's cumulative earnings for the preceding four years!

> *Clearly, the traditional approach to strategic control has a few loopholes— but what are the alternatives? Is there a better way?*

MOVING TOWARD CONTEMPORARY CONTROL SYSTEMS

Josh Weston, CEO of ADP Corporation, captures the essence of what we consider "contemporary" control systems:

> At ADP, 39 plus 1 adds up to more than 40 plus zero. The 40-plus-zero employee is the harried worker who at 40 hours a week just tries to keep up with what's in the "in" basket. He tries to do whatever he thinks he's supposed to do. Because he works his full 40 hours with his head down, he takes zero hours to think about what he's doing, why he's doing it, and how he's doing it. Where does the work go after he does it? Does he need to do it in the first place? On the other hand, a 39-plus-1 employee takes at least one of those 40 hours to think about what he's doing and why he's doing it. That's why the other 39 hours are far more productive.[12]

Here we have, to carry on the analogy, thermostats with the gumption to decide if the present temperature is, in fact, desirable. In such "double loop"[13] learning, the organization's assumptions, premises, goals, and strategies are continuously monitored, tested, and reviewed. The relationships between strategy formulation,

FIGURE 7-3

Contemporary Approach to Strategic
Control

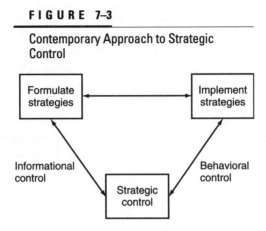

implementation, and control are highly interactive as suggested by
Figure 7–3.

In the contemporary approach, we consider two different types
of strategic control: *informational control* and *behavioral control.* Informational control is primarily interested in whether or not the organization is "doing the right things." Behavioral control is concerned
with the other side of the coin—is the organization "doing things
right" in the implementation of its strategy? Both the informational
and behavioral components of strategic control are necessary, but
not sufficient, conditions for success. What good is a well-conceived
strategy that cannot be implemented, or an energetic and committed
workforce focused on the wrong strategic target?

Informational Control

Informational control deals with the external strategic context and
the assumptions and premises that provide the foundation for an
organization's strategy. The key question addressed by informational control is: *Do the organization's goals and strategies still "fit"
within the current strategic context?* Chapters 2 and 3 addressed the
need to understand the organization's strategic context, monitor
the external environment, and understand and critically evaluate
the collective assumption base of the management team. These activities are important to strategy formulation regardless of the approach to strategic control. The essential difference is this: In the
traditional approach, the understanding of the strategic context

and examination of the assumption base is an *initial step* in the process of strategy formulation; in the contemporary approach, informational control is an *ongoing process* that continuously updates and challenges the assumptions and premises that underlie the organization's strategy. The benefits of continuous monitoring are evident—time lags are dramatically shortened, changes in the competitive environment are detected earlier, and the organization's ability to respond with speed and flexibility is enhanced.

As we noted in Chapter 2, very few organizations have sufficient slack to be able to dedicate full-time resources to ongoing environmental monitoring. Those that are most successful maximize the use of both formal and informal sources of data—with a strong bias toward informal sources and "soft data." Roy Vagelos, formerly the CEO of Merck & Company, liked to swap stories with scientists in the tray line at the company's cafeteria. "That's where I get a lot of my information," he claimed, "the scientists can't wait to tell me what they've just accomplished. And I stay very current."[14] Another example illustrates the potential payoffs in informal sources of information:

In 1980, Ford Motor Company's design chief, Jack Telnack, was approached at work by an unexpected visitor. The man tapped Telnack on the shoulder and pointed to a photograph of the Thunderbird, currently in development. "Do you like these cars? Do you feel proud of them?" he asked. "Would you park one of these cars in your driveway?" Telnack wasn't sure what to say. After all, the visitor was Donald Petersen, the company's president and chief operating officer. At first, he was tempted to stand by the company's design. But he saw honesty in Petersen's face that he couldn't ignore. "Actually, no, I don't like these designs," Telnack told him.

Petersen challenged him to come up with a new model and Telnack responded with a sleek, aerodynamic design—one that would dramatically affect the look of Ford's 1983 Thunderbird and later, the wildly successful Ford Taurus. That one conversation turned everything around. In the 1980s, Ford made a phenomenal comeback, surpassing General Motors in profitability. And like any great team player, Petersen was quick to share the credit.[15]

Our message is straightforward. Unless your firm is competing in a simple and highly stable competitive environment—*are there any left?*—informational control is essential. Assumptions, goals, and objectives must be continually tested and both internal

operations and the external competitive environment must be
monitored to ensure that your strategy continues to be focused on
"doing the right thing."

Behavioral Control

Behavioral control is focused on effective implementation—"doing
things right"—by manipulating the key "levers" of behavioral control: *culture, rewards,* and *boundaries.* The traditional approach to
strategic control emphasizes boundaries and constraints. The contemporary approach relies on a balance among culture, rewards, and
boundaries. We believe there are two compelling reasons for an increased emphasis on culture and rewards in implementing a contemporary approach. *First,* the competitive environment is becoming
increasingly more complex and unpredictable, demanding both flexibility and quick response to its challenges. As firms simultaneously
downsize and face the need for increased coordination and integration of activities across organizational boundaries, a control system
based primarily on boundaries and constraints is no longer feasible,
and the use of rewards and culture to align individual and organizational goals becomes increasingly important. *Second,* the implicit
long-term contract between the organization and its key employees
has been eroded. Today's younger managers have been conditioned
to see themselves as "free agents" and to view a career as a series of
opportunistic changes. As managers are advised to "specialize, market yourself, and have work, if not a job[16]," the importance of culture
and rewards in building organizational loyalty becomes clear.

Maintaining a Balance

A key consideration is the need to maintain an appropriate balance
among the three elements of behavioral control, as illustrated by
the following "rags to riches to rags to riches" story:[17]

In 1954, Frank Stronach set out from Austria with a single suitcase and
about $200 in cash. He ended up in Canada and landed a job as a tool-and-
die maker outside Toronto. He did so well that, within six months, the
owner promised him a partnership in the business. When the offer failed
to materialize, he quit and started his own shop in a garage. Within two

years, he employed 20 workers. His foreman then asked to be a partner. After mulling it over, Stronach figured that if the foreman quit, he'd be left to do all the work. The next morning he suggested, "Why don't we open up a new factory? You'll own one-third of it."

That formula was replicated again and again. By 1990, Magna International, Inc., was a $1.3 billion supplier of auto parts with over 100 manufacturing plants. Every one of its factories was built on the same entrepreneurial model: empower a foreman to run each shop as an independent profit center. As his empire grew, Stronach asked himself, "How can I get the employees involved?" He took the company public, gave the employees shares, and entitled them to 10 percent of total profits. He also shared 6 percent of profits with top management.

In the late 1980s, Stronach "took his eye off the ball." He turned—briefly and unsuccessfully—to politics. Meanwhile, his plant managers continued to pile on debt to grow their business units. In 1990, the debt reached $800 million—a precarious 71 percent of capital—and Magna lost $159 million. The bankers suggested that Stronach step aside and put someone else in charge. Reacting with rage, Stronach assured them that he "would do whatever it takes." Within months, he jettisoned 36 factories, slashed headquarters staff by more than 50 percent, and initiated a plan to drastically cut debt. He imposed new planning and control disciplines. Now, factory managers must get approval for major spending from senior executives, who only approve projects that fit into the overall strategic plan. All debt has been eliminated and new debt is forbidden. Peter G. Godsoe, CEO of Bank of Nova Scotia, claims Magna has "a rock solid balance sheet and lots of capital for expansion."

Despite the new constraints, Magna remains "far more entrepreneurial than most North American companies," says Chrysler's purchasing chief, Tom Stallcamp. Each of the 86 plants remains a separate profit center, and managers retain almost total control. They also have a huge incentive: 3 percent of gross profits. Although Magna pays its managers a base of $60,000 a year, bonuses can top $500,000. "We've made many of them millionaires," claims Stronach.

Since the early 1990s nosedive, things have really turned around. 1995 sales came in at $4.5 billion, more than double the 1990 level, and profits soared to $300 million. As automakers continue to outsource more parts and entire systems of components, Magna is well positioned for the future. In 1994, Magna supplied an average of $150 in parts for every vehicle manufactured in North America—an amount expected to grow to between $195 and $210 by 1997.

Magna International demonstrates the problems associated with relying strictly on a strong culture and motivating reward structure to control an organization. The *informational* aspects of strategic control were neglected—while Stronach was campaigning for Parliament, he was wasn't paying attention—and the rapid accumulation of debt almost sunk the firm. Clearly, in 1990, the time had come to place more boundaries and constraints on Magna's operating managers. The key is that Stronach had the wisdom to *balance* the levers of control. He tightened financial controls to avoid a repeat of the early 1990s without eroding the culture and incentives he had institutionalized at Magna over a long period of time. He exercised sound judgment by not "throwing out the baby with the bath water."

BUILDING A STRONG AND EFFECTIVE CULTURE

What is *culture*? Organizational culture is a system of *shared values* (what is important) and *beliefs* (how things work) that shape a company's people, organizational structures, and control systems to produce *behavioral norms* (the way we do things around here). How important is culture? Very. In recent years, numerous best sellers— *Theory Z, Corporate Cultures, In Search of Excellence,* and *A Passion for Excellence*—have emphasized the powerful influence of culture on what goes on within organizations and how they perform.[18] Collins and Porras argue, in *Built to Last,* that the key factor in sustained exceptional performance is a cult-like culture.[19] You can't touch it, you can't write it down, but it's there, and its influence is pervasive. It can work for you—or against you. Effective leaders understand its importance and strive to shape and use it as one of their most important levers of strategic control.

The Role of Culture

Culture wears many different hats. Culture can be used to focus an organization on the dominant values that sustain its primary source of competitive advantage. Federal Express and Southwest Airlines focus on *customer service;* Motorola and Hewlett-Packard emphasize *product quality,* Rubbermaid and 3M place a high value on *innovation,* and Nucor and Emerson Electric are concerned, above all, with *operational efficiency.* Culture sets implicit boundaries—unwritten standards of appropriate behavior—in dress, in ethical matters, and in the way an organization conducts its business. By creating a framework of shared values, culture encourages individual identification with the organization and its objectives.

Sustaining an Effective Culture

Powerful organization cultures just don't happen overnight. And, they don't remain in place without a strong commitment—both in words and deeds—by leaders throughout the organization. A discussion of the *content* dimensions of an organization's culture—the unique values and beliefs it holds, shares, and emphasizes—is beyond the scope of this book. Rather, our focus will be on the *process*—how a viable and productive organizational culture can be strengthened and sustained. (The more challenging issue of changing the culture, a vital part of transformation leadership, is an important focus of the next chapter). A culture is more organic than mechanical—it cannot be "built" or "assembled." It must be cultivated, encouraged, and "fertilized" if it is to grow and remain viable. Several techniques have proven their worth in cultivating and sustaining a culture:

- Personnel selection.
- Training and indoctrination.
- Ongoing reinforcement.
- Top management's "walking the talk."

These techniques are mutually reinforcing. Each is necessary, but none is sufficient. If any one dimension is missing or insufficiently emphasized, the culture will stagnate or flounder.

Personnel Selection

Effective organizations don't look upon the hiring process as a backwater operation; it must be a priority! Managers at every level need to be involved in hiring to ensure that the organization's dominant values are sustained. Personnel selection is *input* control, in the same sense that the monitoring of ongoing activities corresponds to *process* control and measuring performance is a form of *output* control.

In a *Fortune* interview, David Pritchard, head of Microsoft's recruiting operations, observed that ". . . the best thing we can do for our competitors is hire poorly."[20]. At Microsoft, even Bill Gates gets involved in college recruiting, calling candidates to say, "Hey, we're interested in having you work here." The interview process hones in on the ability of the candidate to think creatively—the hallmark of Microsoft's success. Why does Microsoft ask seemingly off-beat questions such as "how much water flows through the Mississippi River each day?" Pritchard's response:

> We're not looking for the 'right' answer. We're looking for the method . . . We want to see what information they ask for, like the length of the river or the flow rate at certain measuring points. It's a learning process. One of the things we look for is smarts and experience, but we also want to know what they will bring here over the long term. Are they flexible? Can they learn new concepts? In this industry, things are changing on a daily basis, and if you're not capable of learning new things, you won't be successful.

Many leading-edge firms don't focus just on key employees, but view the selection process for *all* employees as a critical activity. At Motorola, every job candidate—even those seeking factory work—goes through three days of interviews. Applicants write a composition and complete lengthy tests in math, problem solving, and the ability to work on a team. Only 1 in 10 makes the cut. Sounds demanding? Not any more than the six sigma quality benchmark for which Motorola is famous.

The personnel selection process is unique for each organization, depending on its needs and circumstances, but these suggestions for winning the battle for top talent are applicable to most situations:[21]

- Make recruiting more than just a staff function—line managers *and* top executives must be involved. The organization's dominant values should be a template for the selection process.
- Involve recruiters in more than recruiting—they need to understand the business needs of the units they hire for.
- Don't rely solely on written tests. It may lead to hires that can answer questions correctly but not think creatively. Teach candidates something in the morning and then ask them about it later in the day. Can they apply or expand on it?
- Follow-up on failures. If new hires depart within 12 months, find out why.

Training and Indoctrination

Training and indoctrination become critical if companies wish to maintain their standards and culture. Motorola's rigorous hiring practices are only the beginning. They also significantly outspend their peers on training and development—4 percent of payroll versus 1.2 percent for all U.S. companies—providing an average of 40 hours of annual training per employee.[22] It pays off for Motorola. Thanks to a competent and highly motivated work force, quality has steadily improved from 7,000 defects per million opportunities for error in 1987 to less than 30 in 1995.

There is probably no more demanding training and indoctrination program in the world than that of the U.S. Navy's SEAL Teams.[23] Here, the culture of excellence and selfless teamwork is literally a matter of life and death. The training is demanding, not only to weed out all but the top candidates, but also to increase team cohesion and effectiveness. Only 3 out of every 10 recruits eventually become SEALs. Let's look at the regimen and we'll see why only a select few make it through:

> After five weeks of rigorous training, Hell Week begins. For five days, the recruits can expect about four hours sleep per night. They will swim endless miles in the cold night waters of the Pacific, paddle rubber boats for hours; run a daunting obstacle course over and over, and perform grueling calisthenics using 300-pound logs while instructors scream insults at them. A couple of days into this, hallucinations are common. Captain Steve Ahlberg, 45, a SEAL and now deputy chief of staff for the Navy's special warfare command, recalls a rather startling experience during his own Hell Week. He saw a giant figure walking across the water and pointed out the phenomenon to his comrades. They all seemed to find it unremarkable.
>
> After Hell Week, 19 more weeks of training remain: 7 weeks of rigorous underwater training, 9 weeks of weapons training, and then 3 weeks of parachute training at Fort Benning. Then, the six-month probationary period begins during which the recruit must prove himself with an active SEAL unit.
>
> One SEAL veteran claims that to get through training, recruits need a black heart—meaning you have to be the sort of person who will do anything to get to where you need to go. And that's the key point. The demanding training weeds out recruits who can't make a total commitment to the group. The sense of all-out teamwork carries through in the field. SEALs never operate on their own—their sense of identity with the group is all but total—and the fact that they have never left a dead comrade behind on a battlefield is a great source of pride.

In this line of work—where there are few boundaries and ordinary rewards are relatively meaningless—culture is everything!

Clearly the rigorous program of training and indoctrination is a unique factor in the development and internalization of the SEAL unit's culture of teamwork and dedication.

Reinforcing the Culture

Every organization has a culture, but even a strong and healthy culture must be reinforced and passed on to others if it is to remain viable. Storytelling is one way effective cultures are maintained. Most of us are familiar with the story of how Art Fry's failure to develop a strong adhesive led to 3M's Post-It notes, but how about the story of inventor Francis G. Okie?[24] In 1922, he came up with the idea of selling sandpaper to men as a replacement for razor blades. That idea didn't pan out, but the technology led 3M to develop its first blockbuster product—a waterproof sandpaper that became a staple of the auto industry. Such stories foster the importance of risk taking, experimentation, freedom to fail, and, of course, innovation—all vital elements of 3M's corporate culture.

Annual reports and speeches by top executives also provide a forum to relate incidents of exceptional employee dedication. The following story from Federal Express's 1993 Annual Report both communicates Fed Ex's "can do" spirit and reinforces the company's dominant value—superb customer service:[25]

> Melody Harrison, a courier based in Jackson, Mississippi, came home to find a message on her answering machine. It was her manager expressing concern that another courier had not returned to the station that day. Melody called the station and directed the dispatcher to contact two area hospitals. Her hunch proved correct. The other courier had been in an accident and was in serious condition at a hospital emergency room.
>
> After determining there was nothing more she could do for her colleague, Melody turned her attention to the stranded packages. She contacted the state patrol to learn the location of the injured courier's van. She was told it had been towed to a city some 40 miles away. Upon arriving there, Melody contacted her manager and got permission to do whatever was needed to retrieve the contents of the badly damaged van. With the key sheared off in the ignition, Melody pried open the doors with a crowbar and retrieved the contents. Because of her effort, 38 pieces of customer freight made it to Memphis on time that evening.

Rallies or pep talks by top executives can also serve to reinforce a firm's culture. The late Sam Walton was well-known for his pep rallies at local Wal-Mart stores. Four times a year, the founders of Home Depot, CEO Bernard Marcus and president Arthur Blank, don their orange aprons and stage *"Breakfast with Bernie and Arthur,"* a 6:30 AM pep rally broadcast live over the firm's closed-circuit TV network to most of its 45,000 employees.[26]

Southwest Airlines' Culture Committee is a unique vehicle designed to perpetuate the company's highly successful culture. The following excerpt from an internal company publication describes its objectives:[27]

> The goal of this Committee is simple—to ensure that our unique Corporate Culture stays alive. . . . Culture Committee members represent all regions and departments across our system and they are selected based upon their exemplary display of the "Positively Outrageous Service" that won us the first ever Triple Crown; their continual exhibition of the "Southwest Spirit" to our Customers and to their fellow workers; and their high energy level, boundless enthusiasm, unique creativity, and constant demonstration of teamwork and love for their fellow workers.

"Walking the Talk"

For better or for worse, managers, especially top executives, serve as role models for their organizations. Consistency in word and deed can serve as a stimulus to cultural cohesion and greater commitment from employees, but *"do as I say, not as I do"* simply doesn't get the job done. Mixed signals can sabotage even the best-laid plans. Reacting to a $271 million loss in 1989, Lone Star Industries Inc. CEO James E. Stewart ordered layoffs, put $400 million of corporate assets on the block, and eliminated the corporate dividend.[28] But the austerity did not apply to Stewart. He had a $2.9 million expense account and flew the corporate jet between his home in Florida and corporate headquarters in Connecticut as he ordered his managers to fly coach. Shortly thereafter, Lone Star, the nation's largest cement company, filed for Chapter 11. Stewart resigned a month later as the board conducted an inquiry into his expenses.

Leadership by example—if it's headed in the wrong direction—can mean real trouble, especially if it involves fraud and cover-ups, as in this example:

United Telecontrol Electronics, Inc., of Asbury Park, New Jersey, was recently hauled into court for violating federal procurement regulations on a
$48 million contract to build launcher rails for the Maverick antitank missile
used so successfully in the Gulf War.[29] The problems were traced to a former
executive, Raymond Herter, who was in charge of the launcher production.

According to prosecutors, the problems began in 1986, when a shipment of forged aluminum lugs produced by a German subcontractor
failed inspection at UTE's plant. UTE was already behind schedule and
facing contract penalties. So Mr. Herter ordered the parts inspected on a
Saturday, when the Defense Department inspectors assigned to the plant
wouldn't be around. The defective parts were segregated and Mr. Herter
ordered a machinist to work at night, after the inspectors had departed, to
grind off and smooth over the cracks and then to prepare a "clean" inspection report. It worked—and the shipment made it on time!

In 1987, when quality problems appeared with another part, Mr. Herter
told the engineers to come up with a way to pass the defective parts. This
problem was easy to solve—just run the good rails through the testing ap-
paratus over and over again and record a different serial number each
time. Defrauding the government seemed simple, and it saved a lot of
money. It became, in effect, a part of UTE's culture.

All went well and no one was the wiser until missiles started falling off
the wings of aircraft when they weren't supposed to. A quality control inspector fired by Mr. Herter blew the whistle and the government began to
investigate. It took several years to crack an elaborate cover-up, but eventually, Herter and a number of his associates were brought to trial and
convicted. The company went into bankruptcy.

Other corporate leaders set a much better example as they
lead their organizations forward and reinforce their dominant
values. David Kearns, CEO of Xerox, consistently "walked the
talk" as he made quality the *new* dominant value of his firm during its remarkable turnaround in the 1980s. His consistency in
words, actions, and strategies during the implementation of
"Leadership Through Quality" sent a firm, steady message to
every employee.

Ken Iverson, Nucor's highly respected CEO, epitomizes his
firm's lean management philosophy and the dominant values of efficiency and low cost.[30] Although Nucor Corp.'s annual sales are
over $3 billion, its one-story headquarters in suburban Charlotte,
North Carolina, is staffed by only 23 people. Missing are lawyers
and public relations officers. He shares his secretary with other

executives and often answers his own phone. When guests come, Chairman Iverson jokingly describes the lunch counter across the street as the "corporate dining room."

Andy Grove, as CEO of Intel, also sets the tone for his organization. To encourage a culture of openness and equalitarianism, Grove—like all top managers—has a cubicle, not a private office. And, when traveling, executives fly coach and rent subcompact cars. Ford Escorts, in fact, have been jokingly referred to as "Intel limousines."

MOTIVATING WITH REWARDS AND INCENTIVES

Typically, people in organizations act rationally, each motivated by his or her own best interests.[31] The collective sum of the individual behaviors of an organization's employees may not, however, result in the best thing for the organization—individual rationality may not always guarantee organizational rationality. Rewards and incentives can often serve as a powerful tool to align individual and organizational objectives.

We're all aware of the potential for conflicts among different functions. Sales wants to customize orders and promises quick deliveries to please customers—much to the chagrin of operations managers who have to deliver the goods. R&D overdesigns products and ignores costs—leading to frictions with manufacturing. Goal conflicts and perceived inequities among managers often lead to detrimental outcomes, as one of our consulting clients learned the hard way:

Deteriorating morale in the field had become a problem in a nationwide tax assessment consulting firm. As it turned out, the compensation plan had the sales staff, which reported directly to a headquarters vice president, and the division managers working at cross-purposes. In some divisions, about the only thing the two groups of executives had in common was an office address.

The sales executives' incentives were based on total revenues, and the sales force lived well—first class air fares, the best hotels and liberal entertainment spending. Division manager incentives were based on division profitability, and they squeezed every unnecessary nickel out of their budgets. Sales expenses, however, were charged against the division managers' budgets, and they had historically run 25 to 30 percent over budget. Volume was growing rapidly, but the division managers were complaining. While the sales force was bringing in more and more business, much of it was unprofitable.

A redesign of the compensation system did a lot to solve the problem. Sales compensation was restructured to take into account not only sales volume, but division profitability as well. Expense control was solved by establishing a new procedure under which salespeople earned no commissions until their sales exceeded their expenses, and the commission rate increased progressively as a multiple of their selling expenses. Division manager compensation was restructured to take into account both growth and profitability. The message was clear: "We're all in this together, guys!"

After the initial presentation of the new compensation plan was completed, the president asked: "Are there any questions?" Silence. Then the company's top salesman raised his hand. "Only one, sir: Since the commission rate is based on a multiple of my expenses, will you cut my salary to a dollar?" In the following year, sales were up nearly 10 percent; sales expenses were flat, and profit margins more than doubled.

Effective reward and incentive programs have a number of common characteristics, and those that are most successful incorporate them all:

- Objectives are clear, well understood, and broadly accepted.
- Rewards are clearly linked to performance and desired behaviors.
- Performance measures are clear and highly visible.
- Performance feedback is prompt, clear, and unambiguous.
- The compensation system is perceived as fair and equitable.
- The structure is flexible—it can adapt to changing circumstances.

While most of these appear obvious, a surprising number of incentive programs ignore these fundamentals. The objectives of most successful organizations are clear to senior management, but they frequently are not broadly communicated, and the link between performance and rewards is often obscure. Objective performance measures are highly visible in most firms, but are the intangibles even considered? At Federal Express, a separate system, based primarily on recognition, targets the intangibles of customer service and extraordinary effort. Recognition can be a powerful motivator when it involves prompt feedback and is linked directly to performance that is "above and beyond." Two different programs are involved:[32]

- The *Bravo Zulu* program—the Navy signal for "well done"—uses modest cash awards and gift certificates to reward employees, on the spot, for outstanding efforts and achievement.

- The *Golden Falcon* award, which includes 10 shares of stock and a congratulatory phone call or visit from a top executive, is triggered directly by a letter or phone call from a customer praising an employee's performance.

The perception that a plan is fair and equitable is critically important, as is the flexibility to respond to changing requirements as an organization's direction and objectives change. In recent years, many companies have begun to place more emphasis on growth, and their organizations have become so "lean and mean" that only marginal returns are available from further cost cutting.[33] Emerson Electric is one company shifting its emphasis, and the compensation program is one of the key levers of strategic control.[34] Planning sessions now focus exclusively on sales, new product development, overseas expansion, and the like, and discussions about profits are handled separately. This approach encourages a culture of risk taking. To ensure that the change takes hold, the management compensation formula has been changed from a focus largely on the bottom line to one that emphasizes growth, new products, acquisitions, and international expansion.

SETTING BOUNDARIES AND CONSTRAINTS

Frequently, when individual and organizational objectives diverge, culture and rewards are not enough and boundaries and constraints become essential. A prison is an extreme example—the inmates are confined because they have failed to conform to society's norms. The guards are paid to enforce norms of acceptable behavior within a (literally) iron-clad system of boundaries and constraints. The procedures of highly bureaucratic organizations are not too different in objective from the constraints of a prison. The essential idea behind bureaucracy is to constrain individual discretion and assert control through rules, regulations, and division of labor. Rule-based controls have their place in organizations with predictable environments, where employees are largely unskilled and interchangeable, or where the risk of error or malfeasance is extremely high (in banking or casino operations, for example) and controls must be implemented to guard against improper conduct. At Chemical Bank, for example, the Reporting and Compliance Department ensures that all new laws and regulations affecting the banking industry are disseminated throughout the organization in order to prevent violations of the laws.

The downside is that organizations that rely too heavily on rules and regulations are inflexible and often suffer from a lack of motivation on the part of employees. An overreliance on rules may lead to difficulties with customers, indifferent performance (doing the minimum to avoid being fired), and constant conflicts among departments and functions ("not my job, man"). Despite the potential downside, boundaries and controls, in combination with other techniques, can serve a vital purpose in organizations:

Josh Weston, ADP's CEO, believes that his firm's long-term success can be attributed to decentralization, motivation, and "strong cultural awareness."[35] He fosters what he calls a "relatively apolitical atmosphere" in order to minimize turf guarding and secrecy, as well as to promote candor. All of ADP's 20,000 employees are called associates for good reason: more than half own ADP stock. They clearly have a vested interest in the firm's success, and culture and rewards play a significant role in ADP's model of strategic control. Boundaries are also important.

Weston backs up decentralization and empowerment with effective controls and a hawkish eye for detail. Approximately one-fifth of the 250-member corporate staff are accountants, who carefully monitor performance in the company's 50 data processing locations around the United States and Europe. Once a month, Weston directs one of the accountants to give him a batch of 40 to 50 randomly chosen ADP accounts payable receipts, which he examines for ways to cut costs. Weston also visits *all* 50 locations at least once a year and requires all senior executives to do likewise. "You can't be aware sitting behind a desk."

This example shows how a balanced mix of rewards, culture, and boundaries can play a key role in a firm's success. Boundaries and constraints can also help to focus an organization's priorities. Eli Lilly and Co. has reduced its research efforts to five broad disease areas from eight or nine a decade ago, providing a narrower and more targeted focus and greater opportunity for competitive advantage and above-average shareholder returns in the remaining areas.

EVOLVING FROM BOUNDARIES TO REWARDS AND CULTURE

In most environments, organizations should endeavor to provide a system of rewards and incentives, coupled with a culture strong enough that boundaries become internalized. The need for external controls is thus reduced. We suggest several ways to move in this direction. First, hire the right people—individuals who already identify with the organization's dominant values and have attributes consistent with them. Microsoft's David Pritchard is well aware of the consequences of failing to hire properly:

> If I hire a bunch of bozos, it will hurt us, because it takes time to get rid of them. They start infiltrating the organization and then they themselves start hiring people of lower quality. At Microsoft, we are always looking to hire people who are better than we are.[36]

Second, training and indoctrination play a key role. In the example of the Navy SEALs, the training regimen so thoroughly internalizes the culture that the individuals, in effect, lose their identity. The group becomes the overriding concern and focal point of their energies. Few external controls are required if the culture is strong and the training is thorough. At Motorola—and as we'll see in the next chapter, Xerox—training not only builds skills, but also plays a significant role in building a strong culture on the foundation of each organization's dominant values.

Third, managerial role models are vital. At Nucor, Ken Iverson's spartan surroundings and skeleton staff send the powerful message that cost leadership is *the* dominant value. Andy Grove at Intel doesn't need (or want) a lot of bureaucratic rules to determine who's responsible for what, who's supposed to talk to whom, and who gets to fly first class (no one does!). He encourages openness by not having many of the trappings of success—he has a cubicle like all the others.

Can you image any new manager asking whether or not he can fly first class? Grove's example obviates such a need.

Fourth, reward systems must be clearly aligned with organizational goals and objectives. Where do you think rules and regulations are more important in controlling employee behavior—Home Depot with its generous bonus and stock option plan, or K mart, which does not provide the same level of incentives?

We will close with the example of Brazil-based Semco, a classic success story that shows how a strong culture and effective reward systems will reduce the need for rules and regulations:[37]

At the age of 21, Richardo Semler took over the family business from his father. Semco was pretty much like any other old-line Brazilian company— fear was the prime motivator, guards patrolled the shop floor, and anyone who broke plant equipment had to pony up money for its replacement. For a while, Richardo followed the tradition of the autocratic ethic and worked relentlessly, but at the age of 25, he had his epiphany. While visiting a pump factory in upstate New York, he collapsed on the shop floor. The doctor pronounced him basically healthy but said he was the most stressed-out 25 year-old he'd ever seen. That experience gave Semler the resolve to transform the company into "a true democracy, a place built on trust and freedom, not fear."

Semler succeeded in creating an organization governed both by democratic principles and the marketplace. When he joined the firm in 1979, it manufactured hydraulic pumps, had annual sales of about $4 million, employed around 100 people, and was on the brink of bankruptcy. By 1995, it generated $30 million in annual revenues, well over $1 million in profits, and produced a wide range of sophisticated products. It's now considered one of Brazil's most sought-after employers, with over 1,000 applications for each opening. Hundreds of U.S. companies such as Mobil and IBM have trekked to Sao Paulo to witness the operation first-hand.

What makes Semco tick? The close, symbiotic relationship between culture and rewards. Semco employees truly run the company. They wear what they want, select their own bosses, and come and go as they please. Amazingly, a third of them set their own salaries. But there is one huge hitch—they must reapply for their jobs every six months. Shop floor workers evaluate their bosses once a year, and if they are consistently graded low, they step down. A strong incentive compensation system also plays an important role—a huge 23 percent of profits are shared with employees. Communications is also a key component. Every employee has access to all of the business' key statistics, including costs, overhead, sales, payroll, taxes, and profits.

Semler also shares his title. Six people, including a woman, rotate as CEO for six-month periods. Although Semler's family owns the company, his vote carries the same weight as everyone else's. According to the head of Semco's durable goods division and one of the rotating CEOs: "Richardo will say, 'if you want my opinion, I can give it to you now or later. But, it's just another opinion.'"

Senior managers receive the same type of upward evaluations as lower-level executives. Semler himself gets good, but not great ratings. Employees complain that he doesn't intervene enough, but Semler responds: "the day I intervene is the day I condemn this entire system. I grit my teeth a lot, and I watch while they sometimes elect managers I would never want to work for. But I trust my employees. They're looking for success as strongly as I am."

STRATEGIC INVENTORY

Honing the informational aspects of strategic control

- Is the planning process sufficiently flexible to permit changes in goals as the evolving competitive environment dictates? In strategies? Are performance targets for operating units adjusted when internal or external conditions change?
- Are both the competitive environment and the internal environment monitored on an ongoing basis? Are both "hard" and "soft" sources of data used effectively? Does the organization rely too heavily on formal reporting mechanisms?
- Is performance judged primarily against predetermined standards? Or are the standards rigorously questioned and frequently updated?
- Is there a tendency for negative information to be filtered out and suppressed as it moves up the hierarchy? Why? How can this bias be eliminated?

Improving the behavioral control aspect of strategic control

- Do employees understand management's goals and objectives? Can they identify with them? Are they motivated to achieve the same goals?
- What are the organization's dominant values? Do they reflect and reinforce the strategic priorities? Does culture play an important role? Do the employees "buy in" to the organization's culture and dominant values?

- Do employees focus on goals and objectives, or do they live within a system of boundaries and constraints?
- Do boundaries and constraints unnecessarily stifle creativity? Risk taking? How can the system of boundaries and constraints be improved? Can some be eliminated?
- Does the organization's culture establish norms of appropriate and ethical behavior? Are boundaries and constraints internalized by culture or does the organization rely primarily on rules and procedures?
- Does the system of rewards and incentives focus and channel the efforts of all employees? Does it align individual and organizational goals? Does it encourage working together or does it put different groups at cross purposes?
- What practices are used to strengthen the organization's culture? Are they effective? Do recruitment and selection procedures focus on dominant values? Is training and indoctrination focused on attitudes and values as well as skills? Are executive speeches, storytelling, and role models used to reinforce values? Do you—and your managers—"walk the talk"?

ENDNOTES

1. Handy, C. May-June, 1995. Trust and the virtual organization. *Harvard Business Review*, 73: 40–50.
2. Lawbook, K. November 14, 1994. Why companies fail. *Fortune*: 64.
3. Simons, R. March-April, 1995. Control in an age of empowerment. *Harvard Business Review*, 73: 80–88. Simons does make the important point that machinelike bureaucracies are very effective when standardization is critical for efficiency and yield, such as on an assembly line; when the risk of theft of valuable assets is high, such as in a casino; or when quality and safety are essential to product performance, such as at a nuclear power plant.
4. Sources for this example include: Baranathan, J., DeGeorge, G. & Maremont, M. October 23, 1995. Blind Ambition: *Business Week*: 78-91; Maremont, M. December 25, 1995. Judgment day at Bausch & Lomb. *Business Week*: 39; and Maremont, M. December 9, 1994. Numbers Game at Bausch & Lomb? *Business Week*: 108–110.

5. For an insightful article on how to incorporate multiple perspectives in evaluating an organization, refer to: Kaplan, R.S. & Norton, D.P. January-February, 1992. The balanced scorecard measures that drive performance. *Harvard Business Review*, 70: 166.

6. This imagery is suggested by Robert Simons. March-April, 1995. Control in an age of empowerment. *Harvard Business Review*, 73: 80–90.

7. The next three paragraphs draw on Goold, M. & Quinn, J.J. 1990. The paradox of strategic controls. *Strategic Management Journal*, 11: 43–57.

8. Quinn, J.B. 1980. *Strategies for Change*. Homewood, IL: Richard D. Irwin.

9. Mintzberg, H. July-August 1987. Crafting strategy. *Harvard Business Review* 65: 66–75.

10. Argyris, C. September-October, 1977. Double loop learning in organizations. *Harvard Business Review*, 55: 115–125.

11. An address by Norman R. Augustine, Chairman and Chief Executive Officer, Martin Marietta Corporation, at the Crummer Business School, Rollins College, Winter Park, Florida, October 20, 1989.

12. Weston, J.S. July-August, 1992. Soft stuff matters. *Financial Executive*: 52–53.

13. Argyris, C. op.cit.

14. Byrne, J.A. and Symonds, W.C. April 12, 1991. Best bosses avoid the pitfalls of power. *Business Week*: 59.

15. Jones, G.A. undated. *On Leadership, No.11 in a series.* CSX Intermodal (with permission).

16. Klechel, W. III. April 4, 1994. *Fortune*: 68–72.

17. Sources for this example include: O'Reilly, B. January 11, 1993. The perils of too much freedom. *Fortune*: 79; Osterland, A. January 31, 1995. Love those musical chairs. *Financial World*: 48–49; Symonds, W.C. and Frey, E. May 1, 1995. Frank Stronach's secret: Call it empowered steering. *Business Week*: 63–66; and von Daehne, N. November, 1995. Kingmaker. *Success:* 16; Markey, Keith A. February 2, 1996. Magna International, Ltd. *Value Line*: 1277.

18. Ouichi, W. 1981. *Theory Z*. Reading, MA: Addison-Wesley; Deal, T.E., and Kennedy, A.A. 1982. *Corporate Cultures*. Reading, MA: Addison-Wesley; Peters, T.J., and Waterman, R.H. 1982. *In Search of Excellence*, New York: Harper & Row; Peters, T., and Austin, A. 1985. *A Passion for Excellence*, New York: Random House.

19. Collins, J.C., and Porras, J.I. 1994. *Built to Last: Successful Habits of Visionary Companies*. New York: HarperBusiness.

20. Lieber, R. February 5, 1996. Wired for hiring: Microsoft's slick recruiting machine. *Fortune*: 123–4.

21. Adapted from Leiber, R. op. cit.

22. Zellner, W., Hof, R.D., Brandt, R., Baker, S., and Greising, D. February 13, 1995. Go-go goliaths. *Business Week*: 69.

23. Lawbook, K. February 19, 1996. Elite teams: Get the job done. *Fortune*: 92–3.

24. Mitchell, R. April 10, 1989. Masters of innovation. *Business Week*: 58–63.

25. *1993 Federal Express Annual Report*: 23.

26. Sellers, P. May 31, 1993. Companies that serve you best. *Fortune*: 88.

27. March-April, 1993. Southwest Airlines Culture Committee. *Luv Lines* (company publication): 17–18.

28. Byrne, J.A., Symonds, W.C., and Silar, J.F. April 1, 1991. CEO Disease: Egotism can breed corporate disaster—and the malady is spreading. *Business Week*: 54.

29. Carley, W. M. February 27, 1996. Bombs Away: A defense contractor gets tough scrutiny for defective products. *The Wall Street Journal*: A1, A6.

30. Zellner, W., Hof, R.D., Brandt, R., Baker, S., and Greising, D. February 13, 1995. *Business Week*: 64–70.

31. See Hrebiniak, L.G., and Joyce, W.F. 1986. The strategic importance of managing myopia. *Sloan Management Review*, 28: 5–14 for an insightful perspective on goal conflict in organizations.

31. *Blueprints for Service Quality*, second edition. 1994. New York: AMA Publications: 30–31.

33. Zellner, W., Hof, R.D., Brandt, R., Baker, S., and Greising, D. February 13, 1995. Go-go goliaths. *Business Week*: 66–67.

34. Lubov, S. August 1, 1994. It ain't broke but fix it anyway. *Forbes*: 56–60.

35. The ADP example draws on Nulty, P. September 30, 1993. Making money like clockwork. *Fortune*: 80, and Weston, J.S. July/August, 1992. Soft Stuff matters. *Financial Executive*: 52–53.

36. Lieber, R. February 5, 1996. Wired for hiring: Microsoft's slick recruiting machine, *Fortune*: 123.

37. Sources for the Semco example include: Fierman, J. February 6, 1995. Winning ideas from maverick managers. *Fortune*: 70, 73; and Semler, R. September-October, 1989. Managing without managers. *Harvard Business Review*, 67: 76–84.

8

CHAPTER

[Mis]leading: Failures of Leadership

It ought to be remembered that there is nothing more difficult to take in hand, more perilous to conduct, or more uncertain in its success, than to take the lead in the introduction of a new order of things. Because the innovator has for enemies all those who have done well under the old conditions, and lukewarm defenders in those who may do well under the new.[1]

Machiavelli, The Prince, 1513

Clearly, times have changed since the 16th century—or have they? Leadership is still mostly about the process of managing change—transforming organizations from *what they are* to what the leader would have them become. And, as Machiavelli observed, the task is far from easy. Consider the example of Boise, Idaho-based Morrison Knudsen:[2]

Founded in the 1920s, Morrison Knudsen, was a consummate builder with such massive projects as the Hoover Dam, the San Francisco–Oakland Bay Bridge, and the Trans-Alaska Pipeline on its corporate resume. Over the years, it had successfully diversified into the construction of auto assembly plants, breweries, power plants, and military bases. It reached out too far, however, in the 1970s. Ventures in land development and shipbuilding went sour as land prices softened and rising oil prices cut demand for oil tankers. Things got progressively worse. By 1987—when the company reported a loss of $60 million on revenues of $1.9 billion—MK's board looked to a change in leadership to reverse the company's declining fortunes. William Agee, a Boise-area native and member of the board, was picked as Morrison Knudsen's savior-designate.

Bill Agee had the credentials. He was a Harvard MBA, the CFO of Boise Cascade at the age of 31, and by 38, the CEO of Bendix, a $4 billion-a-year auto parts maker. His record was impressive, and he presented an image of shrewdness and sound planning in finance and investing. He had little experience in MK's core businesses of construction or engineering, but he offered expertise in both real estate and manufacturing, the two most troubled parts of MK's empire. On the board since 1981, Agee was well aware of the problems facing Morrison Knudsen.

Agee's strategy, as outlined in the 1988 annual report, was to "refocus on MK's basic strengths," but it soon became clear that Agee had not learned from MK's past errors. Rather than focusing on its historical strengths, Agee began to see MK as a vehicle for solving many of the country's infrastructure and transportation problems and he began chasing billion-dollar, high-profile contracts that ventured well beyond MK's areas of expertise. MK bid low on major design-build contracts, hoping to learn the required critical skills and make up for losses on options. This high-risk strategy was badly flawed and the warning signs were abundant, as *Forbes* noted in 1992: "MK may have been bidding too low"; "finding engineering and management staff [and] training the rest of the skilled workers will also be far from simple or cheap"; "Agee has pushed MK into treacherous territory"; and "the company's plate is very full, too full."

MK's first railcar production contract was a disaster. Its inexperienced engineers relied on outdated technology and the adaptation of designs developed by another firm. The task was more difficult than anyone had expected and the customer rejected the first cars it received. MK tried to fix the problems, but it fell farther and farther behind. Despite this performance, the company won (bought?) four more railcar production contracts, worth more than $780 million.

On the surface, financial performance improved, but much of the progress was based on the "smoke and mirrors" of aggressive accounting practices that had raised eyebrows during Agee's time at Boise Cascade and Bendix. These practices included the capitalization of operating expenses, which created the illusion of earnings while the balance sheet deteriorated. Profits increasingly depended on Agee's expertise in buying and selling securities and unrelated assets, which the auditors allowed MK to report as operating income.

Agee reportedly spent much of his time at his Pebble Beach, California, mansion, commuting to Boise in a corporate jet that cost MK $4 million yearly—13 percent of the company's general and administrative budget. He appointed his wife to head MK's $1 million-a-year charitable foundation and spent lavishly on personal perks, including $7,000 for a portrait of himself and his wife and over $10,000 in a single month for landscaping services at his Pebble Beach estate.

Many felt Agee had a propensity to jettison real talent. A little more than a year into Agee's tenure, he fired the CFO, Don Kayser, and Keith Price, an executive vice president, board member, and well-respected MK veteran. One director contended that Agee kept talented managers away from the board: "He'd move people up, but when they got to where we could see them, he'd move them back down. As soon as we liked someone, Bill would say he wasn't a performer." Agee, he concluded, lacked confidence. "He was afraid to have talent around."

Many of the people Agee installed were young and lacked experience. One vice president was 33, another 30, and the treasurer was only 28. One MK executive commented: "They were bright, but they were in no position to argue with him." A rail company executive was much more direct: "His inner circle was made up of sycophants and 'yes men.' People at the next level down caught hell."

MK's 1993 Annual Report reported a "banner year" with "milestone events, new projects of grand proportions and strong financial results," but less than a year later the bubble burst. In February 1995, MK reported that it (1) expected a large loss for 1994 after taking big write-downs on its major construction and transit projects, (2) was in default on its loan agreements, (3) was eliminating its dividend, and (4) was seriously considering the sale of several of its noncore businesses. Despite the bad news, employees at MK's headquarters celebrated—the board had finally seen that the emperor had no clothes, and Agee had been thrown out as CEO!

An analyst at Smith Barney, quoted in a recent *Fortune* article that highlighted America's most admired corporations, wrote MK's epitaph: "Morrison Knudsen's reputation is just shot, and the very few customers they have left are very nervous . . . We don't see any way for them to recover."[3] Morrison Knudsen ranked near the bottom—one of the "least admired" companies— in six of eight categories: quality of management; ability to attract, develop and keep talented people; financial soundness; use of corporate assets; value as a long-term investment; and community and environmental responsibility. If it hadn't been for Kmart and TWA, MK might have had a clean sweep of all the categories! The total return to investors on the S&P 500 for 1995 was 37.5 percent—MK's investors lost 64.2 percent over the same period.

> *So, what went wrong? Did Morrison Knudsen fall victim to external forces and factors beyond its control? Was the company too far gone for a successful turnaround by the time Agee arrived in 1988? Or was it—as it appears—a disastrous failure of leadership?*

DEFINING LEADERSHIP

Before we analyze the mess at Morrison Knudsen, let's take a brief look at the subject of leadership. *Just what is leadership, anyway?* Tough question. Everyone has a definition and an interpretation. Manfred F.R. Kets de Vries, a noted authority, recently observed:

> When we plunge into the organizational literature on leadership we quickly become lost in a labyrinth: there are endless definitions, countless articles and never-ending polemics. As far as leadership studies go, it seems that more and more has been studied about less and less, to end up ironically with a group of researchers studying everything about nothing.[4]

Many would agree. Two alternate perspectives seem, however, to capture much of the contemporary thinking about leadership. One approach, the *romantic view,* "implies a strong faith in the importance of leadership factors to the functioning and dysfunctioning of organized systems."[5] The popularity of this perspective is reinforced by the intense media attention focused on high-level executives, the high levels of executive compensation, and the often significant stock market reaction to announcements of CEO changes. A second approach, an *external control perspective,* argues that leadership is not necessarily the most important factor in an organization's success. External factors that constrain a leader's options and choices are considered paramount—economic conditions, constraints on funding, labor union demands, pressures from shareholders and environmental groups, government regulations and the like.

Both views, of course, have merit. Many leaders, through their personal actions and example, have left an indelible imprint on their countries or organizations. Consider, for example, Winston Churchill's indispensable leadership during World War II, Lee Iacocca's role in Chrysler's turnarounds, and professional football coach Bill Walsh's leadership role in turning around the San Francisco 49ers. Leaders, of course, also face constraints. Effective leaders recognize constraints, but don't permit them to become an overriding focus. They demonstrate their leadership skills by developing creative solutions.

In this increasingly chaotic world, few would argue about the need for leadership—but how do we recognize and encourage it? Let's narrow the focus to business organizations. In an ever-changing environment, is it enough to just keep the organization afloat, or is it essential to make steady progress toward some well-defined objective? In our view, custodial management—maintaining the status quo—is not leadership. Leadership is proactive, goal-oriented, and focused on the management of constructive change. To put it more simply: *Leadership is about the process of transforming organizations or institutions from **what they are** to what the leader **would have them become**.* This simple definition implies a lot: *dissatisfaction* with the status quo; a *vision* of how things ought to be; and a *process of significant change*—a transformation—influenced, motivated, and directed by an effective leader. Warren Bennis, one of the world's most respected leadership gurus, makes an important distinction between leadership and management:

> Leaders are people who do the right things. Managers are people who do things right. There's a profound difference. When you think about doing the right things, your mind immediately goes toward thinking about the future, thinking about dreams, missions, visions, strategic intent, purpose. But when you think about doing things right, you think about control mechanisms. You think about how-to. Leaders ask the what and why question, not the how question. Leaders think about empowerment, not control. And the best definition of empowerment is that you don't steal responsibility from people.[6]

Determining the "right thing" has become increasingly challenging as we move toward the next millennia. Many industries are mature or declining; the global village is becoming increasingly complex, interconnected, and unpredictable; and product and market life cycles are shrinking. Recently, when asked by one of the authors to describe the life cycle of his company's products, the CEO of a supplier of computer components replied: "Seven months from cradle to grave—and that includes three months to design the product and get it into production!" Richard D'Aveni, the author of *Hypercompetition*, goes so far as to argue that, in a world where all dimensions of competition appear to be compressed in time and heightened in intensity, *sustainable* competitive advantages are no longer possible.[7]

Transformational leadership is a complex and difficult undertaking. All kinds of barriers stand in the way—conflicting objectives, organizational fiefdoms, political rivalries, and organizational inertia—to name a few. Things don't always work out as well as planned—sometimes gravity takes over and things come crashing down around the would-be leader's head. Morrison Knudsen's Bill Agee understands. So do Eastman Kodak's Kay Whitmore, Westinghouse's Paul Lego, GM's Bob Stempel, and IBM's John Akers, each of whom failed to achieve the desired results and, as a result, were removed from their position at the top of the organization chart. Other transformational leaders have produced stellar results, including Jack Welch at GE, Lawrence Bossidy at Allied Signal, the late Mike Walsh at both Union Pacific and Tenneco, and Michael Eisner at Walt Disney. Examples of excellence in leadership are also found at lower levels. The story of Craig Weatherup's leader-ship as the head of Pepsico's soft drink operations is an example that illustrates all of the key elements of effective transformational leadership:

In 1990, things were looking good at Pepsi-Cola, PepsiCo, Inc.'s soft drink unit. Earnings were up 10 percent and the business was more profitable in the United States than Coca-Cola.[8] Craig Weatherup, the unit's president, sensed, however, that the future would not be so bright. He was concerned that the market would turn flat and competition would intensify. Recently, smaller companies like Snapple Beverage Corp. had begun to cut into Pepsi and Coca-Cola's domination with fruit drinks, tea, and iced coffee. In Weatherup's view, Pepsi continued "doing things the same old way because that's the way we did things. We had allowed a culture to develop around the notion that we could make it, send it down the chute, and take in the money." But, given the unit's performance, how could he convince his 30,000 people that dramatic and fundamental change was necessary?

Weatherup's response: Create a crisis—everyone in the organization needed to feel a sense of urgency. He called a three-day meeting with his top 11 lieutenants and bluntly told them that he would no longer be satisfied with 10 percent annual earnings hikes—the goal was now 15 percent. Simply setting a goal was not enough, however—the message had to be reinforced! To drive home his point, he handed each manager a model train with 15 percent painted on its side. On the tracks, in front of the train, were 11 tiny figures. It didn't take long for his managers to get the message. He then set out to convince the rest of the organization. Between 1990 and 1992, in a series of meetings that ultimately involved all 30,000 employees, he delivered the message of impending crisis and communicated his vision of a new, customer-driven organization.

Each meeting was opened with Weatherup's version of the "burning platform" story. Several years earlier, a North Sea oil rig had caught fire. One worker, trained to wait for help rather than to jump from the 150-foot-high rig into the icy sea, leaped anyway. Fortunately, he survived. When asked why he jumped, he replied that, after looking up at the approaching wall of fire and down at the icy sea: "I chose probable death over certain death."

For Pepsi-Cola, Weatherup argued that business as usual was the equivalent of certain death. To stress his point, he talked about what he called "customer pain." One story was about his first meeting with David Glass, Wal-Mart's CEO, who told him, "There is nothing about the way your company does business that I like." Weatherup then recited a litany of customer complaints: missed or inaccurate deliveries, ineffective merchandising, and poor communications. After he had convinced them of the crisis, he turned to the solution. He articulated a new vision: Pepsi-Cola would become an organization focused on customer needs and filled with employees who knew how to reengineer the processes by which to do their work. He then backed up his vision with specific proposals.

The meetings were designed to get one layer of the organization to train the next, which in turn would train the next. For example, at the first meeting (with the trains), the 11 managers had three months to learn such techniques as reengineering, continuous improvement, and the mapping of work flows. They trained the next 70 managers who, in turn, had three months to train the next 400 managers, and so on.

Weatherup made other significant changes designed to make Pepsi-Cola more responsive to its customers. He turned the organization chart on its head, putting the customer representatives on top, and cut the number of layers between himself and the reps from six to four. This change was symbolic: "The company [was] changed from an organization . . . focused on satisfying management to one now focused on the customer." COO Brenda Barnes noted that with fewer layers of management "you have to empower people." Field reps now plan marketing and promotion with customers without the need for higher approval, and reps who find a product out of stock call for the item immediately rather than waiting days for the next scheduled delivery.

In another example, a team composed of managers and hourly workers analyzed how the company delivered soft drinks to supermarkets, stores, and restaurants. A lot of time was wasted by having an employee check soft drink stock on delivery trucks at the gates of the bottling plant each morning. Now, the people who load the trucks check their own work, and the trucks get out faster. It's not brain surgery, but Weatherup estimates that this one change gives each of his 10,000 trucks another 45 minutes of extra delivery time each day—enabling them to make more stops and sell more product.

Weatherup's successful transformation at Pepsi-Cola illustrates most of the basic principles that characterize successful organizational change efforts.[9] Although things were going well in 1990, Craig Weatherup was looking ahead—*focusing on the future*. Sensing trouble on the horizon, he *moved quickly* and *created a sense of urgency* with his model trains and stories of "customer pain." He *developed a vision and a plan* for organizational transformation, and *communicated it effectively* through speeches, meetings, and employee training. He challenged the organization with *stretch goals*, *empowered workers* at every level, and *motivated* them to achieve the objectives. Finally, he *institutionalized the changes* and made them an integral part of the organization's culture and business model with changes in organization structure, policies, and procedures. Textbook perfect! And highly successful! The target of 15 percent earnings growth was reached in 1993, and the unit contributed greatly to PepsiCo's sizzling stock performance—roughly a 100 percent increase—over the past two years. Quite a contrast to the disaster at Morrison Knudsen, isn't it?

STRATEGIC TRAP #7: A FAILURE OF LEADERSHIP

In 1988, a failed diversification strategy had Morrison Knudsen on the rocks. When the board turned to Bill Agee as its savior, he pledged to "refocus [the strategy] on MK's basic strengths." Unfortunately, Agee behaved more like a politician than a business leader—that was the first of a long string of broken promises—and he appeared to be more interested in his personal image and power base than in the best interests of the organization he headed. Agee's litany of leadership blunders is the stuff of legends—but what was the fundamental strategic error? And in this case, who made it? Was Agee at fault, or did MK's board make the biggest mistake by selecting Agee in the first place? Let's look at some of the things that went wrong:

- Morrison Knudsen was in trouble and everyone knew it— no need to create a sense of urgency—but what kind of message did Agee send by spending his time in Pebble Beach rather than in Boise?

- Agee's vision? Seriously flawed. Diversification away from the company's strengths was the problem he was hired to correct. Rather than refocus on the firm's core competencies, he made the same mistake again—with disastrous results.

- What were the goals? What was the objective, targets of opportunity? Aggressive bids won big contracts—and Agee took full credit—but the inability to perform at the prices he quoted only showed up years later as the contracts ran out of money before they were completed.

- How about empowering others? He put together a supportive management coalition—by firing experienced finance and operating managers and replacing them with inexperienced young executives unlikely to question his decisions.

- Clear and straightforward communications? Questionable accounting practices boosted earnings and covered up his marketing and operational miscues—hiding the true results from the board, the shareholders, and the financial markets. He held board meetings away from headquarters, limiting board access to the other members of the management team.

- How about leadership by example? He isolated himself from the organization, running the Idaho-based company from Pebble Beach, California, and spending lavishly on his personal perks.

In hindsight, MK's board made a poor choice. Agee clearly failed to transform the organization—and by most accounts left the company in much worse shape than before he arrived. But the fundamental strategic problem was Agee's. He ignored basic principles, failed to provide effective leadership, and thus fell right into Strategic Trap #7.

PRINCIPLES OF EFFECTIVE TRANSFORMATIONAL LEADERSHIP

In an earlier example, we highlighted the fundamental principles that characterized Craig Weatherup's successful transformation at Pepsi-Cola. Four basic principles provide the foundation and are found in most successful organizational change efforts. Successful transformational leaders:

- Move quickly and decisively—and create a sense of urgency.
- Develop and communicate both a vision and a plan.
- Set stretch goals and empower others to act.
- Consolidate the gains by institutionalizing change.

Two important caveats are in order before we proceed. First, these are *principles* of transformational leadership, rather than *steps* in a leadership process. Long-lasting and significant change cannot be accomplished by a sequence of one-time actions. A consistent and comprehensive approach is required. For example, a *sense of urgency* must be maintained throughout the process. Cultural issues implicit in "institutionalizing change" need to be addressed early on and throughout the process. Second, the organization's focus must be fixed on the external objective, rather than on the internal process. Arthur Martinez, chairman and CEO of the Sears Merchandise Group and the force behind its dramatic transformation, observes:

> Any transformation effort must consider what the customer requires. If the customer is not the architect of the transformation, a company may find that it has reinvented itself but has done little or nothing to improve the customer's lot. This can easily happen when a company's transformation efforts are focused internally. Too much time and energy spent on management processes and not enough on processes relevant to the customer's needs is a recipe for trouble.[10]

Now, let's take a look, one by one, at each of the key principles of transformational leadership—keeping in mind that they do not stand alone. All must work together to create a successful transformation.

MOVE QUICKLY AND DECISIVELY—AND CREATE A SENSE OF URGENCY

What a difference a day makes! Effective transformational leaders must move quickly and decisively to seize the initiative and assert their leadership.

In early 1874, an inventor named Elisha Gray transmitted a few faint musical notes over a telegraph wire. And if he could send music, then what next? The human voice. A word. Conversation. The New York Times reported predictions of a "talking telegraph," and the public grew eager for it. Just one year later, Gray believed he had the answer: tin can-like voice chambers connected by a wire and a liquid that could turn vibrations into signals. But inexplicably, he didn't put his idea on paper for two months. And after finally making a sketch, he waited four more days before he went to the patent office. When he arrived, Mr. Gray was told that, a mere two hours earlier, a schoolteacher named Alexander Graham Bell had burst through the door with his own sketch. Of voice chambers. Connected by a wire. The sketches—Gray's and Bell's—were almost identical. The two men were not.[11]

Move Quickly and Decisively

Speed and first mover advantages are critical to the success of technological innovations—or any viable idea. Swift and decisive action is even more important in transforming organizations. Boards can become very impatient when changes aren't made quickly enough to revitalize downtrodden corporations. Just ask John Akers or Bob Stempel, *formerly* the CEOs of IBM and GM, respectively. In contrast, consider Al Dunlap's rapid-fire changes after taking over as CEO of Scott Paper in April of 1994:[12]

- Within hours, he offered three former associates top jobs.
- On the second day, he disbanded the ruling management committee.
- On the third day, he fired 9 of the 11 highest-ranking executives.
- On the fourth day, he threw out four bookshelves crammed with his predecessor's strategic plans.

Mr. Dunlap's blitzkrieg kept going. In a year, he engineered one of the quickest turnarounds in corporate history. It was capped off in July 1995 by Kimberly-Clark Corporation's $7.36 billion offer to purchase Scott Paper. It was also a pretty profitable venture for Dunlap—he walked away with about $100 million. Floyd Hall's 1995 efforts to reverse the slipping fortunes of Kmart illustrate another approach:

Investors were excited when Floyd Hall was tapped in June 1995 to reverse the downward spiral at Kmart.[13] His background seemed to justify such high hopes, having previously headed discount rival Target Stores and Grand Union Supermarkets. And, if a company ever really needed help, it was Kmart. Consider, for example:

- Kmart's core customer is over 55 with an income less than $20,000 and no kids at home. By contrast, Wal-Mart's consumer is under 44, has children at home, and has an annual income just under $40,000.
- Kmart shoppers visit the stores 15 times a year—Wal-Mart's customers make more than twice as many visits. 49 percent of shoppers drive past a Kmart to shop at Wal-Mart.
- Kmart's sales per square foot in 1994 were $185 versus Target's $282 and Wal-Mart's $379.

Within 10 weeks after Floyd's appointment, Kmart's shares spurted 25 percent to hit $16 per share—a 52-week high. The rise in the stock price didn't last. Whereas quick action was required to transform Kmart, the market sensed it was not forthcoming. By March 1996, Kmart's stock had fallen by nearly one half, to about $8 per share.

Confidence in Hall's leadership eroded when it became clear that strong, decisive action was not forthcoming. Investors began to doubt that Hall had a plan. In a late 1995 interview, Hall claimed that there were no "silver bullets": turning Kmart around was "a tall order, but we can do this methodically—department by department." Despite calls from Wall Street to immediately shutter as many as 1,000 stores, Hall planned to close only 200 over three years. The reactions from Wall Street were caustic: "People are wondering if [Hall] is serious"; "Hall has managed to fritter away all the goodwill he had"; and from a mutual fund manager who dumped Kmart shares at a loss: "We weren't convinced a turnaround was imminent, and we didn't want to spend 90 percent of our time worrying about it." *Fortune* even offered Hall some advice:

> Over the six months he has been on the job, he has failed to show that he has a handle on the company's troubles. He lacks a strategy. And he doesn't even seem committed to the supersize task. Inside his office, in the center of his conference table, Hall keeps a Lucite sign that reads NO SURPRISES. Here's some advice to the boss: Kill the motto. Start surprising.

Floyd Hall's foot-dragging approach to the crisis at Kmart reflected the kind of organizational inertia that got Kmart in trouble in the first place. Less than 10 years previously, in 1987, when Hall's predecessor, Joe Antonini, became CEO of Kmart, its sales were twice those of Wal-Mart! But Kmart failed to keep pace under Antonini, and Wal-Mart left them in the dust. Organizational inertia is a powerful force—success breeds complacency, inertia, and resistance to future change. Sumantra Ghosal and Chris Bartlett recently described the process:

> Yesterday's winning formula ossifies into today's conventional wisdom before petrifying into tomorrow's tablets of stone. Such organizational sclerosis prevents companies from adjusting to new market realities or emerging strategic opportunities.[14]

Successful transformational leaders must shatter the tablets of stone and define a new paradigm. Leaders must challenge the status quo if they are to succeed. Yoshio Murata, CEO of Kao Corp., Japan's giant consumer products company, considers "change agent" one of his most important roles:

> Past wisdom must not be a constraint but something to be challenged. Yesterday's success formula is often today's obsolete dogma. My challenge is to have the organization continually questioning the past so we can renew ourselves every day.[15]

Create a Sense of Urgency

Change is greatly facilitated when people throughout the organization share an awareness of a crisis and a need for immediate action. Although it may appear inappropriate for a leader to deliberately create and encourage an atmosphere of fear and anxiety, there is probably no more vital act of leadership than to alert an organization to danger and to recognize that which, in fact, should be feared. Many organizations have suffered more because their leaders failed to recognize a developing crisis or because they mistakenly "protected" their flock from anxiety or stress by not calling their attention to it. But awareness is a two-edged sword—the same message that stirs a sleeping giant to action may also create an unintended and undesirable level of anxiety and stress. Two kinds of anxiety are found in organizations—one is constructive and the other is not.[16] Successful leaders know the difference. The anxiety created by the *fear of change*—of doing something new and possibly making a mistake—must be replaced by the *fear of not changing*—the anxiety of continuing on a course of action that one knows will lead to failure. Consider the advice of the late Mike Walsh, veteran of successful turnarounds at both Union Pacific and Tenneco, the latter while heroically fighting terminal cancer:[17]

> I think the biggest enemy to progress is happy talk. You need to tell your people that if we do not change fundamentally, we are going out of business, and that will create insecurity. The trick is to turn that insecurity into constructive tension. My experience is that people can deal with reality much better than managers give them credit for. If you don't deal with reality, and you paper it over in the name of undue apprehension about creating insecurity, I do not believe you can cause a revolution or major change.

Clearly, credibility becomes a key issue. Without it, little change will likely be effected—except perhaps by outright intimidation. Do you recall how Pepsi Cola's Craig Weatherup effectively communicated the sense of urgency throughout his organization with dramatic stories about troubling feedback from customers? The model trains and tiny figures would likely have had little effect had Weatherup not been armed with an arsenal of relevant facts. Let's look at another leader who instilled a sense of urgency even though—like Pepsi-Cola—the company's current position looked very good:

Peter Lewis is CEO of Progressive, a highly successful Cleveland-based auto insurer that sells policies mostly to high-risk drivers.[18] He was confident that his employees took pride in their relationships with customers, and his people believed that they provided the best service of any insurer in America. However, to convince them that they *had* to change, he communicated in a manner that was guaranteed to capture their attention. Lewis explains: "I told them that our customers hated us."

His comment wasn't totally off the mark. Voters in California had just passed Proposition 103 that mandated cuts in auto insurance rates (that eventually cost Progressive $50 million). Lewis was convinced that drivers were fed up with sky-high insurance premiums: "I said our customers felt like the people in the movie *Network* who were all hanging out of an apartment building screaming: 'I'm mad as hell and I'm not going to take it anymore!'"

With the company experiencing healthy growth, internal resistance was understandably formidable. Competitors had already responded, however, with significant price cuts and were taking market share. To remain competitive, Lewis felt that the company needed both to revamp its claims processes and to lower prices. Nearly one-fifth of the workforce needed to be cut. To convince his people that the cuts were worth it, Lewis launched a profit-sharing plan in 1992 for all supervisors and hourly workers.

The claims system is now faster and more cost effective. Progressive offers an 800 number 24 hours a day, seven days a week. With the 24-hour claims service, if a policyholder calls at 3 AM, a live person takes the accident report. Claims adjusters virtually live in their Ford Explorers, taking calls from central dispatching offices and heading either to the accident scene or the home of the policyholder. The benefits: less paperwork, fewer hours spent by claims adjusters, big savings, more satisfied customers— and fewer lawyers getting involved. Shareholders have also been treated very well—compound total returns exceeded 20 percent over the past 20 years. Net profits in 1996 are projected to be six times the 1991 level.

In order to create a sense of urgency the leader needs, *first*, to communicate the crisis in a simple and straightforward manner. Here, strong statements like "Our customers hate us" or "If we don't change we're dead" fit the bill. When coupled with powerful imagery, like the "burning platform" story, the organization can be energized to question the status quo. *Second*, the leader's assertions must be supported by facts. Hard evidence from customer feedback, new competitors, documented industry trends, and the like, are essential to establishing credibility. Weatherup used the complaints of a significant customer to emphasize his point. Lewis invoked California's Proposition 103 and a competitor's aggressive pricing strategy to establish the legitimacy of his arguments.

Although creating a sense of urgency would appear to be rather straightforward, John Kotter of Harvard University maintains, based on a study of more than 100 companies, that it is not.[19]

Companies fail at this task more than 50 percent of the time. Why? Executives often underestimate how difficult it is to drive people out of their comfort zones or overestimate how successful they have been in communicating a sense of urgency. In other cases, they simply lack patience: "Enough with the preliminaries; let's get on with it." Recall that Craig Weatherup spent *two years* holding three-day meetings to deliver the message to his 30,000 employees. Kotter contends that executives frequently back off too soon. Paralyzed by the potential downside, they fear that the troops may become defensive, morale will plunge, and short-term performance and the stock price will decline—and they will be blamed for unnecessarily creating a crisis.

Perhaps the paralysis of senior management comes from having too many managers and not enough leaders. After all, managers' jobs generally center on minimizing risks and keeping the current system operating. Change, on the other hand, generally demands a different kind of leadership skill. Transformation processes often become stalled unless enough real leaders are promoted or hired into senior-level jobs. Often a change of top management is the dramatic event required to shake up the organization—Gerstner at IBM, Jordan at Westinghouse, Gault at Goodyear, and so on.[20]

Once a sense of urgency is created, the leader needs to communicate a clear sense of direction. It does little good for the troops to believe that they're "up to their ass in alligators," unless they are also confident their leader knows the way out of the swamp!

DEVELOP AND COMMUNICATE A VISION AND A PLAN

The "vision thing" haunted George Bush throughout his failed 1992 reelection campaign. Right or wrong, Bush was perceived by many as the custodian of the status quo—and his challenger played up the contrast by presenting himself as the outsider with fresh new ideas. Clinton won the election, but three years into his term, he was under attack as a back-peddling defender of the status quo. The "vision thing" is a strange animal—just how important is it to transformational leadership? Opinions differ:

> Good business leaders create a vision, articulate the vision, and relentlessly drive it to completion.[21]
>
> *Jack Welch, CEO, GE*

We changed CEOs in early 1993. The new CEO, Lou Gerstner, called me up on his first day and said, "Let's talk about strategy." I went to see him with a long list of strategic issues that had to be dealt with, headed by the topic of vision. He responded, "Let's not worry about vision for now, let's get right down to the issues—the problems that are making this company a poor performer. Let's get to profitability, our software and our hardware architecture, and the guts of our distribution system." And so vision got scratched off the list. I think you know what happened next. Last July, Lou Gerstner told the press, "the last thing the IBM Corporation needs now is a vision."[22]

Pete Schavoir, Director of Strategy, IBM (retired)

Two perspectives. Almost dramatically opposed to each other. The topic of vision is not new. Consider Henry Ford's vision of a car for the common man. Or, Thomas Edison's vision of building *systems*, not just devices.[23] Rather than make a light bulb, he built an entire infrastructure—Edison Light Company, a predecessor to GE—to manufacture and install the equipment required to illuminate the night, from the bulbs to huge coal-fired generators known as dynamos. There is no doubt—visions can serve a vital purpose for organizations undergoing significant change.

Leaders who develop and effectively communicate a clear sense of direction for their organizations create a solid foundation for the development of organizational goals, objectives, and a sense of purpose, and are rewarded with enhanced commitment and participation by their employees. To be effective, a statement of vision must:

- Be simple, direct, and focused on the essentials.
- Be expressed in terms employees and stakeholders can relate to.
- Provide a framework for goals and objectives.
- Focus on the future—and what the organization must do to succeed.

Simple, Direct, and Focused on the Essentials

In 1981, when Jack Welch took over as CEO of General Electric, the company had hundreds of businesses—ranging from aircraft engines to light bulbs to major appliances—but many were marginal performers. Early on, he announced his intentions: GE would keep only those businesses that had, or were capable of achieving, an outstanding competitive position in their industry. The decision rules were simple: the businesses that would be kept had to fit in one of three categories—described with a diagram of interlocking circles, and had to be capable of being either first or second in worldwide market share in their industries.[24]

Express in Terms That Employees and Stakeholders can Relate to

A statement of vision should capture the employees' interest and attention.[25] Bob Allen, AT&T's CEO, was well aware of the technical and marketing challenges of transforming his company from regulated monopoly to market-driven competitor, but he chose to describe his vision in human terms, stating that AT&T was "dedicated to becoming the world's best at bringing people together, giving them easy access to the information and services they want and need—anytime, anywhere." The statement captures AT&T's objectives in a simple, personal language that anyone can understand and that employees can identify with and take pride in.

Provide a Framework for Goals and Objectives

Effective visions not only communicate organizational goals (the ends), but also provide a framework within which the means to those ends can be understood, as illustrated by the following example:

Frank Schaper, a marketing manager at KLM, was brainstorming with his staff during the Olympic Games a couple of years ago.[26] Suddenly, he had an insight: To win the decathlon—the most demanding of all sporting events—you don't have to win all the individual events that make up the contest. "It struck me that airline service is a lot like the decathlon," Schaper says. Published airline service ratings are based on 10 separate items from passenger surveys conducted by IATA, the international air transport association. Like the decathlon, not all of the items are weighted equally. The idea of communicating the airline's annual service plan as a Service Decathlon evolved from this insight. KLM's plan establishes goals for each service category—for KLM to rank first or second on the most critical items and no lower than fifth in any category, with the objective of ranking at the top in overall passenger service by 1997.

The concept of the Service Decathlon provides a framework within which specific goals can be established in each of the service areas—channeling efforts, igniting enthusiasm, and providing direction to employees throughout the organization.

Focus on the Future—What the Organization Must Do to Succeed

Hamel and Prahalad, in their influential book, *Competing for the Future*, argue that effective visions must reflect a sound and well-developed point of view—"foresight"—on what it will take to succeed in your business 10 years from now.[27] They contend that too often visions fail to go much beyond existing products, markets, and technologies and suggest that developing sound visions requires (*a*) a thorough knowledge of customer values (*b*) a willingness to reject orthodoxy and (*c*) an understanding of the organizational competencies required to develop solutions that will meet the future needs of customers.[28]

Develop a Plan

A vision without a plan is nothing but a dream. It does little good to set a direction without a plan for how to get there. Nor are plans, directives, and programs an adequate substitute for an effective organizational vision.[29] In one case, a firm passed out four-inch-thick notebooks describing its change effort. In mind-numbing detail, procedures, goals, methods, and deadlines were spelled out. Nowhere, however, was there a clear and compelling statement of where the organization was heading. Not surprisingly, most of the employees were either confused or alienated.

Communicate the Vision and the Plan

Key to the effective communication of a leader's vision and plan are clarity, persistence, motivation, and involvement. If a vision statement is simple, direct, focused on the essentials, and expressed in terms everyone can understand, it should not be difficult to communicate it with ease and clarity.

Too often, however, organizations attempt to communicate a vision via a single mass meeting, a poster on the wall, or some other form of impersonal communication. It rarely works. The key is straightforward: *persistence.* Recall the persistence that Craig Weatherup at Pepsi-Cola demonstrated with his two-year marathon of demanding three-day meetings. When Lawrence A. Bossidy became chairman and CEO of Allied Signal, he also took to the road, as related in a recent interview.[30]

> In 1991, we were hemorrhaging cash. That was the issue that needed focus. I traveled all over the company with the same message and the same charts, over and over. Here's what I think is good about us. Here's what I'm worried about. Here's what we have to do about it. And if we don't fix the cash problem, none of us is going to be around. You can keep it simple: "we're spending more than we're taking in. If you do that at home, there will be a day of reckoning."
>
> In the first 60 days, I talked to probably 5,000 employees. I would go to Los Angeles and speak to 500 people, then to Phoenix and talk to another 500. I would stand on a loading dock and speak to people and answer their questions. We talked about what was wrong and what we should do about it. And as we talked, it became clear to me that there hadn't been a good top-down enunciation of the company's problem.

Leaders also need to *motivate and inspire* their employees. Take the case of Jamie Houghton, CEO of Corning. He continually and eloquently challenges his organization to synthesize its outstanding technological capability with a commitment to quality—a combination that can make Corning a "world class" competitor. Here's an excerpt from a recent speech—simple, straightforward, and forceful:[31]

> Today, each of us is empowered. Responsible. Both as individuals and as team members. Now, put that fact next to our new goal: "to understand and meet the requirements of our customers better than anyone else." This is now a job for every individual in the company. Even those whose customers are internal can contribute to making Corning more effective—and therefore a superior supplier to our external customers. Our principles remain the same—and they are tough. One is error-free work. It means making so few mistakes that we are now measuring them as parts per million. Many of you will remember that it wasn't so long ago that we were happy to achieve quality levels of 99 percent. That sounds pretty good. But that 1 percent error rate equals 10,000 errors per million! A 1 percent error rate would mean 20,000 lost pieces of mail each hour in the United States. It would mean three or four bad landings every day at major airports. It would mean 5,000 wrong drug prescriptions a month and 5,000 bad surgical procedures a year. And it would mean your heart would beat just fine —except for 87 hours a year! No, thanks. I'll take

an error-free heartbeat, if you don't mind. Error-free work is what will win the day with our customers. It's the only way we can hope to meet their requirements better than anyone else.

Employees must buy in to the vision and make a commitment—become involved. Les Alberthal had a tough act to follow when he took over as CEO of Electronic Data Systems in 1986.[32] The company's culture was a cult of personality—dominated for 24 years by the hard-charging, but often quirky, leadership of Ross Perot. When Perot departed suddenly, after a highly visible spat with EDS's new parent, General Motors, employees were confused and demoralized. Alberthal, a low-key, but effective leader, was not the man to rally the troops with a fiery speech or a new vision. Instead, he chose to emphasize that the strength of EDS was in its people, not its leaders. In one meeting he handed out small mirrors to the assembled employees. "Look in the mirror," he said, "What you see is EDS." And the employees have responded to his vote of confidence. EDS is now a $12.4 billion a year company growing, over the last two years, at 30 percent per year—twice the industry average.

Consider, also, how Paul O'Neill, CEO of Alcoa since 1987, invites commitment and employee involvement in his vision of the new Alcoa:

> As we make the journey together, the operable words and phrases are trust, candor, quantum-leap improvement, vision, values, leadership, customer focus, value creation, practical limits, sharing, learning, empowerment, involvement, ownership, accountability, and communication, communication, communication , and communication.[33]
>
> When I was a young man I worked in Alaska for a construction company and my boss was a grizzled old-style construction superintendent . . . his approach to everything [was] exuberant, excited, energetic, knowing he could make a difference—thrilled about life and his own ability to create things of value.
>
> If next week your job and your role feel differently to you, I'll consider that good news. If you feel you understand the ground rules and your accountability and our expectations better than ever before, that's better news. If you find yourself excited and ready to really move out with this new structure we've provided, I'll consider that my old superintendent has been reincarnated a hundred times over!!! We have the potential to be one of the great companies in the world, measured by any standard. We have more than 63,000 of the best people around the world who share that goal. Let's provide leadership to take us there. TOGETHER, WE CAN DO IT!

The key words are *together* and *we*. No matter how great the crisis, how widely felt the sense of urgency, how clearly communicated the vision—leadership is not about doing it alone. The essence of leadership is getting others involved—communicating a sense of direction, setting goals, and then giving the organization the tools to get the job done. We now turn to the critical issues of goal-setting and empowerment.

SET STRETCH GOALS AND EMPOWER OTHERS TO ACT

> If you don't demand something out of the ordinary, you won't get anything but ordinary results.[34]
>
> *Charles Jones, EDS Management Consulting*

In an increasingly competitive environment, incremental gains are not enough! Organizations need to reinvent themselves and radically change the way they conceive, make, and distribute products. Hamel and Prahalad argue that "Creating stretch, a misfit between resources and aspirations, is the single most important task senior management faces."[35] As organizations transform themselves to face new competitive realities, they have often been forced to downsize, eliminating layers of middle management and giving more discretion and control to workers. According to Lawrence Bossidy, Allied Signal's CEO, "Ten years ago, we thought that if you had four employees reporting to every manager, your managers were overworked. We've discovered that if you have nine, you have less time to manage" and must rely on subordinates to help out.

So, how do you go about setting stretch goals—just what is involved?

There are four important elements involved in the establishment of stretch goals: "stretch," credibility, achievability, and empowerment.

The Element of "Stretch"

Incremental improvements—those that can be achieved by working a little faster or little harder—are not stretch goals. Effective stretch goals must require an organization to change what it does and how it does it in order to deliver its products or services more effectively and more efficiently.

The Element of Credibility

Just as in establishing a sense of urgency, stretch targets need to be clearly and unambiguously linked to corporate goals, and the downside risks associated with not improving performance have to be articulated. Arbitrary targets without a clear link to broader objectives—whether they be growth targets, inventory turns, product development cycles, or manufacturing costs—are a quick and sure way to turn employees off.

The Element of Achievability

Employees must be convinced that the goals are achievable—not impossible. Benchmarking is a powerful persuader. Seeing outsiders excel doesn't just teach managers how, it also acts as a powerful motivator. Implicit peer pressure and organizational pride can often be more powerful motivators than the proverbial carrot and are certainly more effective than the stick.

The Element of Empowerment

The leader has to, in essence, "get out of the way." Stretch targets differ from the old-fashioned top-down management fiat that U.S. companies have spent many years unlearning. The job belongs to the managers in the field, workers on the plant floor, and engineers and technicians in the labs. Let's see how John Snow, the CEO of CSX, a $10 billion-a-year railroad and shipping company, was able to use stretch goals to reach the objective of earning its full cost of capital—10 percent—within two years, and then to exceed it thereafter.[36]

In 1991, Snow realized that such an ambitious goal would force his managers to face the railroad's core problem: its multibillion dollar fleet of locomotives and railcars sat loafing much of the time at loading docks and seaport terminals. Although some subordinates considered the goal impossible, Snow refused to back off. Pete Carpenter, head of CSX's railroad business, decided that reaching such a demanding target required a radical change from the traditional model of centralized scheduling and control. He empowered five supervisors—all volunteers—in an experiment that now serves as a model for the entire company. The group set up an independent profit center at Cumberland for hauling coal for customers in western Maryland. Their goal: to go from breakeven to a substantial profit in a year and eliminate 800 of 5,000 railcars.

The stretch provided the spur to get to the core of the problem: the railroad's practice of running the longest trains possible. At both ends of the route—the coal yards and the port—railcars often were idle for days until enough of them accumulated to form a train. Executives at headquarters had been working at cross-purposes: those in *equipment utilization* wanted shorter, more frequent trains; those responsible for *staffing* wanted longer trains to hold down labor costs. The head of the Cumberland profit center, Ray Sharp, gladly paid for the extra crews to reap the far bigger savings generated by cutting the fleet. He ran trains with as few as 78 cars, but they never sat idle for more than a day.

The results were impressive. Cumberland exceeded the stretch target by cutting 1,000 of 5,000 railcars and 25 of 100 locomotives. Volume increased by 6 percent and profits soared. By replicating the model across the company, CSX eliminated 20,000 of its 125,000 railcars and cut annual capital expenditures for fleet replacement by $200 million. By 1993, CSX was earning its full cost of capital. Between 1991 and 1995, net income nearly doubled on a sales increase of about 20 percent.

Empowerment can also extend to the factory floor. UAW workers at John Deere & Co. have gotten involved in tasks that go well beyond the normal role of union workers—a marked contrast to the recent labor-management problems at rival Caterpillar.

With long-term demand for farm equipment weakening and competition intensifying, John Deere's 1991 sales declined by 11 percent to $6 billion and Deere had a small loss versus 1990 profits of $411 million. Deere CEO Hans W. Becherer felt that the quickest way to adapt to the tougher environment was to reach out to his workforce.[37] Becherer got them involved in a number of nontraditional ways. John Soliz, a 26-year veteran, spent 1993 traveling throughout the Midwest as a Deere pitchman, logging over 7,000 miles speaking to groups of farmers. David Rowe was on the road three weeks out of four, visiting customers and dealers and instructing them in maintenance procedures.

Deere has also gotten its workers involved in cost reduction. At its Davenport, Iowa, plant, cost reduction teams meet weekly to simplify assembly processes and eliminate production problems. Worker participation has helped Deere cut costs and reduce design times by 33 percent over a three-year period. Empowerment has reaped benefits for Deere, and its financial performance has shown dramatic improvement, with 1995 sales up 42 percent over 1991 and record earnings of over $700 million.

Once the leader has gotten the ball rolling by creating a sense of urgency and communicating the vision, and once the organization is beginning to make progress toward its new objectives, the leader's focus must shift to consolidating gains and institutionalizing the changes—making them a permanent part of the organizational infrastructure.

INSTITUTIONALIZING CHANGE

Competitors may understand a company's products, technology, and finances, but they cannot easily replicate management processes that are deeply embedded in a company's traditions and culture. Moreover, once a committed group starts moving in the right direction, it is self-sustaining.[38]

David A.G. Simon, Deputy Chairman-British Petroleum

Institutionalizing change—making it last—is critically important. Transformational change, by its very nature, entails major disruptions throughout the organization, dramatically altering how work is done, and in the process, how people communicate and interact with each other throughout the organization. Institutionalizing change has to do with making these new processes, procedures, and behaviors permanent. The obvious changes may include new organization charts and modified policies, procedures, and work flows. That's usually the easy part. Culture and values are much tougher to change, but unless the organization's culture—the "shared philosophies, expectations, attitudes and norms that knit an organization together"—is also addressed, old habits soon creep back in and the hard-won gains in performance and productivity are soon lost.[39]

It's extraordinarily difficult to change an entrenched culture. Sometimes, it requires a change in top leadership by bringing in individuals who are not bound to tradition and have no vested interest in the old culture. Outside CEOs often have an advantage: Michael H. Jordan of Westinghouse claims that he brings "ruthless logic" to his turnarounds, which lets him "cut through emotions and people's opinions and get down to facts." Randall Robias of Eli

Lilly & Co. says, "I don't have some hidden agenda. I don't bring any emotional baggage."[40] Changing culture and values often may mean terminating many of the "old guard." Dunlap fired 9 of the 11 members of Scott Paper's executive committee in his first week. Within four years after Bossidy took over at Allied-Signal, 75 percent of the top 140 managers were new to their jobs.[41]

The Walt Disney Company probably needed an outsider in the mid-1980s. For years after Disney's death, executives second guessed every major decision, asking "What would Walt have done?"[42] It was almost as if Walt's ghost stalked the halls of the studios in Burbank, as the company's competitive and financial position eroded. When Michael Eisner was appointed CEO in 1984, he brought a new management team—outsiders free of "Disney's ghost." They created a new culture—one that was more sophisticated, adventurous, and ambitious. The company has leveraged the traditional products and set new directions with a number of successful strategic moves. Over the past decade, the revitalized Disney has been one of the top performers on the New York Stock Exchange.

Although cultural change may be the cornerstone of sustaining the potential benefits of transformational changes, it requires much more. Let's consider the case of Xerox Corporation, which found its competitive position seriously eroded in the early 1980s by aggressive Japanese manufacturers.[43] In fact-finding trips to Japan during 1980 and 1981, Xerox discovered that its Japanese competitors could manufacture, ship, and sell copiers for about what it cost Xerox just to manufacture them. Dramatic change was called for. Under the leadership of David Kearns, Xerox embarked on an organizationwide transformation that came to be called "Leadership through Quality." There was resistance initially. One manager responded: "This is the stupidest thing I've ever heard of. It's going to cost millions of dollars. We should spend that money on refurbishing equipment, not something this idiotic." Another equated total quality and its goal of worker empowerment to communism. However, Kearns persevered. Among the "organizational levers" he pulled to eventually make it succeed:

- The company's complex, function-dominated matrix *structure* was revamped into three simpler strategic business units (SBUs) that corresponded to Xerox's principal market segments.

- *Evaluation and reward systems* were changed to monitor how effectively managers supported Leadership through Quality. Subordinates rated their managers on, among other things, how well they "walked the talk." The top 200 managers were required to maintain the highest rating, "role model," to qualify for promotion.

- *An extensive training program* eventually included all 100,000 Xerox employees. A "training cascade" was initiated: employees at each level of management trained their subordinates in total quality management concepts. The five-year process cost $125 million.

- *New standards and measurements* were introduced to make the language of total quality management part of the everyday business process.

- The language and symbols of TQM were *widely disseminated* through training, videotape messages, and company publications and became an essential part of the culture. Top managers insisted Leadership through Quality was not just another managerial acronym but was to be "jealously guarded" as Xerox's unique understanding of the strategy.

- Finally, in 1986, David Kearns *rearranged the order of corporate goals* on company literature to *quality*, return on assets, and market share.

The glue that held the transformation together was undoubtedly David Kearns' leadership. He traveled the world to deliver the message. When asked whether the quality effort would interfere with other priorities, his response was unequivocal: "Quality will not get *in* the way; quality *is* the way. Anyone who cannot understand this distinction would perhaps be better suited for work in another organization." Frank Pipp, head of manufacturing, who had been with Xerox since its inception, recalled that Kearns "never blinked." Pipp says that when it comes to "walking the talk," Kearns was second to none.

The results? In 1993, Kearns reported back to the employees: "Datapro Research named our 1090 the best copier in the world— period! Dataquest ranked Xerox number one in product reliability and service. In our survey of employees last year, 94 percent indicated that customer satisfaction was their top priority. Machine performance during the first 30 days [after installation] has improved 40 percent in four years." Xerox went on to win the prestigious Malcolm Baldridge National Quality Award. Financial performance kept pace. From 1983 to 1989, sales and profits increased over 50 percent to $16.4 billion and $704 million, respectively.

As the Xerox example demonstrates, enduring transformational leadership involves, in effect, pulling many organizational levers. Xerox found its matrix structure too complex and inflexible—an SBU structure provided the needed decentralization and autonomy. Xerox's innovative training programs, reward and evaluation systems, standards, and measurement processes helped to reinforce the message. Finally the culture—shared norms, values, and beliefs—was shaped and molded through continual reinforcement. *Leadership through Quality* was more than part of the culture—it became the culture. And through it all, nothing was more important than the words and actions of David Kearns. He showed persistence, acted in a consistent manner, and "walked the talk."

STRATEGIC INVENTORY

To successfully transform organizations, leaders need to incorporate a number of key principles into their strategies and actions. Do you (and the other executives in your organization):

Move quickly and decisively—and create a sense of urgency?

- Does the organization act and respond with authority in response to a changing environment—or do organizational inertia and bureaucratic processes often bog things down?
- Are issues communicated in a simple and straightforward manner?
- Are the leader's assertions supported by facts?

Effectively develop and communicate a vision and a plan?

- Is the vision simple, direct, and focused on the essentials?
- Is it expressed in terms employees and stakeholders can relate to?
- Does the vision provide a framework for goals and objectives?
- Is the vision focused on the future—on what the organization must do to succeed?
- Is it backed up with a plan for how the vision will be realized?

- Has the vision been communicated with clarity and persistence?
- Does the message motivate employees and stimulate involvement?

Set stretch goals and empower others to act?

- Do your goals demand "stretch"—ask for more than incremental improvements?
- Are they credible—do they relate to broader organizational goals and objectives?
- Are they achievable—can you demonstrate the potential through benchmarking?
- Have you empowered your employees to act so the goals can be achieved?

Take actions to institutionalize change? Have important, long lasting changes been institutionalized by pulling the "organizational levers" of:

- Culture?
- Ordering of corporate goals and objectives?
- Organizational structures and reporting relationships?
- Evaluation and reward systems?
- Standards and performance measurements?
- Training programs?
- Internal communications and publications?

Overall—are you focused on the future (visions, missions, objectives)—or more concerned with today's organizational constraints and control systems?

ENDNOTES

1. Machiavelli, N., *The Prince* (1513). Translated by W. K. Marriott. E.P. Dutton & Co. New York, 1908: 47–48.
2. The sources for this example include: Johnson, S.S. May 22, 1995. Dithering. *Forbes*: 45; O'Reilly, B. May 29, 1995, Agee in exile, *Fortune*:

51–74; Rigdon, J.E., March 21, 1995. Morrison Knudsen's Loss Estimates are Widened: Acting Chairman Resigns. *The Wall Street Journal*:
A4; Rigdon, J.E. February 2, 1995. William Agee will leave Morrison
Knudsen. *The Wall Street Journal*: B1, B11; Stern, R. L., and Abelson, R.
June 8, 1992. The Imperial Agees. *Forbes*: 88–92. We would like to
thank Ms. Connie Bookholt for her input and assistance in the preparation of this example.

3. Tobias Levkovich, quoted by Anne B. Fisher in Corporate reputations: comebacks and comeuppances, *Fortune*, March 4, 1996: 91.

4. The three quotes and paragraph are from Kets de Vries, M.F.R., The
leadership mystique. *Academy of Management Executive* 8(3): 73, August 1994.

5. Meindl, J.R., and Ehrlich, S.B. 1987. The romance of leadership and
the evaluation of organizational performance. *Academy of Management Journal*, 30: 92–109.

6. Loeb, M. September 19, 1994. Where leaders come from. *Fortune*: 241.

7. D'Aveni, R. 1994. *Hypercompetition*. New York: Free Press.

8. This example draws on Dumaine, B. June 28, 1993. Times are good?
Create a crisis. *Fortune*: 123–127 and Byrne, J.A. "Belt- tightening
the smart way. *Business Week*, Special Enterprise Issue, October 22,
1993: 34–38.

9. These attributes are distilled from several sources including: Dolan,
P.F. 1983. A four-phase rescue plan for today's troubled companies.
Journal of Business Strategy, 4: 22–31; Finkin, E.F. July-August, 1992.
Structuring a successful turnaround *Journal of Business Strategy*, 13: 56;
Kotter, J.P. March-April, 1995. Leading change: Why transformation
efforts fail. *Harvard Business Review*, 73: 59–67; and Tichy, N.M., and
Ulrich, D.O. 1984. The leadership challenge: A call for the transforma-
tional leader. *Sloan Management Review*, 4(26): 59–67.

10. Martinez, A.C. May-June, 1995. Transformation. *Harvard Business Review*, 73: 166.

11. Why your competition doesn't have need to fail, only to hesitate.
CSX Intermodal. (company publication).

12. Lublin, J.S., and Markels, A. July 21, 1995. How three CEOs achieved
fast turnarounds. *Wall Street Journal*: B1.

13. Vlasic, B., and Naughton, K. December 4, 1995. Kmart: Who's in
charge here? *Business Week*: 104–108; and Sellers, P. January 15, 1996.
Kmart is down for the count. *Fortune:* 102–103.

14. Ghosal, S., and Bartlett, C. January-February, 1995. Changing the role
of top management: Beyond structure to process. *Harvard Business Review*, 73: 94.

15. *Ibid.*

16. Schein, E.H. Winter, 1993. How can organizations learn faster? The challenge of entering the green room. *Sloan Management Review,* 34: 85–92.

17. Graves, J. December 14, 1992. Leaders of corporate change. *Fortune:* 104–114.

18. Dumaine, B. June 28, 1993. Times are good? Create a crisis. *Fortune:* August 7, 1995: 123–127; Loomis, C. August 7, 1995. Sex, reefer? and auto insurance. *Fortune:* 76–89.

19. Kotter, J.P. March-April, 1995. Leading Change: Why Transformation Efforts Fail. *Harvard Business Review,* 73: 59–67.

20. For an interesting perspective on this issue, see Lesley, E., Schiller, G., Baker, S. and Smith, G. October 11, 1993. CEOs with the outside edge. *Business Week:* 60–62.

21. Tichy, N., and Charan, R. September-October, 1989. Speed, Simplicity, and Self-Confidence: An Interview with Jack Welch. *Harvard Business Review,* 67: 113.

22. Simpson, D. September-October, 1994. Rethinking vision and mission. *Planning Review,* 22: 11.

23. Coy, P. February 20, 1995. Edison: What made light bulbs go on? *Business Week:* 17.

24. Slater, R. 1994. *Get Better or Get Beaten!* Irwin: Burr Ridge, IL: 31.

25. Bartlett, C.A., and Ghosal, S. November-December 1994. Changing the role of top management: Beyond strategy to purpose. *Harvard Business Review,* 72: 79–88.

26. September 18, 1995. Quality happens through people. *Fortune:* 57–58.

27. Hamel, G., and Prahalad, C.K. 1994. *Competing for the Future.* Boston: Harvard University Press.

28. This also draws on Miller, A., and Dess, G.G. 1996. *Strategic Management.* 2nd ed. New York: McGraw-Hill: 389–390.

29. Kotter, J.P. March-April, 1995. Leading change: Why transformation efforts fail. *Harvard Business Review,* 73: 59–67.

30. Tichy, N.M., and Charan, R. March-April, 1995. The CEO as Coach: An interview with Allied Signal's Lawrence A. Bossidy. *Harvard Business Review,* 73: 69–78.

31. Speech by J.R. Houghton, CEO-Corning. "Quality Milestone 1994–Maintaining our Momentum," June 29, 1994.

32. Templin, N. February 21, 1996. Les is more: Under Alberthal, EDS is out of limelight but triples revenues. *The Wall Street Journal:* A1, A6.

33. Remarks by Paul H. O'Neill at the Alcoa Organizational Meeting, Pittsburgh Hilton Hotel, August 9, 1991.

34. Tully, S. November 14, 1994. Why go for stretch targets. *Fortune*: 145–158. This subsection draws heavily on this reference.

35. Hamel, G., and Prahalad, C.K. March-April, 1993. Strategy as Stretch and leverage. *Harvard Business Review*, 71: 78.

36. Tully, S., op. cit.

37. Kelley, K. January 31, 1994. The new soul of John Deere, *Business Week*: 64–66; Siegel, Morton L. February 9, 1996. John Deere Company, Inc. *Value Line*: 1342.

38. Simon, David A.G. January-February, 1995. The role of top management. *Harvard Business Review* 73: 142.

39. Killman, R.H., Saxton, M.J., and Serpa, R. 1985. Five key issues in understanding and changing culture. In R.H. Killman, R.H. Saxton, and Serpa, R. *Gaining control of the corporate culture*. San Francisco: Josey-Bass: 1–16.

40. Lesley, E., and Schiller, Z., Baker, S., and Smith, G. October 11, 1993. CEOs with the outside edge. *Business Week*: 60–62.

41. Tichy, N.J., and Charan, R. March-April 1995. The CEO as Coach: An interview with Allied Signal's Lawrence A. Bossidy. *Harvard Business Review*, 73: 69–78.

42. Bennett, A. April 18, 1990. Pay for performance. *Wall Street Journal*: R7; and Crystal, G. June 8, 1989. Seeking Sense in CEO pay. *Fortune*: 88, 90, 92, 96, 100, 104.

43. This example is based on Dess, G.G., and Miller, A. 1993. *Strategic Management*. New York: McGraw-Hill, 621–639; Kearns, D., and Nadler, D. 1992. *Prophets in the Dark: How Xerox reinvented itself and beat back the Japanese*. New York: HarperBusiness; Kearns, D. May 1990. Leadership through quality. *The Executive*: 86–89; Cohen, D.R. April 28, 1995. Xerox Corp. *ValueLine*: 1138.

9

CHAPTER

A Sound Strategy, Implemented without Error

The best of strategies, poorly implemented, is of little value. A flawed strategy—no matter how brilliant the leadership, no matter how effective the implementation—is doomed to failure. A sound strategy, implemented without error, wins every time.

We begin this chapter by reiterating our belief that most common strategic errors are avoidable. By understanding the mistakes others have made and being aware of what to look for, prudent strategic managers can navigate around the rocks and shoals and plot a safe course to reach their organization's strategic objectives. There's an old saying in the aviation industry: "There are *old* pilots and there are *bold* pilots, but there are no *old, bold* pilots." The moral of the story is simple: the bold pilots eventually make a fatal mistake. Only those willing to learn from the mistakes of others get to be old pilots.

There's a common misconception that, in order to be considered a success, you've got to be number one—the first to market, with the best technology, the most aggressive sales force, and the most creative and inspiring leadership. But is boldness and innovation a guarantee of success? Look around your industry. How many companies are there out there? Hundreds—perhaps thousands. How many carbon copies of Roberto Goizueta or Jack Welch do you see? Were Compaq or Dell the first to market with a PC? No. Apple Computer was first, but a long string of strategic miscues has cast Apple into the role of the perennial also-ran.

Fortune's 1996 list of America's Most Admired Companies includes a couple of up-and-coming technology superstars—Intel and Microsoft—but many of the "most admired" companies such as Coca-Cola, Procter & Gamble, Rubbermaid, Johnson & Johnson and Merck, to name a few, have been around for a while.[1] Their solid strategies, strong brands, and capable organizations have kept them on top for years. And it's not just coincidence that the 11,000 executives, directors, and analysts who participated in Fortune's survey ranked "quality of management" as the most important factor in determining a company's reputation. A closer look at those who ended up at the bottom of the list—Kmart, Morrison Knudsen, and TWA—reveals that each has suffered from one or more significant errors in strategy or implementation in recent years.

The companies that craft a solid strategy—one that avoids the obvious errors—and implement it well, avoiding the most common strategic mistakes, usually do pretty well. Not everyone needs to hit a home run every time they come to the plate. We believe the evidence is on our side—*a sound strategy, implemented without error, wins every time.*

DOING THE RIGHT THINGS . . . AND DOING THEM RIGHT

In the earlier chapters, we focused on some of the most common strategic errors and outlined the steps that should be taken to avoid them. In this chapter, we will take a somewhat different perspective, placing more emphasis on what *should* be done, rather than on what to avoid. In the process, we will integrate and summarize our recommendations for the development and implementation of sound strategies.

In our discussion of leadership, we noted Warren Bennis's distinction between leadership and management: "Leaders are people who do the right things. Managers are people who do things right."[2] A similar distinction can be made about the processes of strategy formulation and implementation. Strategy formulation is about "doing the right things"; implementation is about "doing things right." But, before either strategy formulation or implementation is possible, a comprehensive understanding of the strategic context must be developed, as described in Chapters 2 and 3. Strategy formulation, as we have described it in Chapters 4 and 5, takes place within a conceptual framework defined by the strategic context and involves, first, understanding the sources of sustainable competitive advantage; and second, developing a sound plan—crafting a strategy—to exploit one or more of the available sources of advantage in a way that accomplishes the organization's defined goals and objectives.

Participation in the process of strategy formulation is limited, in most organizations, to a relatively small group of executives and staff personnel. The process of implementation, however, is largely about getting the rest of the organization involved, committed, and headed in the right direction—"making it happen." Chapters 6 through 8 were focused on the key issues of implementation: coordination, integration, strategic control, and the role and processes of transformational leadership. This chapter summarizes our key points from the earlier chapters, focusing first on developing the necessary understanding of the strategic context; second, on ensuring that the organization's strategy is focused on "doing the right things"; and, finally, on leadership and the steps that must be taken in the process of implementation to ensure that the organization is "doing things right."

UNDERSTANDING THE STRATEGIC CONTEXT

Developing an understanding of the strategic context is an essential first step in strategy formulation. The strategic context has many dimensions, and not only the individual pieces, but their many and complex interrelationships and dependencies must be understood. The key elements of the strategic context include:

- Customers.
- Competitors.
- Potential competitors.
- Partners and suppliers.
- Stakeholders: owners, managers, and employees.
- Technology and methods (product, process, delivery systems).

- Political, legal, and regulatory constraints.
- Economic, social, and cultural factors.

Key Questions

Understanding the strategic context means having the answers to a lot of questions. Who are the customers? Who are the noncustomers? Who are the competitors? Who are the key suppliers? Where are the boundaries? What are the rules of the game? What technologies are important to the industry? What technologies will change this industry over the next decade? What are the strengths and weaknesses of our organization? Of our competitors? And, of course, many more.

Defining the Boundaries of the Competitive Environment

One of the most important steps in developing a meaningful understanding of the strategic context is to define the boundaries of the competitive environment. A good place to start is with the value chain. For this purpose, it is important to conceptualize the value chain in its broadest context and without regard to organizational boundaries—explicitly placing the organization into context, along with its suppliers and customers, and focusing on the role each plays in ultimately providing a product or a service to the end user. What are the boundaries of the industry? What market is served? Where is the value added? What products and services does our firm provide? How do they add value for the end user? Why are some organizations customers and others noncustomers? What makes one organization a competitor and another not? What are the key competencies required to compete in this industry? Do all competitors share the same set of skills and capabilities? If not, why not? How broad should the industry definition be? Are our suppliers and our immediate customers part of the industry, or are they outside the boundaries? Does it make sense for them to integrate backward or forward so they can also do what our firm does?

Identifying Key Players and Their Interrelationships

It is not enough to know who the customers, suppliers, and competitors are; their interrelationships and interdependencies must also be understood. Why does a competitor serve one customer and your firm serve another? What is important in their relationship?

Who are your key suppliers? Who supplies the competitors? Are the suppliers the same or are they different? Why? What kind of relationships exist among your competitors? Between your firm and its competitors? Are there opportunities in this network of relationships to strengthen your position—or are there potential threats?

Understanding Your Frame of Reference

It is also important to distinguish between *what is known* and *what is assumed* about each of these key dimensions of strategic context. Perhaps even more important than what an organization knows about its strategic context is what it assumes to be the case. As we noted in Chapter 3, over time the processes of socialization and accommodation within an organization tend to produce a set of broadly shared assumptions and beliefs about the organization and the industry in which it competes. This *dominant logic* or *managerial frame of reference*—assumptions about the mission of the organization, the boundaries of the industry, who the competitors are, and what works and what doesn't—tends to become more important in guiding management decisions than the objective reality it mirrors. As the dominant logic gradually becomes institutionalized as part of the fabric of the organization, it tends to reinforce certain perspectives and exclude others.

Validating Key Assumptions and Premises

Because the managerial frame of reference is the primary context for strategic decision making, it is important to validate this assumption base. Key premises must be identified, made explicit, and periodically validated against conditions in the real world. Is the assumption set internally consistent? Do we understand the importance of each individual premise? How critical is each to our near-term performance? How confident are we that each is valid? How likely is near-term change? How important is each to the viability of our long-term strategy?

Creating a Culture of Environmental Awareness

Many organizations tend, more by default than by design, to insulate and isolate their top managers from day-to-day interactions in the competitive arena. Successful top executives do two things to counter the effects of these tendencies. First, they strive to create a culture of environmental awareness throughout their organizations. They include key boundary-spanners—sales and service employees, purchasing agents, and the like—by sharing the organization's intelligence needs and priorities and by creating processes and incentives to get them involved in intelligence gathering. And they ensure that information flows freely throughout their organizations so critical intelligence gets to the right place in a timely fashion. Second, executives create and use their own informal networks to keep in touch—both within and outside the organization. They rely on informal contacts with customers, suppliers, competitors, and industry peers to keep in touch with the external environment, and they practice "management by walking around" to keep a finger on the pulse of their own organizations.

STRATEGY FORMULATION—A TWO-STEP PROCESS

The formulation of strategy involves, first, the identification and understanding of the sources of sustainable competitive advantage available to the organization. Second, it involves the development of a sound, internally consistent, and implementable plan—crafting a strategy—to exploit one or more of the potential sources of competitive advantage in a way that accomplishes the goals and objectives of the organization. We use Mintzberg's term *crafting a strategy* to acknowledge that the formulation of strategy is more of an art than a "by the numbers" process. In the beginning there is little more than a broad objective bounded by a clear understanding of what is possible and what is not and a sense of direction—how the organization will achieve its objective. The details are usually, however, far from clear.

As we noted in Chapter 4, most organizations that have created significant competitive advantages and sustained them over time appear to rely on a loosely organized set of guiding principles. Within a well-defined sense of strategic context that defines what is realistic and achievable, these organizations identify the available sources of competitive advantage by:

- Understanding the business as a process—focusing on the value chain.
- Expanding the boundaries to include customers and suppliers.

- Identifying potential sources of competitive advantage at each link in the value chain.
- Focusing on the future—emphasizing foresight in planning.

Having identified the potential sources of competitive advantage, successful organizations then go about the process of crafting a strategy that both exploits one or more sources of competitive advantage and seeks to create sustainable advantage by:

- Identifying opportunities and understanding threats in the environment.
- Leveraging the organization's core competencies.
- Adding value in multiple activities and in multiple ways.
- Achieving close integration of value-creating activities.
- Innovating by adding value in new and unique ways.
- Broadening the base through well-conceived diversification.
- Focusing on strengths by outsourcing noncritical functions.

IDENTIFYING THE POTENTIAL SOURCES OF COMPETITIVE ADVANTAGE

Identifying the potential sources of competitive advantage involves a thorough and detailed analysis of the organization and its relationships with suppliers, customers, and competitors. Once again, we recommend that the search for competitive advantage begin by focusing on the business as a value-creating process.

The Business as a Process—Focusing on the Value Chain

Recall that we have defined the value chain as:

> a sequential arrangement of processes or activities that operate on inputs, add value, and collectively produce outputs—a product or service—created for and delivered to an end-user.

The conceptualization of the business as a sequence of value-creating activities forces the strategist to look beyond the artificial boundaries of traditional organization structures and to recognize important internal relationships and interdependencies. Only by understanding *where* and *how* value is created within the organization can the strategist begin to identify the potential sources of competitive advantage available to his firm.

Expanding the Boundaries

Our definition of the value chain also facilitates the conceptualization of an organization's role as an integral part of a larger value chain that, ignoring the limits of traditional organizational boundaries, is expanded as appropriate to include upstream suppliers, alliance partners, intermediate customers in the downstream channel of distribution, and the ultimate end user. In addition to a thorough understanding of the activities that create and add value *within the organization*, managers must also understand how interactions with other organizations in the broader value chain create value for the end user. By conceptualizing the value chain in this way, strategists are encouraged to consider the role of their organization as part of a *larger process of value creation*, providing valuable insights into sources of competitive advantage that are often hidden from those who view the organization as an isolated entity with clearly defined boundaries.

Identifying Potential Sources of Competitive Advantage

The management literature has identified the generic strategies of *cost leadership, differentiation*, and *quick response* as the primary sources of sustainable competitive advantage, with scope or *focus* being another important dimension. As we have described, the across-the-board implementation of one or another of these generic strategies is no guarantee of competitive advantage. Rather, each must be considered, perhaps in combination with others, as a possible approach to creating competitive advantage *at each link in the value chain*. Once one begins to view the business as a process (or as a series of parallel processes), it becomes only natural to assess the organization's strengths and weaknesses (and those of its competitors) in the context of the value chain—identifying potential sources of competitive advantage and areas of relative weakness at each stage in the process.

As they examine each link in the value chain, strategists should seek to determine: (*a*) which activities add customer value; (*b*) how value is created within each activity; (*c*) which relationships among value activities are most important; (*d*) what kinds of competitive advantage can be exploited successfully at each stage in the value chain; and (*e*) how likely it is that the advantage can be sustained over time. For a competitive advantage to have real long-term value, it must be sustainable. We have described four criteria for the evaluation of organizational strengths and resources as potential sources of competitive advantage: Are they valuable? Are they rare? Are they difficult to imitate? Are there few substitutes? If a potential source of competitive advantage can pass these tests, it can form the cornerstone of a viable competitive strategy. If not, it makes sense to keep searching.

The Importance of Foresight

As we have described, an understanding of the strategic context and the sources of competitive advantage *as they are today* is critical to the formulation of a sound strategy. Even more important, however, is a sense of how things are *likely to be in the future*. What changes—in demographics, in technology, in regulation, in consumer tastes and preferences, in sources of supply, in competitive conditions—are likely over the next 5 to 10 years? What impact will these changes have on our organization and our industry? Will our strategy lead us to a stronger or weaker position as the market and competitive conditions evolve? What new opportunities are on the horizon? How can we take advantage?

Remember when you first learned to drive? Or taught your son or daughter? Beginners tend to focus only a few yards ahead, and they must be taught to look farther down the road. Focusing too closely tends to result in erratic steering, bumping into curbs, and high anxiety for the instructor. It's the same with strategy—a longer view tends to result in steadier progress toward the objective. A clear view of what the future is likely to bring is important to the development of a sound strategy.

CRAFTING A SOUND STRATEGY

A sound strategy aligns an organization's strengths with the opportunities that are available in the competitive environment in a way that levers the organization's core competencies and exploits one or more of the available sources of competitive advantage. At the same time it acknowledges the organization's limitations, recognizes the potential threats from competitors and other sources in the environment, and positions the organization to minimize the risks and dangers inherent in the competitive arena. Developing a sound strategy requires that the strategist spot the opportunities, understand the threats, and develop an internally consistent plan to leverage core competencies and exploit multiple sources of competitive advantage across the organization's entire value chain.

Spotting the Opportunity

Perspective is all-important. Understanding the business as a process, focusing on the broader value chain, and identifying strengths and weaknesses at each link in the chain will help the strategist to identify opportunities to develop competitive advantage. Creativity and an open mind are important—many successful strategies have been based on a different perspective, looking at the same facts in a different way, and spotting an opportunity missed by others. Two other key points must also be kept in mind: (1) the only "value" that really matters is value that is recognized by the customer; and (2) competitive advantage is relative to the strengths or weaknesses of your competitors.

It is important to understand the strengths of competitors and how your rivals use them to create advantage. Keep in mind, however, that it is difficult to gain competitive advantage by imitating a competitor's actions, unless you can do whatever he does better, faster, or cheaper. Sometimes opportunities can be found in substitution—as Xerox copies have replaced carbon paper (except for technological backwaters like IRS forms) and personal computers with word processing software have largely replaced typewriters. Sometimes unfilled market needs can be identified—as in the case of Chrysler's minivan—and in other cases, value can be created by doing the same thing quicker and more effectively—as in the example of Dynatec's field service.

Understanding the Threats

Sometimes it is as important to understand the potential threats as it is to spot the opportunities. This is particularly important for firms that have an already well-established position in the marketplace.

Recall what happened to the A.T. Cross Company in the luxury pen market or to Grossman's in the retail building materials business. Any organizational weakness must be considered a potential point of attack for an aggressive competitor. Strategies must consider organizational weaknesses and potential threats and devise actions to counter them.

Leveraging Core Competencies

Sustainable competitive advantages are most often based on core competencies that can be developed, protected, and leveraged across multiple end products or services. Core competencies may exist in special expertise, skill, or experience in a variety of areas—technology, delivery systems, service capabilities, production processes, and so on. Organizations must understand the critical technologies and other core competencies important to the development and enhancement of a sustainable competitive position in their industries, assess their strengths, and determine where they can build and create sustainable competitive advantages.

Exploiting Multiple Sources of Competitive Advantage

Successful strategies may be built on a single competitive advantage, but it is rare. Sustainable advantages most often arise when multiple sources of competitive advantage—differentiation, low cost, and quick response—are combined in a mutually reinforcing and complementary fashion. Again, a thorough understanding of the broader value chain will help in identifying what customers value and tailoring the organization's offering to produce the greatest value for the customer at the lowest cost to the organization.

Using the Entire Value Chain

A competitive advantage based on a value created at a single link in the value chain is vulnerable to competitors who can identify additional opportunities throughout the value chain. Organizations that create differentiation, low cost, or quick response in multiple ways and across multiple links in the chain frequently are able to develop more powerful and more readily sustainable advantages than those whose strategies are focused on only a single link.

Innovating by Adding Value in New and Unique Ways

Firms that identify new and unique ways to create value for their customer often are able to create sustainable competitive advantages. Consider how Paul Orfalea of Kinko's Graphics, Inc. continues to stay a step ahead of the competition by finding new and creative ways to create value for his customers. The key to creating competitive advantage through innovation is in knowing your customer and anticipating rather than reacting to changing needs.

Broadening the Base through Well-Conceived Diversification

Opportunities for diversification that capitalize on core competencies, provide for effective sharing of infrastructures, or increase market power can also create competitive advantage. By broadening the base, organizations can reduce their competitive vulnerabilities, but only if the synergies created are significantly greater (and more certain) than the costs of diversification (acquisition premiums and other costs of consolidation and integration).

Focusing on Strengths by Outsourcing Noncritical Activities

Frequently, as pointed out in our discussion of modular organizations, firms can lever scarce management and financial resources by outsourcing noncritical value activities to specialist firms that can accomplish them more efficiently or capably than they can be completed in-house. Outsourcing is not easy to manage, however, nor is it a sure path to more effective operations. Remember the fate of the Schwinn Bicycle Company, which outsourced key value-creating activities and gave away its competitive advantage.

AVOIDING THE COMMON STRATEGIC ERRORS

Although the guidelines outlined above are relatively straightforward, organizations fall prey to the same common strategic mistakes, over and over again. A few of the most common errors are summarized below:

Blind Spots in the Competitive Vision

When organizations fail to recognize and understand the implications of events and changing conditions in their competitive environment, they are vulnerable to new competitors, new technologies, and market substitutes. Consider how A.T. Cross took its markets for granted and was clobbered by new entrants into the market. Or how Britannica was first to market with CD-ROM technology with their low-end *Compton's Encyclopedia*, but totally missed the opportunity to do the same with their flagship product. Consider how Sega's definition of the boundaries of the competitive arena differed from Nintendo's—and how Sega's broader view helped to catapult them past Nintendo to become the leader in video game technology. Or how Hallmark's loyalty to its traditional channels of distribution caused it to lag behind its nimbler competitors in response to changing market demographics.

Beware the False Premise

Basing a strategy on an initial set of premises that are not supported by the facts or failing to adjust an initial set of assumptions and premises to changing conditions in the marketplace frequently leads to trouble. Although it made sense to Wall Street at the time, Greyhound's attempts to remake a bus company in the image of an airline failed, largely because it was based on unsupportable premises. Raytheon's Beech Starship never got off the ground for similar reasons—although its technology was apparently sound, it made some assumptions about the posture of the FAA regulators that, in hindsight, turned out to be false. And even Microsoft, Lotus, and other computer industry leaders have been taken by surprise by the speed at which the Internet has become a mainstream technology for the masses.

When Strengths Do not Create a Sustainable Advantage

We saw, in the examples of the Japanese automakers, Food Lion, and Apple Computer, that basing a strategy on a strength that does not lead to a sustainable competitive advantage often backfires, especially when that strength is emphasized to the extent that it becomes dysfunctional. GM's attempt, through the NUMMI joint venture, to level the playing field with the Japanese on cost and quality was a success, but it failed to create a competitive advantage for GM when the key sources of competitive advantage in the industry shifted from cost and quality to marketing and other forms of differentiation.

Diversification for all the Wrong Reasons

Diversification that fails to create synergies greater than the incremental costs involved (primarily acquisition premiums) rarely creates value for shareholders. The examples of Lyonnaise des Eaux, Novell, Borden, and the Dole Food Company show how ill-considered diversification strategies based on growth for the sake of growth, egocentric machoism, or portfolio management strategies often create negative synergy and a loss of shareholder value.

EFFECTIVE IMPLEMENTATION—DOING THINGS RIGHT

We now turn to the second half of the problem—the effective and error-free implementation of an organization's strategy. Implementation is about "doing things right," on the assumption that the strategy has identified the "right things to do." Implementation—the process of making it happen—is often the hard part, requiring the long-term commitment of resources, sustained focus, and consistent and committed involvement of the organization's top leaders. As the emphasis shifts from strategy formulation to implementation, the whole organization must become involved, and as it does, coordination, integration, strategic control, and top management leadership must take center stage.

COORDINATION, INTEGRATION, AND STRATEGIC CONTROL

The implementation of strategy must take place within an organizational framework designed to ensure effective coordination, integration, and strategic control. *Coordination* refers to the management activities by which consistency in goals and objectives is achieved among individuals and functions, both within organizations and across organizational boundaries. *Integration* is concerned with issues of process—systems, procedures, and working relationships that determine how effectively participants and diverse organizational components work together to achieve the common goal. *Strategic control* refers to the management tools and techniques used to steer the organization consistently in the direction of its defined objectives. Successful strategic management requires an appropriate mix of these elements; all are essential, and a judicious balance must be maintained among them. Our guidelines for the development of an appropriate framework for the implementation of strategy begin, as in the case of strategy formulation, with the understanding of the strategic context.

Understanding the Strategic Context

The development of an effective framework of coordination, integration, and strategic controls begins with an understanding of the strategic context—although in a somewhat narrower view than was considered in the formulation of strategy. As the definition of strategy narrows the focus, the number of potential customers, suppliers, alliance partners, and competitors that must be considered is lessened. It is important, however, particularly when considering the requirements for coordination and integration of key activities in the value chain, to focus closely on the relationships with suppliers, customers, and alliance partners. Many organizations fall into the trap of conceptualizing their role in the larger scheme of things too narrowly, defining and understanding their business only in the context of those activities under their direct operational or strategic control. By failing to take proper account of the contributions of other organizations to the product or service delivered to the end-user, they fall into the trap of relying on the traditional model illustrated by the example of the ill-fated baggage system for the Denver International Airport. The traditional model emphasizes task specialization, hierarchical structures, and clear definitions of authority and responsibility that delineate organizational boundaries and avoid redundancies. It is also notoriously rigid and inflexible—the organizational architecture and the associated control-oriented managerial mindset create barriers that frequently stand in the way of effective coordination and integration—and it increasingly runs into problems in complex and dynamic environments.

Tearing Down the Barriers and Redefining the Boundaries

A new management model, the boundaryless organization, has been proposed as an alternative to the traditional model. The boundaryless organization seeks to create flexible, porous organizational boundaries and to establish communication flows and mutually beneficial relationships with customers, suppliers, and other external constituencies. As noted, it's largely a matter of perspective—recognizing that your own organization doesn't stand alone but is rather one of several links in a larger value chain involved in creating and delivering of value to the end user. The definition of an effective framework for coordination and control involves two separate steps: (1) designing an organizational architecture by defining, structuring, and implementing critical relationships among the key players; and (2) selecting and implementing an appropriate set of tools and techniques for coordinating goals and integrating value-creating activities, both within and across organizational boundaries. In addition to the traditional model, we described the *modular, virtual,* and *barrier-free* models as the building blocks of organizational architecture, to be used individually or in combination to provide a structure within which key relationships can be defined and implemented. Communications; culture; shared values; horizontal organization structures, systems, procedures, and human resource practices; and information technologies are among the tools and techniques available for enhancing coordination and integration.

Contemporary versus Traditional Approaches to Strategic Control

The traditional approach to strategic control is rigid, sequential, and involves a single feedback loop. Strategies are formulated and goals are set, plans are implemented, and performance is measured against the predetermined goal. Although simple and easy to implement, the traditional approach is inflexible and the long time lag between goal-setting and performance measurement limits the usefulness of the approach in dynamic and rapidly changing environments.

In the contemporary approach to strategic control, both the premises of strategy formulation and the results of strategy implementation are monitored more or less continuously. *Informational control* monitors both premises and the current strategic context to ensure that the organization's strategy continues to be focused on "doing the right things," while *behavioral control* focuses on ensuring that the organization is "doing things right."

Essential Elements of Strategic Control

Effective strategic control requires the use and balancing of three separate elements or "levers" of behavioral control: culture, rewards, and boundaries. Each of these elements plays a different role in the developing and implementing of an effective system of strategic controls—alignment and balance among them is essential. If culture, rewards, and boundaries are not consistent, they will work at cross purposes; if one or more dimensions are neglected or overemphasized, the resulting distortions may render the entire system dysfunctional.

Culture and Rewards versus Boundaries

Traditional organizations have relied heavily on boundaries and constraints—rules, policies, procedures, and the sanctions of enforcement—to exercise operational and strategic control. As firms downsize and eliminate layers of management, and as the marketplace requires greater flexibility and responsiveness, increased coordination and integration of activities across organizational boundaries is essential. Reliance on boundaries and constraints as the primary means of strategic control may no longer be feasible, and the use of rewards and culture to align individual and organizational goals becomes increasingly important. In addition, as the implicit long-term contract between the organization and its key employees has fallen by the wayside, the importance of culture and rewards in building organizational loyalty is enhanced.

Monitoring is expensive—and pure overhead—and many organizations cannot afford the costs. Culture and rewards are often less costly, although they involve investment of a different kind. The increased use of culture and rewards requires different kinds of behavior from top executives. Increasingly, the development and reinforcement of culture involves managers in personnel selection, training and indoctrination, and the ongoing reinforcement of organizational values through their writings, speeches, and leadership by example. Well-designed rewards and incentives can do a great deal to align individual and organizational objectives and to ensure that the entire organization is focused on "doing the right things." Although culture and rewards have much to recommend them as more flexible and more desirable levers of strategic control, these positive reinforcements must be carefully balanced with a judicious mix of boundaries and constraints to ensure that things don't get out of hand.

THE VITAL ROLE OF LEADERSHIP

The role of leadership is crucial in the effective implementation of strategy. We have focused on leadership primarily in the context of organizational transformation: leadership is about the process of transforming organizations or institutions from *what they are* to what the leader *would have them become*. We noted that most successful transformational leaders:

- Move quickly and decisively and create a sense of urgency.
- Develop and communicate both a vision and a plan.
- Set stretch goals and empower others to act.
- Consolidate the gains by institutionalizing change.

A Sense of Urgency

Successful transformational leaders must often "shatter the tablets of stone" and define a new paradigm for their organizations. Inertia is a powerful counterforce. Change is greatly facilitated when people throughout the organization share an awareness of a crisis and a need for immediate action. Although it may appear inappropriate for a leader to deliberately create a sense of crisis, there may be no more vital act of leadership than to alert an organization to danger and get it moving in the right direction.

A Vision and a Plan

The leader needs to develop a vision and a plan and then to communicate both broadly and effectively throughout the organization. An effective statement of vision is simple, direct, focused on the essentials, and communicated in terms employees can understand. It also must be focused on the future and what the organization needs to do to succeed, and it must provide a framework within which goals and objectives can be developed. A vision, by itself, is little more than a dream. The vision—to be credible—must be backed up with a plan that shows the organization how the leader intends to reach the objective.

Stretch Goals and Empowerment

The next task of leadership is to challenge the organization by setting stretch goals and then to empower it to achieve them. Effective stretch goals require an organization to change what it does and how it does it; incremental improvements are not enough. Effective stretch goals must be credible—clearly linked to broader objectives—and perceived as achievable. Finally, the leader must, in essence "get out of the way" and let the solutions bubble up from the shop floor.

Institutionalizing Change

As changes begin to take hold, the leader must act to institutionalize them by incorporating them into the culture, reward systems, and the structures, policies, and procedures of the organization in a way that makes them permanent. Change must take place across the organization—in all areas and in many different forms—if it is to be permanent and effective.

"Walking the Talk"

One of the most effective techniques available to the transformational leader is personal example. Almost without exception, successful leaders have been observed to consistently "walk the talk," lead by example. They never waver in their conviction that the vision and the plan are the right things to do. Inconsistency between words and deeds, the "do as I say, not as I do" approach, will undermine the best of strategies. On the other hand, some of the most effective leaders—David Kearns at Xerox, Lawrence Bossidy at Allied-Signal, Ken Iverson at Nucor, and Andy Grove at Intel—lead and consistently reinforce their commitment, over and over again, by personal example (and it works!).

AVOIDING THE DUMB MISTAKES

As in the formulation of strategy, implementation has its own set of common strategic errors. We recall a few from our earlier examples:

Failures of Coordination and Integration

Reliance on the traditional organizational model—based on hierarchical structures, task specialization, rigid organizational boundaries, and traditional control systems—often leads to failures of coordination and integration. Internal barriers, such as those described in the Frox example, often stand in the way of effective integration of interdependent activities and lead to functional suboptimization or long delays in accomplishing nonroutine tasks. Barriers created by the traditional external boundaries of organizations tend to impede the coordination and cooperation required among the multiple entities involved in complex projects like the design and construction of the Denver International Airport.

The Breakdown of Traditional Control Systems

The traditional approach to strategic control, with its reliance on rigid and predetermined goals and feedback control mechanisms, is often inadequate in complex and dynamic environments, as illustrated by the example of Bausch and Lomb. Reliance on traditional control systems often produces unintended and undesirable consequences, as illustrated by the examples of Western Electric and the company acquired by Cooper Industries.

Failure to Balance the Levers of Strategic Control

The examples of Bausch and Lomb and Magna International illustrate the adverse consequences of an unbalanced approach to strategic control where the overemphasis on one or more of the "levers" of strategic control and the neglect of another causes an organization to spiral out of control.

Failures of Leadership

The example of Bill Agee at MK really says it all! His vision was flawed and his plan was inadequate. The example he set was inconsistent with the direction he had dictated. Rather than empower his managers, he fired those that were widely considered to be the best and replaced them with "yes men," effectively consolidating his power. Communications—even with the board—were obfuscated with questionable accounting practices and limited access to his other managers.

Others were equally ineffective. How about Floyd Hall's "swift and decisive" foot dragging at Kmart? Or James Stewart's "do as I say, not as I do" example at Lone Star Industries? Or Raymond Herter's pattern of unethical behavior that became part of the culture at United Telecontrol Electronics? Leaders must lead—and if they lead in the wrong direction their organizations frequently follow them, like lemmings, over the cliff.

IN THE FINAL ANALYSIS

In the final analysis, the role of leadership is critical. But effective leadership does not necessarily involve high-profile charisma or risky strategic innovations. Effective leaders do not necessarily have to lead the organization to a new frontier "where no one has gone before." Rather, effective leadership is more frequently about maintaining a steady hand on the tiller—ensuring that the organization is "doing the right things" and avoiding the common strategic errors. It's also about building an effective framework of culture, incentives, and strategic controls to ensure that the implementation of strategy is effective and that the organization "does things right" and avoids making the dumb mistakes. A recent profile in *The Wall Street Journal* of Lester Alberthal, CEO of Electronic Data Systems, makes the point most effectively.[3]

When Alberthal took over at EDS in 1986, he had a tough act to follow. EDS's founder, Ross Perot, was a high-profile, charismatic leader who had built the organization from scratch and sold the company to GM for more than $2 billion. The writer notes that "unlike Mr. Perot, who quit EDS over battles with its parent, General Motors Corp., Mr. Alberthal hasn't rescued any hostages or run for president." Characterized as "uncomfortable in the limelight and a lackluster public speaker," Alberthal notes that he has always done what was necessary to make EDS grow and to "make sure that our performance is impeccable." In his first three years, Alberthal made no strategic changes, but focused on shoring up the company's relationship with its largest customer, GM, by providing top-notch customer service. Once that problem was put to bed, he began to focus on growth—and the results have been spectacular. In nine years under Alberthal's low-profile leadership, EDS's revenue has tripled to $12.4 billion and the market value of GM's Class E shares, which represent its EDS investment, is eight times greater than when Perot left the company. Recently, EDS and GM agreed to spin off GM's investment and make EDS a separate public company, free to grow and pursue its own objectives in rapidly growing market for imformation systems and services. By focusing on the basics, implementing a sound strategy, and avoiding costly errors, Les Alberthal and EDS have made our point: *A sound strategy, implemented without error, wins every time.*

END NOTES

1. Fisher, A.B. March 6, 1996. Corporate Reputations: Comebacks and Comeuppances. *Fortune*: 90–98.

2. Quoted in Loeb, M. September 19, 1994. Where Leaders Come From, *Fortune*: 241.

3. Templin, N. February 21, 1996. Les is more: Under Alberthal, EDS is out of limelight but triples revenue." *The Wall Street Journal*: A1, A6.

INDEX

Achievability, elements, 215
Acquisition, 101, 105, 107, 122, 165
  premium, 106
Administrative systems, 16
ADP Corporation, 171, 186
Advertising, 46, 47, 150
After-sales service, 83
Alcoa, 213
Alignment, 164, 167
Alliance partners, 18, 31, 156, 239
Alliances, 51
Allied Signal, 198, 212, 214, 218, 243
AM General Corporation, 46, 52
Amenageur des villes, 102
America OnLine, 50, 51
Amoco, 119
AMT International Industries, Inc., 55–56
Anheuser-Busch, 122
A&P, 76
Apple Computer, 22, 49, 73–76, 140, 149, 152, 226, 237
Arbitrary goals, 6, 168–171
Arms-length relationships, 139
Armstrong World Industries, 125
Asset utilization, 39
Assumption base, 51, 59, 60–61
Assumptions, 52–54, 59, 63, 64, 171, 172. See also Key assumptions
A.T. Cross Company, 2, 10–11, 13, 22, 235
Atarimae hinshitsu, 88
AT&T, 21, 51, 152, 210

Balance, 164, 167
  maintenance, 174–176
  sheet, 171
Bankruptcy, 39, 41, 182
Bargaining position, 111
Barrier-free approach, 147, 159
Barrier-free model, 240
Barrier-free organization, 146, 152–155
Barrier-free type, 160–161
Barriers, 131–162, 240
Basset-Walker division, 116
Bausch & Lomb, 165–168, 170, 244
Beech Aircraft, 43–45
Beech Starship, 2, 43, 44, 237
Behavioral control, 172, 174, 241

Behavioral norms, 176
Beliefs, 53–54
Benchmarking, 215, 221
Blind spots, 5, 21–27. See also Competitive vision
Blockbuster Entertainment, 101
Boeing Aircraft Equipment (BAE), 132, 133, 135
Borden, 120–123, 238
Boston Consulting Group (BCG), 109, 110
Boundaries, 241–242. See also Functional boundaries
  evolution, 187–189
  expansion, 80–82, 232
  redefining, 240
  setting, 185–187
Boundaryless behavior, 143
Boundaryless organization, 142–144, 159
Boundary-spanners, 62, 64, 230
Bravo Zulu program, 185
Bristol-Myers Squibb, 93
British Airways, 142
Bureaucracies, 164
Bureaucratic processes, 220
Business cycle, 27
Business environment, 3
Business leaders, 5
Business model, 40
Business reengineering, 157
Business units, 112, 139
Businesses
  adding, 101–130
  process, 79–80, 231–232
Buyer-supplier relationships, 158

Cabot Corporation, 110, 111
Canon, 142
Capital Cities / ABC, 101
Capital expenditures, 86
Capital requirements, 160
Cash cows, 110
Cash flow, 109
Caterpillar, 89, 90, 216
Cessna, 43, 45
CD-ROM technology, 11
Champion International, 124
Change, fear, 206
Change, institutionalization, 200, 202, 217–220, 242, 243
Chargebacks, 171
Chemical Bank, 186
China Bicycle Company, 150
Chrysler, 29, 30, 127, 142, 149, 153, 154, 158, 234

Coca-Cola, 198, 226
Cognitive taxonomies, 18
Commercial success, 23
Common culture, 156–157
Common infrastructures, sharing, 115–117
Communication, 62, 158, 201, 211, 213, 240, 245
Compaq Computer Corp., 50, 56, 149, 226
Compensation system, 184
Competencies, 228. See also Core competencies
Competing objectives, 138
Competition, 9, 21, 28, 47, 57, 71, 107, 198
Competitive advantage, 5, 47, 114, 124, 159, 198, 234, 235, 237, 238. See also Long-term competitive advantage
  creation, 67–99
  multiple sources, exploitation, 235
  sources, identification, 231–233
  sustaining, 91–94
Competitive arena, 16
Competitive conditions, 233
Competitive environment, 9, 13, 14, 21, 24, 29, 54, 69, 71, 76, 77, 79, 174, 214. See also External competitive environment; Global competitive environment; Near-term competitive environment
  boundaries, 62
  boundary definition, 228
  dynamics, focus, 87–88
  focus, narrowing, 16–17
  understanding, 15–20
Competitive position, 13, 210, 235
Competitive problems, 48
Competitive rivalries, 14
Competitive space, 19, 31
Competitive strategy, 5, 6, 31
Competitive success, 22
Competitive vision, blind spots, 9–36, 237
Competition, 38
Competitor information, 31, 32
Competitor intelligence, 10, 15–20, 30
  processes, 32
Competitor offerings, 84
Competitors, 2, 15, 16, 18, 27, 30–32, 45, 48, 53, 55, 58, 60–63,

Competitors (*continued*) 71, 86, 87, 115, 127, 207, 212, 227, 228, 234, 239. *See also* Japanese competitors; Regional competitors
Compton's Encyclopedia, 11–13
Compuserve, 50
Computer manufacturers, 25
Computer-aided design (CAD), 86
Constraints, 185–187, 242
Consumer debt, 27
Consumer marketplace, 52
Consumer products, 94
Consumer tastes, 233
Consumers, 22, 46–47, 114, 143
Continental Airlines, 133
Contract management, 135
Control, 62. *See also* Behavioral control; Informational control systems, 71, 171–176, 244
Cooper Industries, 124, 170, 244
Cooperation, 38, 125
Coordination, 134, 141, 146, 238–242. *See also* Inter-divisional coordination
  ensuring, 144–146
  failure, 244
  management tools/techniques, 155–158
Core competencies, 37, 55, 60, 111, 119, 120, 127, 147, 159, 160, 231
  capitalization, 112–115
  leveraging, 235
Core customer base, 41
Core processes, 6, 137
Core products, 112
Core strengths, 115
Core values, 53
Corning, 212
Corporate assets, use, 195–196
Corporate diversification, 107
Corporate parenting role, 123
Corporate strategies, 106
Cost control, 68, 69, 71
Cost culture, 71
Cost leadership, 77, 78, 86, 88, 187, 232
Cost position, 91
Cost reduction, 48
Cost savings, 73
Cost structures, 60, 119
Cost/benefit tradeoffs, 92
Cost-cutting, 75
Cost-reduction opportunities, 81
Credibility, 206, 215
Critical, definition, 19–20
Critical intelligence, 230
Critical technologies, 16
Cross external organization, 146
Cross-docking, 92

Cross-functional integration, 138, 144
Cross-functional teams, 153, 157
Cross-training, 157
CSX, 142, 215–216
Cultural factors, 228
Culture, 167, 174, 176, 179, 217, 240–242. *See also* Cost culture; Effective culture; Organizational culture
  barriers, 127
  building, 176–183
  changing, 218
  evolution, 187–189
  reinforcement, 180–181
  role, 176
Customer feedback, 207
Customer functions, 16
Customer groups, 16
Customer interests, 38
Customer needs, 16
Customer pain, 200
Customer relationships, 93
Customer representatives, 199
Customer satisfaction, 84
Customer service, 87, 91, 176, 180
Customer value, 232
Customer-driven, 18
Customer-driven organization, 199
Customers, 14, 15, 22, 31, 32, 41, 53, 55, 60, 62, 63, 80–82, 111, 118, 127, 139, 143, 156, 227, 228, 230, 239
Customer-service associates, 40
Customer-supplier relationships, 81
Customer/supplier relationships, 95
Cycle time reduction, 144

Data processing, 148
Day-to-day interactions, 229
Dealer network, 46
Delivery logistics, 86
Delivery systems, 235
Delivery technologies, 63
Dell Computer, 56, 74, 149, 226
Demographics, 23, 233. *See also* Market demographics
Denver International Airport (DIA), 131–137, 239, 244
Deregulation, 38
Design, 48, 85, 154
Development spending, 48
Differentiation, 73, 77, 78, 82, 88, 90, 159, 232
Disaster, aversion, 21–27
Disney Corporation, 101, 107, 117, 198
Distribution, 31, 47, 80, 91, 117, 150

Diversification, 7, 101, 106, 109, 112, 118, 165, 201. *See also* Corporate diversification; Strategic diversification
  guideline implementation, 123–127
  strategy, 121, 127, 200
  valid reasons, 111–119
  wrong reasons, 107–111, 238
Dole Food Company, 2, 103–105, 238
Dominant logic, 54–59, 229,
Donnelly Corporation, 80, 81
Downsizing, 40
Downstream activities, 70, 88
Due diligence, 120, 123
DuPont, 126
Dynatec, 89, 90, 234

Eastman Kodak, 198
Economic conditions, 196
Economic factors, 228
Economic uncertainty, 27
Economies of scale, 120
Edison Light Company, 209
Effective culture, sustaining, 177
Ego-centric machoism, 107–109, 238
Electronic data interchange (EDI), 153, 158
Electronic Data Systems (EDS), 213, 245, 246
Eli Lilly and Co., 187, 217–218
Emerson Electric, 123, 176
Employee interests, 38
Employees, 2, 14, 154, 178, 200, 209–210
Empowerment, 4, 214–217, 242, 243
Encyclopedia Britannica, Inc., 11–13, 237
End products, 56, 112
End user, 63, 80, 138, 145, 232
Engineering, 139
Entrepreneurial organizations, 29, 141
Entrepreneurs, 28
Environment, 14–21, 30–34, 55, 139. *See also* Competitive environment; External environment; Strategic environment
Environmental analysis, 21
Environmental awareness, 30, 32
  culture, creation, 31, 229–230
Environmental responsibility, 196
Error-free implementation, 7
Essentials, focus, 209–210
Ethical behavior, 167, 190
Expertise, 140

External boundaries, 244
External constituencies, 143, 161
External control perspective, 196
External environment, 59, 63

FAA, 44, 45, 52, 137, 237
False premise, 237
Federal Express, 155, 176, 180, 185
Feedback, 169–170, 185, 240, 244. *See also* Customer feedback; Performance feedback
Financial restructuring, 41
Financial sensitivity analysis, 61
Financial soundness, 195
Financial success, 27
Focus, 19, 77, 78
Food Lion, 2, 67–73, 76, 79, 88, 237
Ford Motor Company, 29, 30, 142, 173, 183, 207
Foresight, importance, 233
Foundation, 59–62
Frame of reference, 37, 38, 229. *See also* Internal frame of reference; Managerial frame of reference, 229
Frox, 140, 141, 244
Functional boundaries, 140, 141
Functional departments, 18, 139, 146
Functional diversity, 138
Funding, constraints, 196
Future, focus, 200, 211

General Electric (GE), 94, 109, 120, 142, 143, 158, 198, 209
General Motors (GM), 29, 30, 47–49, 52, 81, 142, 154, 203, 213, 237, 238, 245, 246
Generic strategies, 77, 78
Generic value chain, 79
Geographic domain, 138
Geographic locations, 18
Geography, barriers, 126
Gillette, 10, 114
Global competitive environment, 164
Global markets, 160
Goal conflicts, 183
Goals. *See* Arbitrary goals; Stretch goals
   communication, 156
   framework, 209–211
   setting, 170, 214
Golden Falcon award, 185
Government regulations, 196
Greyhound Lines, Inc., 2, 38–42, 45, 52
Growth, 107, 215, 238

Gulf & Western, 76

Hallmark, 24, 237
Harley-Davidson, 115
Harvard University, 106, 207
Hewlett-Packard, 115, 176
H.H. Cutler, 116, 119
High-risk strategy, 194
High-technology firms, 9
Historical information, 57
Hitachi, 21
Home Depot, 25, 26
Honda, 72, 73, 80, 81
Horizontal organizations, 123–127, 157, 240
Horizontal structure, 125, 161
Horizontal systems / processes, 157–158
Human resource practices, 158

IBM, 25, 49–51, 142, 149, 150, 152, 188, 198, 203, 208
Illusion of progress, 42
Implementation, 6, 170, 172, 227, 238. *See also* Diversification
Inbound logistics, 79, 82
Incentive programs, 184
Incentives, 167, 242
   creation, 230
   motivation, 183–185
Incremental value, 111
Indoctrination, 178–180
Industrial engineering, 170
Industry analysis, 76, 77
Industry boundaries, 16, 77
Industry domain, 16
Industry environment, 14
Industry growth rate, 109
Industry leadership, 13
Industry taxonomy, 18, 60
Information
   free flow, 31–33
   processing, 124
   systems, 93, 125
   technologies, 158, 240
Informational control, 172–174, 240–241
Infrastructures, 111, 127, 194, 236. *See also* Common infrastructures; Shared infrastructures
In-house development, 50
Innovation, 74, 176
   value adding, 88–90, 236
Integration, 134, 141, 146, 238–242
   ensuring, 144–146
   failure, 244
   management tools / techniques, 155–158
Intel, 183, 243
Intelligence process, 32, 34

Intercompany accounts, 171
Interdepencies, 134, 136, 145, 231
Inter-divisional coordination, 153
Internal barriers, 30, 244
Internal consistency, 61
Internal disagreements, 55
Internal frame of reference, 59
Internal relationships, 231
Internet, 49–52, 57, 58, 237
Interrelationships, 125
Inventory turns, 215
ITT, 76

Japanese competitors, 47
Java, 50
John Deere & Co., 216–217
Johnson & Johnson, 142, 226
Just-in-time (JIT), 81, 86–87

Key assumptions, 62, 229
Key competencies, 62
Key players, 19, 228–229
Key premises, 229
Key questions, 228
Kinko's Graphics, Inc., 27, 236
Kmart, 196, 204, 205, 226, 245
K-minus concept, 90
Knowledge base, 60
Kohlberg, Kravis, Roberts & Company (KKR), 121, 123

Labor-management coopera-tion, 158
Labor-management problems, 150, 216
Layoffs, 181
Leadership, 37, 196–200, 226. *See also* Transformational leadership
   defining, 196–200
   failure, 6, 193–224, 244–245
   role, 242–243
   skills, 197, 208
Leading-edge firms, 178
Lean production techniques, 47
Learjet, 43, 45
Legal constraints, 228
Lexus, 83, 84
Lone Star Industries Inc., 181, 245
Long-term competitive advantage, 5
Long-term contract, 241
Long-term strategy, 229
Long-term viability, 110
Lotus Development Corporation, 50, 237
Lyonnaise des Eaux, 101–103, 105, 238

Machine performance, 219
Magna International, Inc., 175, 176

Malcolm Baldrige National
  Quality Award, 219
Management, 41, 45, 226
  challenge, 143
  coalition, 201
  decisions, 53, 229
  leadership, 238
  model, 142–144
  organization, 62
  quality, 195, 226
  system. *See* Yield
    management systems
  team, 42, 54, 55
Managerial frame of reference,
  229
Manufacturing, 75, 139, 154
  consistency / reliability, 83
  costs, 215
  efficiencies, 116
  operations, 148
Markdowns, 25
Market conditions, 23
Market demographics, 237
Market dominance, 21
Market forces, 56
Market life cycles, 197
Market opportunity, 140
Market power, 111, 118–119, 122
Market research, 30
Market segments, 218
Market share, 29, 72, 110, 116,
  219. *See also* Relative market
  share
Market value, 106
Market-driven, 18
Marketing, 16, 48, 79, 84, 139,
  154
Marketing channels, 111
Marketing resources, 122
Marketing skills, 111
Marketing strategy, 41
Martin Marietta Corporation,
  170
Matsushita, 21
Mazda, 94
MCI Communications Corp, 51,
  152
Mega-merger, 4
Mega-stores, 26
Mental model, 14, 17
Mercedes, 73
Merck & Company, 173, 226
Mergers, 105, 106, 120
Microsoft, 49–52, 94, 104, 108,
  152, 177, 187
Mission, 55
Mission critical, strategic
  challenge, 1–7
Mistakes, avoidance, 244–245
Modular approaches, 159
Modular model, 240
Modular organization, 146–150
Modular type, 160

Monitoring, 62
Morrison Knudsen (MK), 2,
  193–196, 198, 200, 201, 226,
  244
Motorola, 93, 94, 142, 152, 176,
  178, 179
Movement, 203–205
Moving target, one-shot view,
  77
Multifunctional teams, 144
Multimedia product, 12
Multiple activities, value
  adding, 82–86
Multiple streams, 113
Mutual objectives, 156

Near-term competitive environ-
  ment, 16
Near-term performance, 20, 61,
  229
Netscape Communications
  Corp., 49, 51
New United Motor
  Manufacturing, Inc.
  (NUMMI), 47, 48, 237
Nintendo Co., 21, 29, 56, 237
Noncompetitor, 18, 62
Noncore functions, 148
Noncritical functions,
  outsourcing, 90, 236
Noncustomers, 19, 32, 62, 228
Novell, 108, 109, 121
Nucor, 176, 182, 243
Nutmeg Industries, 116, 119

Objective environment, 13
Objective reality, 14
Objectives
  communication, 156
  framework, 209, 210–211
One stop shopping, 24
One-dimensional strategy, 5
Operating budgets, 169
Operating expenses,
  capitalization, 194
Operating performance, 61
Operational efficiencies, 111, 176
Operational tasks, 69
Operations, 75, 79
Opportunities, 30, 233, 234. *See*
  also Cost-reduction
  opportunities; Service
Opportunity. *See* Market
  opportunity spotting, 27–30,
  234
Oracle, 49
Organization, 211. *See also*
  Barrier-free organization;
  Management; Modular
  organization; Virtual
  organization
    dominant logic, 54
    functional breakdown, 18

strengths / weaknesses, 33
  structures, 231
Organizational architectures,
  145–155, 239, 240
Organizational boundaries, 131,
  137, 138, 145, 151, 156, 160,
  238, 239
  barriers, 126
Organizational coordination,
  159
Organizational culture, 176
Organizational entity, 139
Organizational forms, 17
Organizational goals, 209
Organizational inertia, 208
Organizational levers, 218, 221
Organizational loyalty, 241
Organizational performance, 61,
  82
Organizational politics, 30
Organizational specialization,
  139
Organizational systems, 157
Organizational transformation,
  242
Organizational vision, 211
Outbound logistics, 75, 79, 148
Outsourcing, nonstrategic
  functions, 144

Paradigm, 42
Parallel processes, 232
Partners, 60, 227
Patience, 208
Peers, 53, 215
Pepsi-Cola, 122, 198–200, 206,
  212
Performance expectations, 44
Performance feedback, 184
Performance measures, 184,
  185, 221, 240
Personal experience, 53
Personnel selection, 177–178
Perspective, 234
Plan, 242–243
  communication /
    development, 208–214
Planning, foresight, 231
Planning cycle, 62, 169
Political constraints, 228
Political infighting, 55
Porter, five forces model, 76
Porter, three generic strategies,
  78
Portfolio analysis, 109
Portfolio management, 109–111,
  238
Portfolio planning approaches,
  109
Premises, 53–54, 59, 62, 171, 172.
  See also False premise; Key
  premises
Pricing strategies, 119

Prioritization, 19–20, 61
Problems, 37–66
Process reengineering, 144
Process-oriented view, 79
Proctor & Gamble, 115, 116, 226
Procurement processes, 111
Prodigy, 50, 51
Product cost, 48
Product development cycles, 215
Product development resources, 23
Product development time, 155
Product life cycles, 197
Product lines, 115
Product quality, 176
Product technologies, 63
Production, 16, 150
    schedules, 169
    systems, 23
    technologies, 60, 63
Productivity, 154, 217
Productivity enhancements, 123
Product-market characteristics, 17
Product-market scope, 138
Product-service offering, 19
Profit objectives, 170
Profitability, 42, 88
Project complexity, 138
Promotion, 47
Purchasing patterns, 16

Quality, 48, 182
Quick response, 232

Raytheon, Co., 2, 43, 45, 52, 237
Real estate investment trusts (REITs), 105
Receivables, 166
Reengineering, 4
Regional brands, 122
Regional competitors, 41
Regulation, 233
Regulators, 44
Regulatory constraints, 228
Relative market share, 109
Research & development (R&D), 74, 75, 113, 139, 150, 155, 183
    alliance, 152
    expertise, 111
Resources, 140
Restructuring, 22
Retailers, 20, 26
Return on assets, 219
Revenues, 112, 166
Reward structure, 175–176
Rewards, 167, 174, 241–242
    evolution, 187–189
    motivation, 183–185
Risk taking culture, 185

Risks, 48
Romantic view, 196
Rule-based controls, 186
Rules of the game, 9

Sales, 79, 84
Sales expenses, 182
Sales force, 31, 225
Sales quotas, 169
Scale economies, 39, 48
Scott Paper, 203, 204
SEAL, 179, 180, 187
Sears, 51, 202
Securities and Exchange Commission (SEC), 166, 167
Sega Enterprises, Ltd., 21, 29, 56, 117, 152, 237
Self-managed teams, 155
Senior management, 184
    paralysis, 208
Service, 79, 84
    capabilities, 235
    opportunities, 6
    strategies, 157
    tactics, 20
    technologies, 63
Shared costs, 115
Shared infrastructures, 120, 157
Shared philosophies, 217
Shared values, 156, 240
Shareholders, 7, 11, 38, 105, 201, 238
    pressure, 196
Shaw Industries, 118–120
Short-term goals, 151
Short-term perspective, 58
Silicon Graphics, 49, 152
Social factors, 228
Socialization, 53, 229
Sony Computer Entertainment, Inc., 21, 93, 94, 126, 152
Sorting out process, 19
Sound strategies, 7, 225–246
    creation, 233–236
Southwest Airlines, 86, 94, 176, 181
Speed, 88, 89
Sprint, 51
Stakeholders, 17, 60, 209, 210, 227
Stand-alone entity, 110
Static analysis, 77, 78, 87
Status quo, 197, 207, 208
Status symbols, 83
Stock performance, 200
Strategic alliances, 150, 159
Strategic business units (SBUs), 109, 110, 161, 218
Strategic context, 14, 144, 145, 159, 172
    understanding, 31, 227–230, 239

Strategic control, 7, 134, 135, 146, 148, 151, 163–192, 238–242
    contemporary approach, 240–241
    elements, 241
    levers, balancing failure, 244
    traditional approach, 240–241
Strategic criteria, 61
Strategic direction, 61
Strategic diversification, 121–123
Strategic environment, 144
    focusing, 13–15
Strategic errors, 3, 7, 58, 76, 131, 132, 168, 201, 244
    avoidance, 236–238
Strategic failure, 3, 6
Strategic inventory, 32–34, 62–64, 94–96, 127, 159–161, 189–190, 220–221
Strategic investments, 92
Strategic management, 3, 134, 239
Strategic manager, 2
Strategic model, 51
Strategic objectives, 61, 149–151, 225
Strategic outsourcing, 4, 90
Strategic partnership, 135, 144
Strategic plans, 203
Strategic priorities, 189
Strategic success, 6
Strategic traps, 5–7, 13, 52–53, 71–76, 105–107, 137–138, 168–171, 200–202
Strategies, 4, 21, 23, 37–66, 169, 171, 235, 236, 240. *See also* Generic strategies; Porter; Pricing strategies; Sound strategies
    building, 59–62
    single dimension, overemphasis, 77–78
Strategists, 59, 168
Strategy formulation, 171–173, 227, 238
    process, 230–231
Strategy-making, 6
Strengths, 76–77, 237–238
    focus, 90, 236
    identification, 82
Strengths, Weaknesses, Opportunities and Threats (SWOT) analysis, 76, 77, 82
Stretch, elements, 214
Stretch goals, 221, 243, 242
    setting, 214–217
Structure, providing, 32
Subjective environment, 13
Substitute technology, 11, 25
Success, 211

Success-oriented schedule, 135
Sun Microsystems, 49–51, 140
Supplier-customer
    relationships, 151
Suppliers, 14, 17, 31, 32, 53, 60,
    62, 80–82, 111, 118, 127, 139,
    143, 153, 156, 227, 229, 230, 239
Support activities, 79
Sustainable advantage, 237–238
Synergies, 22, 111, 114, 117, 118,
    123, 127, 238

3M, 113, 114, 176, 180
Takeover premiums, 106
Target market, 141
Targeted customers, 17
Task specialization, 164
Team members, 126, 156
Teamwork, 179
Technological innovation, 83
Technological obsolescence, 148
Technologies, 45, 48, 56, 113, 117
Technology, 4, 28, 44, 55, 227,
    233, 235
    environments, 49
    resources, 20
Tenneco, 198, 206
Threats, understanding,
    234–235
Time, 101
Time Warner, 152
Tokyo Electric Power, 142
Top-down management, 215
Toshiba, 152
Total quality management
    (TQM), 4, 144, 219
Toyota, 47, 48, 72, 73, 76, 83, 142
Traditional approaches, 76–78
Traditional model, limitations,
    138–142
Trailways, Inc., 39, 42

Training, 178–180
Transformational leaders, 198,
    205, 242
Transformational leadership,
    177, 220
    principles, 202
Trial and error, 53
Turf battles, 120, 139
Turnarounds, 204, 206
Turnovers, 3
TWA, 196, 226

Unbalanced controls, 6, 168–171
Union Pacific, 198, 206
United Airlines, 132, 133
United Telecontrol Electronics,
    Inc. (UTE), 182, 245
Upstream activities, 70, 88
Urgency, 242, 220, 242
    creation, 203–208
U.S. consumer goods market, 19

Validation, 61
Value
    adding. See Innovation;
        Multiple activities
    long-term investment, 196
    subtracting, 101–130
Value activities, 82, 84, 149, 233
Value chain, 60, 79–82, 85, 86,
    90, 94, 139, 230, 233, 239. See
    also Generic value chain
    activities, 124
    focus, 231–232
    link, 232
    usage, 235–236
Value creation, 123, 232
Value pricing, 48
Value-added services, 28
Value-creating activities, 79, 82,
    95, 231, 236

    integration, 86–87
Value-creating process, 231
Values, 38, 217
    changing, 218
Vertical hierarchies, 148
Vertical structures, 158
VF Corporation, 116, 119
Viacom, 101
Virtual approaches, 159
Virtual model, 240
Virtual organization, 147,
    150–152
Virtual organizational types,
    146
Virtual type, 160
Vision, 242–243
    communication/develop-
        ment, 208–214

Wal-Mart, 19, 26, 27, 92, 93, 181,
    199, 204, 205
Wang, 76
Warner Communications, 101
Waterman S.A., 10
Weaknesses, identification, 82
Westinghouse, 124, 198, 208,
    217
Winner's curse, 58
Win-win deals, 151
WordPerfect Corporation, 108,
    121
Work ethic, 91
Work groups, 18
Workforce, 172
World Wide Web, 49–51

Xerox Corporation, 28, 140, 142,
    182, 218–220, 243

Yamaha, 21
Yield management systems, 40